My Life
GLORIA
HUNNIFORD

My Life

GLORIA HUNNIFORD

JOHN BLAKE

Published by John Blake Publishing,
An Imprint of Bonnier Publishing
3 Bramber Court, 2 Bramber Road,
London W14 9PB, England

www.johnblakebooks.com

www.facebook.com/johnblakebooks 🅵
twitter.com/jblakebooks 🅴

First published in 2017
This edition published in 2018

Parts of this narrative were first published in the author's earlier book,
Next To You (Penguin, 2006), and are reproduced with thanks to her original
publishers. Also thanks to Lynda Lee-Potter's interview with Gloria Hunniford,
which first appeared in the *Daily Mail* on 5th May 2004.

ISBN: 978 1 78606 831 6

British Library Cataloguing-in-Publication Data:

A catalogue record for this book is available from the British Library.

Design by www.envydesign.co.uk

Printed in Great Britain by Clays Ltd, St Ives plc

1 3 5 7 9 10 8 6 4 2

Papers used by John Blake Publishing are natural, recyclable products made from wood
grown in sustainable forests. The manufacturing processes conform to the environmental
regulations of the country of origin.

Every attempt has been made to contact the relevant copyright-holders, but some were
unobtainable. We would be grateful if the appropriate people could contact us.

John Blake Publishing is an imprint of Bonnier Publishing
www.bonnierpublishing.com

*This book is a tribute to the gorgeous memories
of my mum and dad – May and Charlie – my sister Lena,
brother Charles, my beautiful daughter Caron and the
ongoing memories created by my family – sons Paul and
Michael, husband Stephen and the extended Hunniford/
Keating/Way families.*

CONTENTS

FOREWORD BY CLIFF RICHARD   1

PROLOGUE   3

CHAPTER 1   A PINT-SIZED SINGER FROM
PORTADOWN   7

CHAPTER 2   DAFFODIL TEAS AND MEAT SUPPERS   25

CHAPTER 3   MAKING WAVES AND MAKING BABIES   55

CHAPTER 4   BOMBS, BULLETS AND BARRICADES   75

CHAPTER 5   A TASTE OF HUNNI   97

CHAPTER 6   MOVING THE BIG PIECES   121

CHAPTER 7   BREAKING THE BOUNDARIES   141

CHAPTER 8   STARDUST MEMORIES   167

CHAPTER 9   LOVE AND LOSS   195

CHAPTER 10   THAT'S GLO-BIZ   215

CHAPTER 11   THE SECOND TIME AROUND   229

CHAPTER 12   LOSING CARON   251

CHAPTER 13   A RECOVERY OF SORTS   279

CHAPTER 14   I'M STILL HERE, HUNNI   301

ACKNOWLEDGEMENTS   327

FOREWORD

It's at times like this, when writing a foreword for a friend, that I find it difficult to age a friendship. I mean, how long have I known Gloria?

It feels like forever. And yet it feels like only yesterday that she managed to get a 'scoop' interview with me when I was visiting Northern Ireland. I can't even remember exactly when that was, and I had no idea of course that later we were to become close friends.

People used to say that they had heard Gloria interview me and I would say that she had *never* interviewed me, that we had merely had conversations, many of which took place during her BBC Radio 2 afternoon shows.

Gloria is one of the easiest people to talk to and I admire her, not only for that, but also for her commitment to the job of 'interviewing' people from all walks of life. She makes it look so easy, but I have learned by getting to know her over these years that the 'ease' comes from ridiculously early mornings (4am) when she meticulously studies the background of her upcoming guests. Hence, when they meet later she is already comfortable with them.

Even when Glo was dealing with the most horrific years of her life – her daughter's battle with cancer – she continued her appearances with the bravest of faces. When I was dealing with the worst years of my life, Gloria was always there for me.

I feel sure that after reading this book you will discover what I and all her friends already know, that Gloria Hunniford is a devoted wife, mother, mother-in-law and grandmother, and to me and many others, a loyal friend, all while being an incredibly busy, respected and beloved TV presenter.

Cliff Richard
July 2017

PROLOGUE

What a journey it has been.

Even that wide-eyed, ambitious ten-year-old girl from Portadown, County Armagh would never have believed that sixty-seven years later she'd still be in show business and have received an OBE from Her Majesty The Queen at Buckingham Palace.

I've had the absolute pleasure of interviewing some of the greatest stars of our time including Bette Davis, Charlton Heston, Doris Day, Gene Wilder and David Bowie – not only was it thrilling to meet such idols, but some even became great friends, like Cliff Richard and Julio Iglesias.

It's completely remarkable to me that 2017 marks my seventieth year in the business and yet I still have the same passion, drive and desire as when I started. Work keeps me sane, informed and interested in the world, and so long as people want me, I plan to keep on going.

But, of course, it's been far from plain sailing. As the expression goes, I was an overnight thirty-year success. In those early days as a young singer, it was hard graft and sometimes dangerous for a woman, touring round cabaret venues and hotels late at night in Northern Ireland at the height of the Troubles. I had quite a few hair-raising experiences. As a young news reporter, I did a 'live' report from the centre of Belfast involving a petrol tanker packed with 500lbs of IRA Semtex and later that day I was sat with the bomb disposal expert's wife as we watched him diffuse the bomb – all of it happening on 'live' TV – and of course he saved the centre of Belfast from being blown asunder. Later I also reported on the bombing of the Abercorn restaurant explosion that tragically claimed the lives of two young women and injured over 130 people – not exactly what you'd expect a twenty-nine-year-old working mother to be doing in 1969.

Back then it was much harder for women to not only break into the media, but any kind of prominent position. I guess it was a mixture of naivety, gumption, hard work and being in the right place at the right time that landed me those early days at BBC Belfast and Ulster Television. They were hugely exciting times as it was really the start of television as we know it today – it was all 'live' broadcasts, high adrenalin and seat-of-the-pants action, but hugely exciting and the best training one could get. Even today, I'd much prefer to do a 'live' show than a pre-recorded one, 'warts and all'.

In fact, I was the first woman to land her own nightly programme on Ulster Television and later the first female to get her own daytime show on BBC Radio 2. Amazingly in 1982 the BBC didn't even have a woman's toilet on the studio floor, which made for some interesting mid-news bulletin pee breaks. It's not that I ever saw myself as a women's rights trailblazer or someone who had to fight the gender gap, but if I helped change perceptions in some small way, then that is certainly a bonus. I simply knew what I wanted and went for it.

I've had incredible professional highs, but also terrible personal lows in terms of losing my beloved daughter Caron to breast cancer at just forty-one years old. It not only completely tore the family apart, but landed me in the deepest, darkest black hole. Some days were so dark that I thought I'd never return to my former self; I genuinely thought that I'd never laugh again. At the time, my youngest son Michael told me that it felt he had not only lost his sister, but his mother too. It was obviously also incredibly hard for my husband Stephen, but I was so consumed with grief that I was incapable of thinking about anybody else. Over a period of three years, I slowly dragged myself back to some semblance of normality. But more of that later...

There are unforgettable memories from Hever Castle in Kent, which has become my spiritual home since I came over from Northern Ireland. Stephen and I had a real fairy- tale wedding there in 1998; Caron and her husband Russ also married there in 1991 and then just two years ago, my older son Paul married the gorgeous Lisa there, and she has brought so much to our lives.

Tragically of course, St Peter's Church in Hever Castle is also where Caron is buried so, as you can imagine, there is a real mixture of emotions when we recall all these memories over a twenty-year period (in the best man's speech at Paul's wedding, Caron's husband Russ said, 'Now we only need Michael to tie the knot here and we'll have four weddings and a funeral'). We often visit Hever Church at the weekend, where we tend to Caron's graveside and then have lunch together in the King Henry VIII pub opposite, which has been an inn since 1597;

Hever has become an incredibly special place for us.

Nowadays, I live a happy and contented life in Sevenoaks, Kent with Stephen and my two gorgeous Cavalier King Charles Spaniels. I'm still broadcasting on average four days a week and have just been recommissioned by the BBC to make several television programmes over the next two years, which will take me up to almost eighty (that's hard to write let alone say out loud!). Proof though that the industry is not in fact that ageist after all...

I often reflect upon my career and some of the exhilarating and different moments, like meeting the Mafia's Godfather at the exclusive Las Vegas Country Club, and later that night watching Sammy Davis Jr in cabaret at Caesars Palace and being entertained and cooked for by him in his vast apartment. Or, having interviewed Rod Stewart and, knowing Caron was a big fan, racing my car from Belfast to Dublin after my nightly TV show to catch the finale of his gig – it was worth it just to sing along to 'Do Ya Think I'm Sexy' and go backstage afterwards. Spending time with Doris Day at her hotel on Pebble Beach in California and kicking sand with her and her grandson was certainly a standout moment. As was performing in the *Royal Variety Performance* while my mum was still alive, and getting her front-row tickets for the show. She was so proud, and even prouder when I went to interview the Duke of Edinburgh at Buckingham Palace. Now I have the honour of receiving an OBE from Her Majesty The Queen, and oh, how I would have loved to take my mum to Buckingham Palace.

Sometimes I have to pinch myself that all these incredible things have actually happened. Getting here has certainly been a mix of sheer perseverance and a great big dollop of luck.

Here's how it all happened...

CHAPTER ONE

A PINT-SIZED SINGER
FROM PORTADOWN

Slowly and laboriously, I dragged the chair over to the kitchen shelf. I was about five years old and I remember so desperately wanting to get as close as I could to the big old Bakelite radio we had stored up there, to make sure the people on the other side of it could hear me.

I clambered on to the chair and, balancing on my tiny little legs, took a deep breath and started: 'East is East and West is West and the wrong one I have chose…'

I stood there for hours, as I so often did, singing my heart out to the radio. *Surely*, I thought, *if I could hear them, then they must be able to hear me*, and then the people at the BBC would say, 'Who is that person singing "'Buttons and Bows"?' and snap me up. I'd spend hours standing on that chair and singing into the speaker. Funnily enough, it was to be many years before the BBC finally came knocking at the door…

* * *

I was born on 10 April 1940 in my parent's front bedroom at 94 Armagh Road, a pebble-dashed terraced house, two-up, two-down with an outside loo, in Portadown, a small market town in semi-rural Northern Ireland. I was clearly a major disappointment to my sister Lena, whose birthday it also was and who had been hoping for a puppy. She probably thought of me as a complete nuisance for years.

I suppose I was always the show-off of the family and gregarious from the start, perhaps something to do with the fact I was the middle child: Lena, short for Helena, was seven years older than me, and as my mother, May Hunniford, had been just nineteen when she had her, they were more like sisters than anything else. My brother, Charles, was born seven years after me and, as the only son, was the apple of my dad's eye. In fact, when we started learning about sex, we'd say, as children do, 'Gosh, our parents only did it every seven years!'

I'd been born with a tongue-tie – a small abnormality in the form of a restrictive piece of skin under the tongue – so I was taken to the family doctor, who snipped it with a special pair of silver scissors. After that, there was no stopping me when it came to chatting and singing, apparently. Later, my mum even told Des O'Connor this on a special Mother's Day episode of his chat show. With perfect comic timing, she said, 'You know, Des, I sometimes wonder if we did the right thing in snipping it!'. But she was no slouch in the chatting stakes herself, having neighbours and friends gather round the black range in the kitchen, gossiping away about everything and all to the tune of their knitting needles, clicking to the clacking of their tongues. The kitchen was

Mum's domain and I have fond memories of listening to *Take Your Pick*, *Workers' Playtime* and *Variety Bandbox* on the radio, or settling down with *Rupert* or *Girl's Own* annuals or *Little Women*, my favourite book.

My father, Charlie Hunniford, was head of the household and a big disciplinarian, but not physically – he never hit any of us. He had left school when he was barely fourteen, but he could paint and write poetry, and worked as an Advertising Manager by day and a magician by night. In fact, he was magical in every sense of the word and not only a great dad but a very talented man; he was even a member of the Magic Circle. From a young age I was absolutely fascinated by all his tricks, and used to beg to go and stand side stage at the various concerts he performed at around the country. He kept a huge loft in the garden for his homing pigeons – and one dove, which he used in his magic act. My favourite trick of his, though, was the razor-blade trick: he'd put all these sharp blades into his mouth along with a rolled-up ball of thread and then, to a drum roll, draw them out dramatically one-by-one on a string. He would never tell me how he did it – after all, as a member of the Magic Circle he was sworn to secrecy – so as soon as he was out of the house I would rummage in his tricks cupboard to see if I could discover the secret. But I never did work it out. Dad could do so much, he even taught me how to knit. Mum didn't have the patience, so she taught him and he taught me.

My mum was an incredible home-maker, though, and a wonderful cook; her cake tins were always full of delicious temptations which she managed to rustle together, even during this period of rationing, in part thanks to the plentiful supplies of chickens, eggs and fruit from my granny's farm four miles away in the country. I've certainly inherited Mum's love of cooking, although I'm not nearly as good as she was. Now I only have to smell bread in a bakery and I'm right back in her kitchen.

I remember, we would all squeeze around the kitchen table where there was always a steaming pot of tea, hot bread straight from the oven, with butter oozing through it and the thick-spread jam Mum made from strawberries and raspberries, which we grew in the garden. We were never allowed to fill the teapot half-full because, as Mum said, 'You never know who might pop in'. The door in those days was never locked, from early morning till late at night.

The parlour was used only on high days and holidays, so we ate in the kitchen, too. You have five meals in Ireland: breakfast, lunch, afternoon tea, dinner and then supper. If we'd gone to bed without supper, my mum would have thought we were ill. At half nine or ten, she'd make sandwiches and open cake tins, and this huge array of food would be put out. On Saturdays, Mum made fourteen different kinds of bread, including apple bread, treacle-bread, tea cakes, wheaten and soda farls, which she would shape into small triangles and put on the griddle. Breakfast was an Ulster fry-up: soda farls with bacon, eggs and potato bread. Everything she baked she shared with neighbours.

It's extraordinary to think of the amount of food she shovelled in! Cooked breakfast, cakes, bread, constant feeding…Yet, as a family, we were thin as rakes. When I was at school, I had the nickname 'Birdlegs' because they were just so thin. It's only in later years, of course, that you suddenly realise you were actually pretty fortunate. Thin legs are probably one of my best assets now, probably one of the better parts of me that's left. Of course I sometimes rode a bicycle twenty miles a day back then, which must have helped.

Even when I'd started school, there was no question of us staying there for lunch, which means that, essentially, Mum was cooking for the five of us all day long. Quite how she did it, I'll never know – our fridge was just a wooden box with a locking mesh in front, high up on the wall outside where Mum stored her meat and cheese.

Sometimes I wonder if she ever tired of the routine: Monday would be for washing, and Mum would wash everything by hand in a big tub with hot water from a gas boiler outside by the pigeon loft, and just a washboard for ringing out the dirty water – how I hated coming home from school on a wet day, clothes spread everywhere around the range on clothes horses. I can't stand the damp smell to this day. Tuesday would then be taken up with all the ironing, Wednesday would be for visiting with friends (especially a lifelong friend called Mrs Bond – although they knew one another for decades, they always addressed each other as Mrs Hunniford and Mrs Bond; they never used their first names) and then there would be all the other weekly tasks: changing the sheets, cleaning and dusting, and so on... In those days a woman's work was literally never done.

Once a year there would be an agricultural show held in the grounds of Portadown Football Club near where we lived. Farmers would show cows, chicken, sheep and pigs and there would be a huge marquee where baking and cooking went on, a sort of Northern Irish version of *The Great British Bake Off*. Both Mum and Lena would put in a lot of entries, submitting between twelve and fifteen items each. They'd be baking for days in advance. Judging took place the night before the show opened and Lena acted as a scout, sneaking in and finding out how Mum had done. She'd report back and if the outcome was good – 'You had five firsts, three seconds and two highly commended' – Mum would show up the next day and swan around the place, lapping up the glory. If she didn't do so well she wouldn't go at all!

My childhood accounts a great deal for my work ethic. When you are brought up with the Ulster ethic, you work. Historically, it has a very good record of few strikes and strong workers and that's the way we were raised. If my mother came along and saw me sitting in a chair doing nothing, she would say, 'Why are you sitting there not really doing very much? Go and play.' Or if we were reading a book she'd say, 'Go off and do something. When you're old you can sit in an armchair but not now'. These were innocent times and we were practically shoved out of the house after breakfast and never came back until lunch or dinner. We had great freedom, but we were always busy. I have always known what work is – I've always liked my work and I still have a zest for it. To this day, I'm very bad at relaxing, because I still hear my mother's voice saying, 'Go off and do something'.

★ ★ ★

We were a Protestant family in Northern Ireland and very typical of the times. There wasn't much to do except go to the pictures, as we called them. We were lucky we had three cinemas in Portadown, which changed their programme three times a week so we saw a lot of movies. Then, every Saturday morning there was the 'big picture' and the 'wee picture', usually Cowboys and Indians, and Laurel and Hardy. We looked forward to those outings every week. I also dragged my mum to the movies the odd evening but she moaned for weeks about having to sit in the front row craning her neck as I lapped up *The Glenn Miller Story* starring James Stewart and June Allyson. Little did I think that one day I would meet them in person. But wait, I'm going ahead of myself...

In Portadown, as in many similar towns, Protestants lived at one end of the town and Catholics on the other. It was the same with our schools too. I wasn't forced to go to church but I went five times on a Sunday – junior service in the morning, followed by senior service, then in the afternoon it was Sunday School and the evening service was after that, which was then followed by a prayer meeting. In case you think I was obsessed with religion, it was only because everything was closed on a Sunday so this was the only way I could meet up with my pals and of course the boys!

We never had babysitters: my older sister would look after me and then my younger brother too when he was born. But if that didn't work, Dad had priority to go out as the man of the house and Mum could only go out if he stayed in. If she wanted to go to, say, the Women's Institute, she couldn't if he was at his pigeon club. It was a macho life back then and I grew up with it, so to this day a little part of me still thinks that jobs are divided like that, between men and women.

At one point, my mother wanted to take a 'little job' in my cousin's bakery but I remember my dad declaring, 'No wife of mine will ever work. I will provide for the family.' That's how it was. Women were responsible for keeping the cupboards full of food and making sure the children were well-fed and well-slept; men put the bins out and worked in the garden. At the time, I couldn't understand my mum's accepting attitude to it all and can recall, when I was a little older, once asking her, 'Why don't you ever stand up for yourself?'.

'In the end, what does it matter?' she replied.

My first husband, Don, was very helpful and always did his bit around the house and with the children, but a part of me accepts that in Ireland, overall, it is still quite macho.

Mum really was happy and fulfilled in her role as a home-maker though and she was a fantastic mother to come home to. She was also the peacemaker and the only thing that ever seemed to faze her was thunderstorms. She was terrified of them:

'Get away from that window!' she'd tell us. 'Don't let the lightning hit you!'

She would take out every plug in the house, presumably because she thought it would get to us through the electricity sockets, and would shoo us under the kitchen table or into the cubbyhole under the stairs.

She was a wise woman though and I think ahead of her time in so many ways. A philosophy of my mum's has stood the test of time. If ever I had an argument with a friend or broke something precious, she'd ask, 'Is there anything you can do about it? Can you mend it, stick it or apologise? If you can, do it, don't leave any stone unturned. On the other hand if it's out of your control, let it go – it's negative energy.' Do you know, I still follow her advice today. Her other lovely phrase was, 'In life, you should always buy a good pair of shoes and a good bed because if you're not in one, you're in the other.'

Dad wouldn't tolerate bad behaviour in the house, either. Once, when I ignored his instructions not to touch the range because it was so hot and lingered a little too close by, he touched my finger briefly against the searing heat to teach me a lesson. On another occasion, I got a severe telling-off when I was playing by Dad's pigeon loft when the steps were slippery from the rain.

'Gloria, now, don't climb those steps, you'll fall,' he warned.

Of course I did climb them and I did fall and when I ran into the kitchen crying, I got very little sympathy but I certainly learned a lesson.

There was one sin above all that he would not tolerate: bad language. One night I had just had a bath and was sitting with sopping wet hair when I said, 'Oh frig.'

Dad froze.

'Sorry?' he said.

'Oh frig,' I repeated a little unwisely, not realising it was a swear word.

'Out!' he shouted, pointing at the door. I had never seen him looking so angry before.

'Why?' I asked disingenuously. 'I don't understand.'

'We don't use that kind of language in the house. Now get out!'

'Charlie, you can't send her out,' my mother protested, worried about my dripping wet hair. 'It's turning cold and she'll catch pneumonia.'

'Out, out, out!' roared my father.

I had to go and take shelter with a neighbour until Mum came to smuggle me back inside and straight up to my bedroom. Dad was just the same to Lena and my brother Charles too: on one occasion, after we'd got a black-and-white television, Charles refused to go to bed. Dad's solution was to make him sit in front of it all night and he wouldn't let Charles leave when he tried to sneak to bed at 2am. It was only around 2.30am that he finally relented and let my brother go to bed.

But I was very close to my father. One thing that I remember very strongly was that one-to-one relationship on a Saturday morning, which was precious to me. We were a cycling family – I was given my own bicycle one memorable Christmas – so he and I would cycle down to this little ice cream shop called Bacci's, run by this Italian family, for pineapple ice cream. It was actually just ice cream with a bit of crushed pineapple mixed through it, but I thought it was the greatest thing I had ever tasted. But even better was having Dad all to myself on those outings, with Lena and Charles at home.

I truly had a joyful childhood and marvellous parents; I always knew I was loved, which, as you get older, means so much. Of course, all of this was before the Troubles began, and back then the only frightening aspect to life were the B-Specials, the Ulster Special Constabulary, which had been formed in the 1920s to deal with the growing issue of Irish Nationalism. I was terrified of them. They used to have shiny red torches and I heard stories that if you didn't stop for them, they'd shoot you. If we were ever coming home late at night I used to quake at the thought of what would happen if the driver didn't see them and didn't stop.

I was too young to remember much about the Second World War but I do recall the blackout curtains and trying on the gas masks, which we kept in a cupboard by the bed. I already mentioned that my father was a pigeon fancier and, even during the war, he tracked them every weekend in races. The drawback I remember as a child was that we weren't allowed to have pets in case they scared the pigeons when they were landing! I have very vivid memories of a huge truck arriving on a Friday to pick up baskets of pigeons, which were then driven to the start of the race. I still find it incredible that these birds would be dropped off as far afield as France and yet turn up at our loft the next day. The timing was crucial and my dad wouldn't waste a second to take the rings off the pigeons and in to the clock to register their time. It was only later that I realised my dad's hobby played a far more important role: there was a soldier permanently based on my dad's pigeon loft, where it turned out he would send secret messages to the forces on the front line in France. In return, Dad was given meal for his pigeons by the Ministry of Defence. At the end of the war, a letter arrived from a brigadier thanking my dad for this and for the pigeons, so a teenager hobby became a worthwhile war effort. In fact, in 2005, we were invited to a National Flying Club dinner at the House of Commons where, to my surprise, the MC stood up and talked about a silver cup which my husband Stephen had organised, engraved with the words 'In memory of Charles Hunniford', which has since become an annual prize. How proud my dad would have been, his cup launched in the House of Commons.

* * *

Perhaps my favourite childhood memories are of Christmas. By tradition, we went to my paternal grandparents' farm on Christmas Eve. They lived about a mile away from us and all the family would congregate there in the small sitting room. One year my Granny Hunniford gave me a fairy doll with flaxen hair, wings and a white satin dress dotted with silver sequins – I can remember it even now and in fact kept it for years. I'd fallen asleep on the settee clutching my doll, and then I was woken up to walk the mile home. It was a frosty

17

night and fir trees sparkled with a dusting of snow-like frost. My father broke off a branch and when we got home, he put it in a pot in the parlour by the open-lit fire then clipped little candles in holders to it and hung the doll over the top like an angel. I thought I'd never seen anything so beautiful. Then we hung up our stockings by the fireplace, watched over by my fairy on our improvised tree, twinkling in the light of the candles. Bliss!

My dad was always up for a bit of a joke and that night he built a man in the parlour out of old pillows and sheets, dressed with a hat and scarf, and drew a cord round its waist back to his bedroom. When he heard us go downstairs early on Christmas morning, he pulled the string making the man's arm shoot up – and sending us shooting back up the stairs like crazy. We were delightfully scared that Christmas and certainly never forgot it.

Granny and Grandad Hunniford didn't have a very big house but their sitting room was entirely taken up by the most enormous gleaming mahogany table, which my grandad lovingly polished every day. All manner of life went on round that table and every Sunday night the family played whist. It was tradition. In fact, I knew I'd arrived in the card stakes when my mum said to me one time, 'Could you take over my hand while I help with the supper?'. I ended up as a pretty good whist player. They were happy times. I remember chats with my grandad so well; he was an ex-serviceman with many gleaming medals and he used to march proudly in the yearly parade in Portadown, displaying that military upright straight back. He lived until he was ninety-six; he swore it was the tot of whiskey he drank every night that kept him going!

I had a fantastic relationship with all of my grandparents.

Sadly I never knew my maternal grandfather as he died before I was born. My mother's mother, Granny McCann, meanwhile, was an imposing figure; a statuesque woman with a strong-looking face, always wearing ruby and diamond rings, and with a collection of ruby glasses and fine antique furniture. She lived on a farm at the end of a meandering lane four miles outside Portadown so every Wednesday and Saturday without fail she'd visit us in town and sit at the parlour window, watching everyone go by. This she loved because she lived in a dead-end road and few people passed her window, but she expected my poor mother to know everyone who went past the house, 'Who is that, May, who is that?' she'd query regularly.

We'd visit her on the farm and used the donkey she kept in the orchard for our games of Cowboys and Indians. In fact, in 2016 I returned to my granny's farm after sixty-two years for a TV programme. I can't tell you how emotional it was. The structure of the house outside was still the same, and although the inside had been redesigned, the long hall that ran across the front of the house was still there and I could still visualise the old butter churn in one of the rooms where Granny made milk and cheese. Some of the other rooms off the hall had been turned into bedrooms, but I could still see how they once were, with stores of the food and animal feed.

We loved the haymaking season on the farm, when it always seemed to be sunny, in my recollection at least. The long grass was cut and laid out to dry; huge pitchforks tossed the hay and it was made into haystacks. Granny would make her way through the hayfield, carrying a huge double-lidded wicker basket, lined with red-and-white gingham and full of mouth-watering goodies straight from the oven: hot bread dripping with butter and fairy cakes covered in runny icing, accompanied by farm mugs of steaming tea. Food never tasted so good.

The most exciting moment came when the haystacks were moved to the hayloft: my mum's brother, Uncle Geordie drove the tractor which pulled the hay shift and we would load the stacks and then jump on the end to drive back to the farm. There were no safety regulations back then; we thought it was such great fun.

Granny had a great, stone-flagged kitchen with an Irish pine dresser and an inglenook fireplace that was so big we could stand in the middle of it and look up and see the sky. There was a giant cast-iron contraption across, from which two huge black cauldrons hung over the flames, one used to make bubbling soups or stews and the other to boil potato skins or slops for the pigs and chickens. In the evening, we would light oil lamps or candles, and we'd sit around and gossip in the flickering light. Often, one of the neighbours, Jack, would come in and chew tobacco and when he was done, he'd spit his tobacco with unerring aim right into the middle of the fire. Heaven help you if you got in his way.

Sometimes we stayed overnight and when I was a small child Granny would come with me to the end room where I slept, because the shadows created by the single oil lamp shining down on to the big sacks of baking flour and wheaten meal would make me afraid. But once I was there I would climb into the huge antique brass bed and snuggle down under the soft feather eiderdown and be off to the Land of Nod.

One day, when I would have been around ten years old, I remember coming home from school and I knew something was wrong straightaway. Granny had died of a stroke.

That was the first time I had encountered death and I didn't really understand what was going on. Mum was usually such a sunny person, but her face was crumpled with pain and she wept for days. I felt almost as desolate seeing her like this as I did about Granny and we all wept with her, for her as much as for Granny. I remember Lena and I made endless cups of tea, while Dad made hot whiskey toddies, the traditional Irish remedy for absolutely every crisis, no matter how dire.

At that time in Ireland it was quite normal to stand the coffin up in the corner of the room while the neighbours came in to socialise, in the form of singing and dancing. Granny was actually laid out in the bedroom and as was the custom at that time we were all expected to go in and pay our own last respects. Lena held my hand as we climbed up to the room, holding a candle to light our way as we neared the old four poster.

'Doesn't she look so peaceful?' Lena said.

I didn't want to see her like that at all, though. I wanted her back, coming to see us every Wednesday and Saturday.

Granny's friends also came to pay their respects and put on a bit of a hooley in the farmhouse kitchen. As a small child, this was particularly hard to understand; I just saw that they were eating and cracking jokes and I wanted them all to go home.

As it was my first experience of seeing a dead person I just didn't want Granny to leave us. Who would visit us now in Portadown every week and give me the odd two and sixpence to spend on white socks or ice cream?

★ ★ ★

We didn't have a lot but I always knew we were luckier than most. While, at home, I shared a double bed with my sister, my brother slept in a single bed in my parents' room and at night Dad would go and lie down beside him to help him to get to sleep. In fact, I remember when we got electricity in the house. Having previously been used to the old gas mantles on the walls and lighting them every night, we thought we'd gone to Hollywood!

Of course, back in those days no one would dream of going on holidays abroad and I never knew anyone who went to Italy or Spain. Instead, we used to take our trips to the little town of Newcastle, in County Down, where, as the Percy French song had it, 'the Mountains of Mourne sweep down to the sea'.

Growing up in Portadown, this small Irish Sea town was our nearest resort, and it was always a treat to go there. We normally stayed in a caravan, so small we had to get up from bed in the morning to slot in the table to eat off. But one particular time – my dad must have had a better year than usual – we were able to stay in a B&B opposite the beach. I must have been eight or nine at the time, and I thought we'd become millionaires!

Every year though, good or bad, we got new knitted swimsuits for our holidays, usually navy and white-striped – of course, when we got into the water they became so heavy they began to sag. Dad never had a car, so we would travel there on the steam train. In Mum's suitcase she would have more home-baked breads and cakes than she would clothes. But oh, the expectations we had on that train journey!

In the mornings, we would usually have a cooked breakfast and then walk into Newcastle, which was about a mile away, where we'd stay on that beach, rain, hail or shine, with a packed lunch and, if we were lucky, an ice cream. There was a wonderful hotel there called the Slieve Donard, and I used to say to my mum:

'Please, please can we go into that hotel and just have a cup of tea?'

'No, darling, that hotel is only for posh people,' she'd reply.

We never did go in (though I've made up for it since and stay there regularly now – I always think my mum would have liked to have seen that I made it).

Dad yearned for further horizons, though: I find it poignant now that he used to fantasise about Alan Whicker's job. He even looked a little like Alan Wicker, with his glasses, suave moustache and slightly greying hair.

'Look at the travel you'd get, the people you'd meet. A journalist, that would be the job for me.'

And he was right; I've experienced that ever since.

He was a big dreamer and I think this was where his love of magic came from, and where I got my flair for performance. I was definitely the show-off in the family; I would enter the competitions held on a great big bandstand on the beach, and sing. I won a few, for which the prize was a pound, which we thought was luxury. When we got home, Dad persuaded the pianist at the shows he performed his magic in to teach me some songs…and, as a seven-year-old, my life was to take a course I could only have dreamed of.

CHAPTER 2

DAFFODIL TEAS AND MEAT SUPPERS

My dad belonged to the Mid-Ulster Variety Group, which was an amalgam of all sorts of entertainers, ranging from comics and accordion players, to singers, dancers and magicians. Before the concert began, the ladies of the community would set up trestle tables throughout the hall and teas would be served: sandwiches, scones, cakes, apple tarts, all washed down with gallons of tea served in great silver urns.

The tables would be groaning with vases of daffodils during the spring, and they became known as Daffodil Teas during that part of the year; otherwise they were called Meat Suppers. These were all together more formal affairs: sit-down knife and fork dinners, lit by Tilley lamps, with Irish stew or ham and salad, the ham cut so thinly you could see the pattern on the plate.

Despite the simple food, the hammy old jokes that were

sometimes a bit cheesy, the occasional collapse of a trestle table and entertainment that was sometimes a little bit amateur, the audience loved it, laughing and cheering until tears ran down their cheeks. The mood was so very good-natured and the people so open-hearted that even now they bring a smile to my face.

When I was a little girl, of course, they were glamorous too and I saw them sitting in the audience before I actually started taking part myself. I begged Dad to take me along and he sometimes even let me watch from the wings, open-mouthed in awe at the beautiful women in their sequins and all the lovingly polished musical instruments. The compère, George Nixon, would come on and introduce the troupe: then they'd all sing 'Happy Days Are Here Again'. A fiddle player or an accordionist called Joe McVeigh would come on, followed by some slapstick comedy, such as shoving a hot water bottle down the trousers. Two sisters would tap dance to the 'Lullaby of Broadway' in their rainbow tulle dresses, which I longed for; someone would recite 'Albert and the Lion', there would be a tenor, a comic, a couple of bell-ringers called Ken and Eddy Bush and perhaps a schoolteacher, McKay Kenny, reading from one of the great poets, to provide a highbrow touch to it all.

But for me the undoubted star of the evening was Dad. He'd be there in his top hat and tails, performing sleights of hand that I could never work out, even after hours of poking around in his magic tricks cupboard when he was safely out of the house. And then one night he suddenly asked, 'How would you like to come up on stage when the group sings the National Anthem?' My heart was pounding when I climbed up and, holding on to Dad's hand, belted my heart out on stage. The sound of my voice ringing out, followed by applause from the very generous audience, convinced me this was 'my future'. All that singing into the wireless and winning those seaside talent competitions had paid off. I knew what I was going to do in life.

My official debut came on 9 April 1947, the day before my seventh birthday, in Cloncore Orange Hall in Portadown. I was dressed in yellow taffeta, with a few silver sequins – all we could afford – scattered around the frill of the neck and I was hoisted on to the stage by Dad. My first number was 'Powder Your Face With Sunshine', which I performed complete with hand gestures and a non-stop beam on my face, then followed up with 'A – You're Adorable, B – You're So Beautiful', until I had exhausted the alphabet. I was loving every second of it and felt completely at ease: by the time I got round to 'Buttons and Bows' I really didn't want to leave the stage.

Someone produced a hat and there was a quick whip-round. I had earned the princely sum of seven shillings and sixpence, a fortune. It was my very first fee.

Soon I was singing on the public stage in churches, schools and concerts across the whole of Ireland. I was making a bit of money and when I was ten, I brought in £8 one week, which was quite a lot for a child to be earning at that time. I was fortunate to be able to keep it all and I remember buying new sandals and a mock suede jacket for £4 out of my earnings.

I had become quite the seasoned performer when I was still a very young girl. And I think that early experience of performing is why I have little or no fear of an audience now. There are some presenters who can broadcast to 10 million people but couldn't face 100 of them in person but I have never been like that. I suppose the concerts got me used to my own voice introducing my songs.

We would parade like a modern-day troupe of wandering troubadours through village halls, church halls and schools throughout Northern Ireland. This was in the days before television and so we were wildly popular, setting ourselves up in the biggest building in the village and using whatever was available in order to perform.

Often the venues lacked the most basic facilities. Frequently there were no loos, so I would have to use a field, someone coming to watch over me, or as we put it back then, 'keep dick'. The dew-drenched grass would soak my long satin dress, something I would try to ignore when I got up on stage. Sometimes there would be a proper stage in situ and sometimes we'd have to make one up out of trestle tables. We'd always hope there would be a piano ready for us too; sadly, at times there would be nothing and we'd have to get some of the burliest men in the village to haul a set of ivories out of a local house in order to allow us to perform.

I soon became addicted to performing. Every Saturday morning I jumped out of bed at the crack of dawn and rushed down to the shops, because that was when the new sheet music came in. My grandchildren would say, 'What is sheet music?', but it really was the equivalent of picking up a new CD nowadays. From there I'd race on to Gail Sheridan, the concert party pianist, and we would rehearse the new numbers.

The first time I ever watched television was at my neighbour Mrs McCracken's house, who was the first person on our road to have this exotic contraption; in fact, the whole street crowded into her front room to watch the Queen's

Coronation. I visited her a lot and I got my inspiration for my costumes by watching *Come Dancing* on her big television. I wasn't really interested in the dancing: it was the thousands of sequins on the dresses that I loved. I would sit mesmerized as the light caught all the sparkles as the dancers twirled around, and I would try to imagine having to sew or stick all the glitter on. Then I'd take my ideas to my dad's sister, Auntie Myrtle, who would make my stage clothes: she worked magic on her sewing machine and could make an exact replica of anything I'd seen on the show or any cuttings I showed her from a fashion magazine, right down to the starched net petticoats. In fact, she was so clever that she would've fitted into any haute couture atelier in Paris.

I also bought some silver tap shoes tied with bows and white ankle socks. Even back then I was aware of the importance of appearance and how I should look the part.

However the money and attention made me a little too pleased with myself at times.

'Mum, I need new socks and vests,' I said on one occasion.

'I'm sorry, Gloria, I can't afford it this week. You'll have to wait.'

'Well then,' I retorted, tossing my head back. 'I'm going to buy them myself.'

I was lucky Mum didn't give me a slap!

As you may have guessed, I was very independent from a young age and by now, with the fees I was earning, I was looking after myself. I liked the feeling of being able to pay my way. I'd worked most of my life and never expected anyone to work for me; it applies even now.

★ ★ ★

It was around this time that I came home from school one day to find a gorgeous tall man with white hair standing at our front door.

'Who's that?' I whispered to Mum.

'Gloria, this is your Great-uncle Jim.'

He was my mum's uncle and he truly was a lovely man: he had emigrated to Canada forty years earlier and no one had heard of him since then. Now he'd come back to find his old family. Jim lived in a place called Gananoque, near Kingston, Ontario. He had made good for himself: he had an electrical contracting business and was quite wealthy. In post-war Northern Ireland his stories about Canada sounded incredible, so much so that I became obsessed with it. He told us about towering mountains, limitless prairies, Eskimos and Indians (as they were known back then) and what an enormous country it was. Then came the *pièce de résistance*: he opened his bag and out tumbled aromatic fruits, nuts and all manner of sweets. There was still rationing in place in Northern Ireland and from that moment onwards, I always associated him with the land of milk and honey.

Jim stayed with us for a couple of months and on Sundays he took me to the Quaker meetings. They had come from a Quaker family, although Mum gave it up when she got married to Dad. I was fascinated as the congregation sat in complete silence, until suddenly someone would get up and say a prayer, or sing a song, or quote a passage from the Scriptures.

'Why don't you sing?' Uncle Jim whispered.

'I'm used to an introduction,' I said in a panicky whisper.

'It doesn't work that way here,' he reassured me. 'When there's a silence, just do whatever moves you.'

And so after a little while, I stood up and sang a hymn I'd learned in Sunday School. Uncle Jim looked so pleased and proud that I sang a few more. It always amused me that nothing happened until 'the spirit moved them' but I have always had great respect for the Quaker Movement, which is constantly generous with their warmth and invitations back to lunch after church.

After that Uncle Jim took a real interest in me and as the end of the summer approached and he prepared to go back to Canada, I heard him talking to my mother.

'You know, Gloria has great potential, May. Why don't you let her come back to Canada with me? I'll educate her – I promise you she'll have all the very best opportunities.'

Not realising just how far away Canada was I was absolutely thrilled at the idea but Mum was adamant: absolutely not. No Irish mother would be letting her young daughter go all the way across the ocean and so the answer was a firm no. I ran to my bedroom and burst into tears. Didn't she know she was ruining my life? I didn't realise then that Canada would feature in my future far sooner than I could have imagined...

★ ★ ★

But back to then: I settled into a routine of singing and school, and that was pretty much the way it was to be for the next six years. We went everywhere on our bikes or our roller skates, which were just metal wheels tied to our existing shoes. When we travelled around with the troupe, all of us would cram into the few available cars and I would sit on Dad's knee in the back of an old Morris 8. With his encouragement I kept a record of what I did in my Show Work Book: 'Lisbellaw, Wednesday, 12 January, 1951,' one entry starts off. 'Sang "Happy Wanderer",

"This Ole House", "The Little Shoemaker". Wore my white organza dress. In luck! Paid 15 shillings!'

I was sometimes out performing up to five nights a week, occasionally not getting home until 2am. Mum would always be waiting up for me with a cup of tea and sandwiches, peering anxiously through the Venetian blinds at the parlour window until we returned. She'd put me in my pyjamas and tuck me into bed, and then she'd wake me up five hours later to send me to school. I knew Mum worried about me being out so late at night – like me she was worried about the B-Specials in the border areas of Armagh, Fermanagh and Tyrone. They would flash torches in our faces and demand, 'Who are you? Where have you been? Where are you going?' Their main role was to keep the peace around the border, but now they were also on the look out for smugglers. Southern Ireland had been neutral in the Second World War and unlike in the North, there was no rationing.

And yes, we did stock up on goods from across the border: instead of needing a coupon, as we did in the North, we could just walk into a shop in the South of Ireland and buy what we wanted. We had plentiful supplies of chickens, eggs and fruit from my granny's farm, but there was a lot we couldn't get. Like all children I adored sweets and chocolate, and there was a variety in the sweet shops that was unfathomable in the North. It was like walking into an Aladdin's cave. There were all types of chocolate and sweets and, in particular, marshmallow Easter eggs, which I loved. My pals at school loved them as well. Dad's magic box, meanwhile, came into its own: the secret panel which on stage concealed his doves, scarves and card tricks was now filled with butter, sugar and bacon.

With no magic box other than Dad's I remember my mum on a train trip back from Dublin hiding her treasured new shoes in her rather large knickers. When the train crossed the border customs men boarded and searched. Then – tragedy struck. They discovered Mum's secret and she was marched off and told to hand over the shoes. She was far more offended at losing the shoes than the embarrassment of being hiked off the train! Oh yes, we knew all sides of smuggling over the Irish border.

I often look back at this time in terms of my own children and think, would I have let them travel around the country at the age of eight or nine? I don't think so, but I was supervised by my dad and somehow or other it was just different back then. Sometimes I wasn't going to bed until one or two in the morning, and I was up at seven for school the next day, but it didn't seem to do me any harm. In fact, it probably stood me in good stead for the future.

★ ★ ★

It wasn't all plain sailing, though. Just after I entered my teens, Portadown was invaded by an army of American evangelists, led by Billy Graham. My friends and I were fascinated by the colourful revival tents, rousing gospel songs and charismatic preachers, delivering their message in that hypnotic American drawl, so very different from my own Church of Ireland church and the Quaker meetings Uncle Jim had taken me to.

That first revival meeting in a local packed Presbyterian church made a huge impact on me. A commanding figure in a new black silk suit strode out to an audience of zealous converts, eager hopefuls and sceptical curiosity seekers, which at that point included us, and issued a message of hope, mercy and forgiveness, delivered with confidence and bravado. We had been raised on guilt in the hell, fire and brimstone tradition of Protestant churches of Northern Ireland. This seemed so much more uplifting to me, and there was certainly a tinge of glamour because they all came from America.

The preacher called upon the congregation to accept the Lord as our personal saviour before all our friends and neighbours.

'Come forward,' he said. 'Cleanse your souls, wash yourselves in the blood of the Lamb.' I felt myself involuntarily rising and walking forward, my feet scarcely touching the ground. I got to the front of the church and at that moment, I was 'born again'.

Back at home that night, I explained it to my tolerant mum and dad, who seemed to take it quite calmly.

'Fine, if that's what you want,' said Mum. 'Just as long as you realise what you're doing.'

I swallowed.

'Of course, you know I can't sing any more,' I said.

'Why not?' asked Dad.

'I couldn't possibly carry on going to public entertainments.'

My parents wisely didn't say too much as I immersed myself in prayer meetings and Bible study. All that joyous dancing and singing was in the past as they were made out to be terribly sinful – I must have been quite unbearable.

Gradually, though, I began to notice that some of my fundamentalist friends had been sneaking off to the pictures in Belfast. Movie-going might have been a sin in Portadown, but not, it seemed, in a big city far away. Dad bided his time and then one day said, 'Don't you think God gave you your voice to sing with?'

He was absolutely right.

* * *

I quickly went back to singing – to the delight of my mum and dad – and attracted some attention through my performances with the Mid-Ulster Variety Group and now I began to broaden my horizons, singing with some dance bands, which were huge business in Ireland at the time.

My ambitions were getting grander and my success only made me more determined so I began to push even more boundaries.

My parents didn't want me to go to grammar school because we didn't have that much spare money and they thought uniforms and books would cost too much. Instead, they wanted me to do a secretarial course at the local college like my sister. But, again with big ideas, I fought tooth and nail for the opportunity to go to our highly regarded grammar school in Portadown. By now I was semi-professional and was earning good money but I always wanted to have an education – I was definitely a modern girl. So when my parents said we couldn't afford the uniforms and books, I just said haughtily that I could pay for them myself with my singing fees.

But for some reason my talent on stage didn't seem to spill over into my studies at Portadown College, and that was despite the fact that they had a good drama and music department. I was only ever once asked to sing in Assembly and that was 'She Wears Red Feathers And A Hooley-Hooley Skirt', which had been a hit for Guy Mitchell. It was an odd choice and perhaps the reason I wasn't asked to sing again.

I enjoyed my time at school though. One of my classmates was Mary Peters, the former Olympic gold medallist (no wonder I always came last in sports at school!). She was later to recall, on *This Is Your Life*, the time that I beat her in a non-stop talking competition that went on for eleven and a half hours! Is it any wonder I went into broadcasting?

One of my best friends back then was called Anne Downey and together we broadened our horizons by secretly reading 'dirty books', which we considered to be decadent beyond belief. One of these was *Lady Chatterley's Lover*, which she would sneak out of her locker and we'd giggle over it in her sitting room, using her geography books for cover. Alas for her, the next morning Anne came late into Assembly without realising the book was sticking out of her blazer pocket, with the title clearly visible to the rest of the school. Late afternoons in detention became a regular feature for her after that.

However, by the time I was fifteen, my time at the college was nearing its end. I had done well in my junior levels and passed in all fifteen subjects, but when I showed my results to Dad, he said, 'You're not going on to the senior level, are you?'

'Of course I am,' I said, but I could sense there was trouble brewing.

'Do you want to be a teacher? No. Do you want to be a doctor? No. Well then, what's the point? You've had your four years there. Look, if you go to technical college there's a course for grammar school students where you don't concentrate on the academics but the secretarial skills. That will stand you in very good stead. Look at your sister.' Lena was by now working in a top solicitor's office.

It was clear Dad had my best interests at heart – he'd left

school early himself and had done wonders for his family, but I was still terribly disappointed. My headmaster Donald Woodman was horrified: when he learned that my parents were planning to send me to Portadown Technical School, he cycled to our house to make his protest in person.

'Mr Hunniford,' he cried, as he burst through the door, his long black cloak billowing behind him, 'I am frankly horrified to learn that Gloria won't be coming back to do her senior certificate. I just don't believe it. This girl is university material. Why are you saying she can't return?'

'Because she's been at grammar school for four years now and we think it's time for her to move on to technical college and do other things.'

'But this is absurd!' cried my headmaster. 'She could go on to university, she could do anything!'

But my father was not to be moved. I cried myself to sleep at night and my friends all commiserated but there was nothing I could do. Remember, in those days you did what your parents told you and my dad was certainly the boss of the household.

As it happened, the skills I learned at Portadown Technical College were to serve me well in my future career. I learned shorthand, typing and book-keeping, all of which I used when I became a journalist and, unlike grammar school, the college encouraged me to sing. I was cast as the judge in Gilbert and Sullivan's *Trial by Jury* and managed to bring the show to a halt. This wasn't with my singing, mind, but because as I was in the middle of 'For I am a judge and a good judge too,' I threw a heavy tome at the clerk of the court and knocked him senseless! Thankfully, Colin Baxter lived to sing another day and continued to be a great family friend.

Then my big break came when, aged sixteen, the singer

with The Fred Hanna's Show Band fell ill and they asked me to step in at the magnificent City Hall, Belfast. Now I had arrived! This was in quite a different league from the small town locations in which I'd previously performed. I'd never even been in the City Hall before that: I'd only seen it from the bus, looking through the windows at the imposing building with its marble staircases, balustrades and a ballroom complete with chandeliers. Auntie Myrtle returned to the sewing machine and created a beautiful pink strapless ballgown with a tiny waist and big skirt covered in embroidered rosebuds. I earned £16 for two nights' work – it felt like winning the lottery.

★ ★ ★

Although I had been disappointed to have to leave school, there were other compensations and my horizons were widening. By now I was sixteen and had started going to dances at the Savoy Ballroom in Portadown centre, a very glamorous local venue with glittering mirror balls hanging down from the ceiling – just like *Strictly*. It was a very formal affair: the boys would come up to you and ask, 'Would you like to dance?' It was considered terribly rude to turn anyone down, so if there was someone you fancied, you'd place yourself in their line of vision. There was a dark-haired boy that I'd seen at school called Desi, a good sportsman who was a bit older than me, and I'd fancied him for some time. He'd never paid any attention to me previously, but when I dolled myself up in Aunt Myrtle's latest creation to go to the dance, he finally began to notice me.

After flirting and dancing at the Savoy, finally the thrilling night arrived when he 'left me home'. We walked hand in hand back to my house on the edge of town and shared our very first kiss as we lingered at the gate.

Unfortunately I was an hour and a half late. To my dismay, I heard my mum yell from the front door, 'Gloria, come in this very minute!', leaving me wanting to die of embarrassment.

But it didn't dampen my feelings, nor his. Desi was my first love and there were many more kisses to come.

Owning a car was a luxury that no-one I'd known before then could afford, but Desi's father had a Morris Minor, which seemed the height of sophistication to me and all my friends. Desi, to his great credit, taught me to drive, which gave us the opportunity to have a quick grope in the back of the car. But that was the furthest you would ever go back in those days. So lacking were we in our sexual education, some of us thought a girl could get pregnant through her knickers! From the time of being a young teenager my dad's words rang loudly in my ears: 'Save yourself for the man you eventually marry'. And that's exactly what I did.

I was still singing whenever I could but, after I graduated from college, when I was still just sixteen, I was eager to go out into the world of work. My first summer job was as a shorthand typist for the Eagle Star Insurance Company, where I'd been headhunted by a man called Andy Trotter. I worked with a girl called Margaret Titterington and we had a grand time together: when Andy was out we'd get fish and chips from across the street and then frantically try to get rid of the smell before he or anyone else (namely the clients) returned. When it was sunny we'd sit with our heads stuck out through the sash windows to try and get a tan and, as Margaret had just got married, she liked to keep tabs on my own romantic life.

Desi was still around, but so too was a tall and slim young man by the name of Jack McNally. He first turned up to ask about a motor policy, but before long his visits were becoming increasingly regular, with the motor policy totally forgotten about. We became great friends and ultimately Jack was to inherit a beautiful farmhouse and acreage in a village called Richhill in County Armagh. It was very different from my own family's small two-up two-down and I used to love visiting Jack and his family, taking walks through the fields and enjoying the sensation of space, while he carried out his farming duties nearby.

His mother had created a beautiful garden, complete with gorgeous bright red geraniums trailing around the conservatory, and Jack and I used to sit in there with our cups of tea, teasing each other that if our relationships didn't work out then we would end our days lying in bath chairs in the conservatory.

In the event Jack married a great girl called Flo, a marriage that was a very happy one, and they made a great life together in that beautiful house. As I get older I increasingly think about how important young relationships and friendships are and continue to shape my life.

However, back then I was out in the big wide world and I wanted to make the most of myself, especially when it came to clothes. I had always loved fashion and Auntie Myrtle's sewing machine was in constant use as she made dresses inspired by the fashions and trends that Margaret and I would cut out of glossy magazines. I was still singing and now I also had a regular salary so I could afford something more on the odd occasion when I was able to splash out. There was a very upmarket shop called Renee Meneely just below our office and a long-suffering sales assistant used to let me, a scrawny little sixteen-year-old, try on beautiful ball gowns made of silk and satin and taffeta and all manner of luxurious materials that I could only dream about.

One day I spotted a particularly beautiful dress with yards and yards of skirt over lots of net petticoats, and a boned strapless top with a freestanding frill at the bust line. It had a cream background with beautiful splashes of orange flowers, the most stunning and sophisticated gown I had ever seen. I went into the shop every day for a week to try it on and I finally decided that I had to have it: it took weeks and weeks of wages to pay for it but it was worthwhile. Auntie Myrtle never really forgave me for buying from a shop but it was one of the most gorgeous dresses I have ever owned in my life. I wore it to singing engagements and parties, and kept it in the loft for many years afterwards. And one day a long time later, I was utterly thrilled when my daughter Caron, who had always teased me about my conventional tastes, wore it to her very first formal dance.

★ ★ ★

And so my life looked set to follow a conventional path: a job until I married and had children and settled down as a good Ulster housewife. Instead, it was to take a very different turn.

I had never forgotten my Uncle Jim's visit to Northern Ireland when I was nine years old, though, and he'd stayed in touch; he'd sent countless letters asking me when I was going to come out to Canada, something I had been fantasising about for years. And then, when I was seventeen, a friend from Portadown emigrated there. He became a Canadian Mountie, and he would send me letters talking about his new life and photographs in his magnificent Mountie uniform, firing my imagination. It all sounded too thrilling and romantic for words and I became absolutely obsessed.

I'd been saving my money quietly on the side – it didn't all go on beautiful silk dresses! – and as I approached my eighteenth birthday, I made up my mind: I was going to emigrate to Canada. I had never been out of Ireland before – the furthest I'd been was just over the border to Dundalk or Dublin with the troupe but I decided to leave on the now infamous '£10 passage', as it was known then.

I summoned up all my courage and went to talk to Mum and Dad.

'I'd like to go to Canada,' I said.

'How long for?' asked Mum.

'Maybe six months – or perhaps a year,' I said, before quickly pointing out that I would be perfectly safe, in the bosom of my extended family, and that I was a working girl now, who could look after herself. On reflection, I'd have been petrified if my children or grandchildren wanted to do that at the age I was! Though neither of my parents were thrilled, they eventually gave in on the understanding that I would only stay until Christmas.

'We don't want to get a letter saying you're staying another two months and then another two months...' said Dad.

Dad and my younger brother Charles came to see me off. They were standing on the quayside as the ship set sail and I saw Dad break down in tears as we moved off. I got quite a pang: what had I done? But I had to swallow that and embrace my decision.

Apparently Charles missed me quite a lot after I'd left; I used to help him with his homework and Lena was already long gone from the family home, so now it was just him. When we were much older, Charles told me that he thought our parents had done the right thing in letting me off the leash and sending me out on my own with just $50 in my purse to take me to my new life.

Not that I was thinking along those lines at all at the time: it was all a huge adventure and I was soon to see sights I could only have imagined before.

As I had never left the shores of Northern Ireland, even the trip from Belfast to Liverpool was exciting. Then I transferred on to the ocean-going *Empress of Canada*, and headed for our final destinations: Quebec and Montreal. It was an ambitious thing for a seventeen-year-old to do and was so exhilarating, but for the first few days I suffered very badly from sea sickness. The Irish Sea was so rough I was even wondering if I could get in touch with my parents to somehow come and get me but fortunately, on the third day, a member of the crew intervened. I was sharing a cabin with a few girls for the journey and he told one of my room mates, a girl called Janet Barker, 'Listen, if she doesn't get up on deck she'll be in that bunk for the rest of the voyage.' It was good advice. I felt better as soon as I had a whiff of the sea air – and the ship's doctor gave me a dose of seasickness pills and an injection, which quickly sorted me out. I often think back on being that cosseted seventeen-year old, sharing a cabin with total strangers – I'd never known such freedom!

There were lots of young people on the boat actually, including a gang of boys from New Zealand. Once I had recovered, we'd all play games together, running around the ship, teasing each other and telling stories.

It took seven days to reach Canada and I remember celebrating my eighteenth birthday at sea, with the crew throwing me a party, and organising a cake, party and even presents.

It was a long journey but to date it was the best holiday I'd ever experienced. There were fancy dress parties and cinema screenings, and while I'd constantly gone to the flicks back at home, those films were all several months or even several years old. Now, on the ship, it felt like we were watching a series of Hollywood premieres. It was wildly exciting to see *Gigi* before it ever got as far as Portadown and it became a firm favourite of mine. Then all eyes were on its star, Leslie Caron, and little did I know that I would meet her and name my daughter after her.

There was so much to do, too. It was luxury. The cuisine was also new and exciting: I'd never seen such things as lobster stroganoff, chocolate mousse and parfait, along with exotic fruits such as papaya and pomegranate. It was a long way from our Northern Irish fare and my lovely mum's home cooking.

★ ★ ★

It was spring when we approached Canada and the *Empress* was the first ship to sail up the St Lawrence River after the icebreaker ship, which meant we passed massive, towering icebergs. Everything was just on such a huge scale, and quite overwhelming for a small-town Irish girl like me. The captain would call us to the deck to watch the frolicking seals and dolphins as we sailed towards Quebec.

Finally the ship docked and we got off, at long last stepping on to dry land with wobbly legs after a week at sea. I was with the girls from my cabin and we all went in to a pub where everyone was shouting at us in French. It was only later we realised it was a men-only bar! Nothing daunted, we went on to explore the walled French city, which was still covered with inches of snow, and then toured Chateau Frontenac and the old town. After a week spent bonding at sea, the group of us felt like soulmates as we explored this incredible new world.

We then got back on the ship and sailed on to my final destination, Montreal, where I was picked up by my great-uncle, who vouched for me at Immigration – 'guaranteed me' as it was known. I felt sad to be leaving my new-found friends, though we all wished each other well and promised to stay in touch.

Uncle Jim was as tall and handsome as I'd remembered, but he couldn't believe how much I'd grown – the last time he'd seen me I was only a nine-year-old child.

We drove southwest along the St Lawrence River, and I was just beginning to understand the size of this brave new world: we had been travelling in the car for two hours when he showed me a map.

'How big is Ireland?' he asked.

'Oh,' I said, 'big. It would take you three to four days to drive it.'

He then pointed to Lake Superior.

'You know what? You could put the whole of Ireland into that lake and still have room left over.'

It was the first time I realised how small Ireland was and that I was over 3,000 miles from home.

A few hours later we were in the main city of Kingston, and then we carried on to Gananoque, known as the Gateway to the Thousand Islands. Jim's daughter Beth lived there in a beautiful house with her children who were near my age, and it had been decided that I should spend a couple of days there to get my bearings.

I actually got off to a rather shaky start as I was suffering from a bad throat infection. Fortunately, Beth's husband was a doctor but, even so, I felt ill and homesick. I missed Mum and Dad and our house; I wanted my own bed.

And then I got a dreadful shock. 'We live so far from Kingston and you have no car,' said Uncle Jim. 'To meet people your own age, we think you should stay in the YWCA in Kingston.'

I was aghast. Uncle Jim had spent a decade trying to get me to come to Canada, now he was going to push me into a type of boarding house. What would I say to Mum and Dad? He'd promised to look after me, why was he doing this? I felt abandoned.

But Uncle Jim really did have my best interests at heart.

'Gloria,' he said, as gently as he could, 'we live in a very remote area with virtually no one your age. You'd have no friends. How would you get work? Whereas at the hostel you'll have a wonderful and active social life. And of course you'll visit us all the time, on weekends and holidays. We'll still do all the things we talked about.'

In the end I had no choice and it turned out to be the best thing he could have done. I moved to the YWCA, where I shared a room with a Canadian girl called Elizabeth Allen, with whom I shared my woes.

'I'm from the Emerald Isle and I'm 3,000 miles from home,' I said miserably.

'Well I'm 3,500 miles from home and I live in Canada,' she replied. 'Vancouver is on the West Coast.'

That cheered me up instantly and certainly put things in perspective. I knew quite quickly that I'd done the right thing in moving. Kingston was a great university city and I got a job in an equity company calling out figures in the actuarial department – whatever that might mean. I'm not sure I understand it to this day. My Irish brogue caused myriad problems: the girl I was calling out the figures to just could not work out what I was saying.

I would call out 'eight eighty-eight', in my strong Northern Irish accent, and of course she could not understand. To Canadians it sounded like 'Ate, Atey, Ate,' so she would reply, 'What do you mean??' and have to look at my book to understand.

'Oh, you mean *eight*!'

But everyone was very nice about it and there was a good-humoured atmosphere in the office.

I was learning fast about my new home and understanding that life was very different from Northern Ireland, something my new colleagues recognised as well. In the monthly office magazine, they wrote me a good-natured welcome that said so much: 'Gloria must hail from a very small village – the other day she got lost on the way to work and almost didn't get here. She lives about four blocks from the office!'

Probably one of the biggest differences though was the lack of religious divide. In Portadown, Protestants and Catholics were divided. There were still big tensions between the two communities in Northern Ireland at this time in the fifties but in Canada there were none. It was a revelation. In Kingston no one asked about my religion – they couldn't care less.

It turned out to be a huge turning point in my life and broadened my horizons forever because I realised for the first time that Protestants and Catholics could live together. I was meeting new people from all over the world: Germans, Czechs, Italians and Poles, and we were all working happily alongside one another.

Spending the day reading out numbers was a little mind-numbing, though, and so I started looking for another job. I saw an ad for an accounts assistant at Old Fort Henry military base, a tourist attraction that employed university students during the summer. I remember Uncle Jim worrying that I didn't have enough experience but, undaunted, I applied for and got the job. There were 135 male students and only 35 girls, so that to me was a good ratio. I wore the uniform – a red blazer, white shirt and navy skirt – and remember feeling so proud as I walked to the bus every morning.

I was appointed by the Ontario-St Lawrence Development Commission at a Clerk 2 level on $230 dollars a month, which felt like a fortune, and it was a great thrill to walk through the great stoned archway of the amazing 1832 restored fortress. My male colleagues in the parade square were kitted out in a full dress uniform made in England, complete with bearskins, red woollen jackets and polished black boots – I was grateful to be a woman at that point, as it must have been unbearable at times as the temperature was over 100 degrees that summer.

My office overlooked the square and I remember the constant sound of fife and drum bands and the occasional firing of cannons.

One day, not long after I started, I was told I had a *really* important job on the day the Queen was due on a state visit: I wondered to myself, as I was the token Brit, if it was to be handing over flowers? But no, I just had to test the pen Her

Majesty was going to use to sign the visitors' book to make sure it was constantly working! In the event the closest I got to the Queen that time round was to have my picture taken in the chair she sat in.

* * *

My social life back then was first class, full of corn boils and wiener roasts, with the delicious food cooked on open fires. And there were young men aplenty, including one in particular called Henry Knotek, whose family came from Czechoslovakia. His mother used to take great delight in trying to fatten me up with goulash and dumplings.

Henry went on to become one of the most successful lawyers in Ontario and a life long friend. In fact, many decades later my first husband Don and our children spent the summer with them – but more about all that later.

I missed singing on stage but I actually ended up singing on television, thanks to the job in Fort Henry. The girl opposite me in Accounts used to sing on a Canadian show on the local TV station, CKWS, called *Lunchbox* and invited me along to see her perform. She knew about my background, so she introduced me to the producer.

'This is Gloria, who comes from Ireland. She sings as well.' The producer looked interested.

'Do you know any Irish songs?' he asked.

I needed no further encouragement and launched into 'Forty Shades Of Green', and was immediately given a slot on the show... although, to be honest, any Irish immigrant who could sing in tune and had a repertoire of Irish songs would have been in demand. You've never seen anyone learn so many Irish songs in such a short time!

Even so, within weeks I was a firm fixture and from that I was offered a programme of my own on another station, this time radio. It was my big introduction to broadcasting.

I hosted a fifteen-minute weekly request show, in which I sang, backed up by a trio of piano, bass and drums, listeners' requests. I loved it.

'Mrs O'Hanlon from Marysville would like to hear "When Irish Eyes Are Smiling" so here it is!'

Those days singing into the Bakelite radio seemed to be paying off at last, and bearing in mind we only had the BBC back home it seemed extremely indulgent to have 10 TV stations and 15 radio stations in Kingston alone.

★ ★ ★

If I had stayed in Canada, my life might have taken a very different turn, because it was here, at the age of eighteen, that I met my first really serious boyfriend.

The Royal Military College was very near the fort and one day we saw that they were advertising for cheerleaders. Eleanor and I applied and soon got in.

'The female has invaded the RMC in the distracting guise of cheerleaders,' fretted the college magazine, but Eleanor and I were soon yelling our chants with the best of them.

I was the one on top of the pyramid as well – how I ever got there still mystifies me – and I even remember one of the cheers:

> Yell out the cheer
> Reach for a C
> Here come the boys
> From the RMC

A boom a lak – a boom a lak
Boom a lak a bee
Chick a lak – chick a lak
Chick a lak a chee
A boom a lak
Chick a lak
Chick a lak a chee
RMC Whee-ee-ee
What's the matter, can't you take it?
Can't you Alabamy shake it?
Can't you boogie to the right?
Can't you boogie to the left?
Shouting RMC
Fight – fight – fight

One of the members of the football team we were supporting was Walt Moore, the most strikingly handsome man I had ever seen. He was a football hero and I was a cheerleader; could you get a bigger cliché? But I was madly and properly in love.

It was the real thing. Our courting was very innocent by today's standards: we dined by candle light, went ice skating, pony trekking and deep sea fishing. I met all Walt's college friends and was taken to numerous football banquets and teas, and I was introduced to the North American college tradition of being 'pinned': it was a beautiful circular diamond-studded pin with the college crest on it, and receiving it was one step away from being engaged.

I wrote excitedly to Mum and Dad, but they were very, very concerned.

For a start, they wanted me to come home – I was only

supposed to be there a few months, remember. And secondly, they could tell my relationship with Walt was serious and they were very worried about pre-marital sex. I had been raised in hellfire and brimstone Northern Ireland and bearing a child out of wedlock was totally unacceptable, even scandalous. But they really didn't have to worry – it had been so deeply ingrained in me through my childhood that even before Dad wrote to me with his concerns, I had always adhered strictly to the rigid codes of sexual behaviour that I'd been brought up with: we would go so far but never the actual deed.

And though Dad was worried, he was actually very thoughtful and considerate. I still have the touching letter he wrote me, urging me to stay chaste. I received it just before I was heading home for Christmas:

'I understand you've met this boy and I know how feelings can run high, particularly with the pain of parting. But remember, keep yourself intact. Don't ever give in.'

And I didn't. In those days you did as your parents told you, partly out of fear and being a good Irish girl. By the time I got the letter, Walt had actually asked me to marry him, but I still stayed chaste despite wanting to do what other teenagers were doing.

As Christmas was looming, I kept my promise to my parents: after nearly nine months in Canada, I went back to Portadown to see them, money in my pocket for the return trip. I was only planning to spend a few months there and then return to Canada in April for Walt's graduation. In fact,

I was so certain that I was returning, I left two-thirds of my clothes behind.

The return trip was to be my first time in a plane and I was glad when we landed at Dublin Airport. I took the train to Dublin station, where I had arranged to meet my mum and dad. As they were a fraction late, I spied them across three platforms before they noticed me, so I stood up and shouted across to them (as they reminded me), 'Hi Mum, Hi Dad' in a Canadian drawl and chewing gum at the same time. Later, they told me they couldn't believe I'd arrived back with an accent!

It was wonderful to be reunited with my family and to be back home. Mum and Dad were thrilled to see me and my brother told me, years later, that I seemed much more assured and sophisticated, wearing my smart Canadian clothes.

However, when I told them that Walt had proposed, Mum became very visibly upset. She became convinced that she would be losing me forever and I'd be even further away on the other side of the Atlantic: after college, and having trained as a pilot, Walt was planning to move back to Vancouver, even further away than Kingston. I'd be 6,500 miles from home then.

In the event, my clever dad took matters into his own hands and spotted a job that he was pretty sure would keep me in Ireland. He was right, but I've often thought that if I'd gone back and married Walt, I'd have been a pilot's wife now living in Vancouver, with a very different life to the one I had. It was a path not taken, but the right choice. Fate had intervened – as it was to do a number of times in the future.

CHAPTER 3

MAKING WAVES AND MAKING BABIES

'So, Gloria,' asked Dad, 'what are your intentions then? We're so glad to have you home but are you thinking of going back to Canada?'

For once in my life I was completely lost for words. The truth was that to begin with, I'd had every intention of going back to Canada. But I was afraid to say so and in any case I was beginning to wonder what I really wanted to do. I'd landed a temporary job back home to make a bit of money for Christmas presents, selling Rhode Island Reds in a chicken factory, but that wasn't going anywhere, and it hardly compared to having my own radio show in Kingston. But being home was making my decisions a lot less clear.

Dad pretended to look unconcerned.

'You know,' he said casually, 'while you were away, Ulster Television opened up in Belfast? And look, they're searching for people to work for them. Here's an ad I saw in the paper for a production assistant. While you're making up your mind about what to do, why don't you apply?'

And so I did. I am a big believer in fate and I decided that if I got the job, then I was meant to stay in Ireland. If I didn't then my future clearly lay across on the other side of the world.

Even so, fate sometimes needs a helping hand and I was pretty determined that I would land the job. I turned up to the interview in the best fashionable dress I'd bought in Canada topped off with a white leather fur-lined hooded coat and matching boots. I wanted my look to say something other than 'local', that I was an experienced traveller with just the hint of a Canadian accent. *After all*, I thought, *I was semi-professional once and I'd been on radio and television before.*

As it happened, I didn't get the job.

It was settled: I was going back to Canada.

★ ★ ★

But fate quickly showed its hand again when Ulster TV offered me a position in the sales department and so, I thought, *I might as well take that just for now: it sure beat selling hens.* Belfast was only 30 miles from Portadown, and I could stay with my sister Lena in the week as she had moved nearby a few years earlier.

My boss was called Basil Lapworth and nicknamed me 'Hunni', a name that has stuck to this day. But on my first day the managing secretary, Brum Henderson, needed someone to work as his secretary, so I stepped in. I was determined to make a good impression and sat there, my notepad open, ready to take shorthand, when Mr Henderson opened his mouth.

'Felicitations,' he began.

And from there it went from bad to worse: Mr Henderson was a wordsmith and turned out to be one of the most verbose man in all of Ireland, never using one simple word when ten complicated ones would do. I was getting increasingly nervous as I tried to scribble down everything with my rusty shorthand, afraid to let him know I wasn't quite keeping up. Later that night I settled down with Lena, who was much better at shorthand than me, to try to make sense of it. We cut it by about a third in length, and the next day I gave it to Mr Henderson, who never noticed a thing.

I told him once, 'I'm the best subeditor you ever had.'

He was equally helpful in return:

'Never marry for money,' he said, 'but do your courting where there's a bit of it around.'

Major names in the entertainment industry at that time – including Joe Loss & His Orchestra, Emilie Ford & the Checkmates, and Acker Bilk And His Paramount Jazz Band – were beginning to visit Ulster Television and for the first time I was mixing with the big glossy names I'd loved as a child. And then, when I'd only been working there for six weeks, I was asked if I'd like to take the role of production assistant after all.

'Had there been two appointments at the time you would have got it,' I was told. 'Are you still interested?'

I most certainly was and now, finally, I had to make up my mind.

And so I wrote to Walt and told him I wasn't coming back. It was a really tough and upsetting decision to take because

I was being torn in all directions. In love with this gorgeous man but at heart a bit afraid of living so far away permanently, plus the pull of my family and the pull of TV. After one letter in return expressing his disbelief and disappointment, I never heard from him again.

I often wondered what life would have been like living in Vancouver and married to a pilot.

* * *

In Ulster, a whole new world – and vocabulary – was opening up to me. It was 'darling' this and 'luvvie' that, and all the while I was learning my new trade. The two network directors brought in specially to launch Ulster Television (UTV) were Michael Kent and John Scholtz-Conway, who had a habit of calling us all darling, including his wife Terri. She was often in the control box when he was working and when he said, 'Darling, can I have a cup of tea?' we'd both jump up to make one.

In those days everything, and I mean everything, was 'live'; there were no recording facilities at all. It taught me everything I needed to know about broadcasting: I learned how to read a clock and back time, which meant I had to know the timings for the items and the programme to the very second and at the same time call the camera shots. I had to collate information, captions and camera directions. At 4.30pm we ran an hour-long women's show called *A Matter of Taste* and at 5.30 sharp, I'd grab all my captions, theme tunes, timing notes and contracts and race upstairs to my office, dump it, grab the next set of notes for the 6pm news programme and be off. I recall that countdown so clearly: 10, 9, 8, 7, 6, 5, 4, 3, 2, 1, up!

It was high pressured beyond belief but stood me in good stead to this day.

Commercial breaks were different back then, too – not always the 30 to 60-second ads seen today but sometimes mini-dramas lasting between 10 and 13 minutes, known as 'Advertising Magazines':

'Good morning, John, would you pass me those delicious Kellogg's cornflakes?'

'Why sure, Donna. And I'm certain you'll want some Tate & Lyle sugar on those. Say, Donna, did you happen to notice this terrific Robinson & Cleaver jacket I'm wearing to work today?'

Somehow the actors managed to keep a straight face and remember their lines.

There were only about 60 of us working there at the time, but many went on to have great careers, including Anne Gregg, who did the BBC *Holiday* programme, and Ivor Mills, who became a national newsreader for ITN. It was John Scholtz-Conway who discovered singing star Roger Whittaker, who was going nowhere fast in England at the time, but who became an international star after being brought over to Northern Ireland. I went on to interview him frequently, and for decades he used a clipboard he'd pinched from me.

The comedian Frank Carson also got his first big break on UTV, hosting a variety programme entitled *Come On On On On In*. Based in a humble Irish kitchen, Frank would introduce 15 guests a week, with an entertainment budget that stretched to just £100. I always remember that because I typed the contract.

One of the floor managers was Derek Bailey, who became

a very well-known arts director and producer, and who started the same day I did (he told me he sent out letters every week for a year to try to get the job) and he taught me a very valuable lesson early on.

One evening, he was directing the sports coverage when I was on duty and on my break a number of us went to a local pub with the very salubrious name of Dirty Dicks. Someone suggested I have a Tia Maria, which I thought very sophisticated (and had never had it before.). Indeed, I liked it a lot and then had a few more. By the time I returned to the studio everything was a blur – I couldn't even see the stopwatch, never mind do the timings. Afterwards Derek took me aside and said, 'Let this be a lesson to you. In this "live" business of TV one slip-up means disaster. People are depending on you. Don't ever drink before a show again.'

I did remind him that he was the one who bought me the drink. However I never repeated that mistake again and to this day I never ever drink before a show.

★ ★ ★

My parents would have liked me to live at home but I was nearing my twenties and my whole life was opening up before me, so a couple of friends, Suzy Gibson, also from Portadown, and her friend Liz McFetrich, decided to share a flat in the university area of Belfast. We had a large living room, complete with a piano (the scene of many a party) but only one bedroom, which had three beds crammed together: there was no floor space at all and I had to clamber over everyone else's beds to get to my own. There was no heating of course and we would wear very unsexy flannelette pyjamas and a cardie, while we went around with rollers in our hair, face cream and hung our nylons in the shower. There was no privacy but we were having the time of our lives.

We weren't there long before we moved to a slightly bigger place in a posh part of Belfast called Wellington Park. There was still only one bedroom but at least a bit more space between the beds. On Tuesday nights we would go to Maxim's Dancehall in central Belfast: we'd have a couple of bottles of Merrydown cider in the flat before we went out, at five shillings each, and a packet of ciggies. The cigs were not for me because at the early age of thirteen, I smoked five woodbines in a row and made myself so ill I fortunately never got hooked.

Eventually we were turfed out of that flat: it was a nice neighbourhood after all and the neighbours had had enough of our rowdy parties. But luckily I was rescued by another friend who I knew from school, Felicity Carrier. Flick's grandfather owned Wade's Ceramics and her parents ran the Northern Ireland branch based in Portadown; they let us stay in their elegant Belfast flat in Lennoxvale Gardens. This was real gracious living, surrounded by art and elegance way beyond my two-up two-down in Portadown. Flick's mum, Iris, taught me all I know about antiques and kindled a lifelong love of them. Flick remains a great friend to this day – sometimes I think the pals you make friends with when you're a teenager remain the strongest.

The UTV crowd were all young and lively and we spent all our weekends and holidays together. There were dinners and parties; pony trekking and fishing, including one memorable deep sea fishing trip off Donaghadee, during which I was so ill I spent the day lying flat on my back with a string attached to my toe. It was the only way I could fish! And my horizons were widening all the time: I was being exposed to 'exotic' new foods such as curry and spaghetti, neither of which Mum would have dreamed of serving up, and for the first time I was learning about wine. I used to order Nuits St Georges, very much impressing my new group of friends, who didn't realise this was the only wine I knew!

I had moved on from Walt and had a couple of boyfriends but nothing that serious until one day a new cameraman called Don Keating appeared on the scene. Don was nicknamed 'poetry in motion' because of his fluidity with the camera and had been brought over from ABC in Didsbury, Manchester.

It was hate at first sight. I thought he was arrogant as he spoke with an English accent.

'He's a bit off hand, isn't he?' I asked my friends.

Don didn't seem too impressed with me either and promptly took up with the make-up girl, which for some strange reason irritated me intensely. Very odd.

But it turned out that we couldn't avoid one another. We were part of a crowd of young people going around together and so, despite our apparent best efforts, we got to know each other. I discovered that Don was actually Irish and came from Youghal in County Cork, where he'd lived until the age of eight and where his father ran a hotel business. After that went belly up the family moved to Manchester, where they supplied kosher food for the Jewish community, which seemed a bit strange for a Catholic family.

Don enjoyed football and cricket and nearly joined the Navy until it seemed fate had played a hand in his life too. On the day he was due to sign up, he pulled back the curtains, saw a full force gale blowing and decided not to go to sea. Instead he joined ABC Television in Didsbury and learned his trade as a cameraman in the treacherous waters of 'live' TV.

And they could be very treacherous indeed. He told me about one unforgettable television programme in 1958:

'We were doing an armchair theatre one-hour drama called *Underground in the Aftermath of a Tube Explosion*. All was proceeding normally until the beginning of the second act, when one of the three leads, Gareth Jones, abruptly keeled over. This wasn't in the script so [assistant cameraman] Mike Kent rushed over and with the help of one of the prop boys dragged the guy out to the scene dock. We then heard that this poor fellow gave a death rattle and, incredibly, he expired right there in Mike's arms.

'By that time the third act had started and in the midst of the opening scene, when the actors were supposed to be sleeping, poor Mike was running madly about the set calling for a doctor.'

Don heard the director, Ted Kotcheff, crying out over the radio, 'There's somebody in shot, there's somebody in shot. Get that idiot outta shot!'

The entire third act was of course total ad lib. The remaining two leads busked the entire drama, which was complicated dialogue. Simply extraordinary!

Later, it turned out that poor Gareth had died of a massive heart attack and strangely enough his character had been due to suffer a heart attack in the play. The broadcast has since become the stuff of legend.

* * *

By this time Don and I were finally beginning to admit that we had feelings for one another and I began to realise I was falling deeply in love. After a year and a half of dating, when I'd just turned twenty-one, we decided to get married. There was just one problem, and it was a big one: Don was a Catholic.

It was 1961, but the taboo against Protestants and Catholics marrying in Ireland at that time was so great, it was almost like whites and blacks marrying in the American Deep South – it was totally forbidden territory. I dreaded telling my parents, who had never even met Don at that stage, as I was so scared they would find out his religion. I knew the consequences.

When my dad travelled to Belfast to meet with Don, and for him to ask for my hand in marriage, he was as angry as I'd thought he'd be.

'Do you realise what you're saying?' he demanded. 'You can't marry a Catholic. I'm a member of the Orange Order. What would the neighbours say?'

'Look, it's just an accident of birth–'

'I couldn't show my face again at another meeting. I couldn't walk in the Twelfth of July parade. What would the Orangemen think?'

'But I really want you, my parents, at the wedding. You're my parents. Wait till you meet our UTV priest, Father Hugh Murphy – he's such a wonderful, liberal man.'

'You're asking your mother and me to sit in a Catholic church? And see our daughter married by a Catholic priest? What are you thinking?'

'But Don's an *English* Catholic, it's nothing like as rigid...'

But Dad was adamant.

'Gloria, look here,' he said. 'If you marry this chap, I cannot and will not go to the wedding on principle.'

I'd always admired my dad's high principles but it was

heart-breaking now; I just knew my mum wouldn't be allowed to go either.

'I'm sorry, Gloria,' she said. 'I certainly can't go if your father won't.'

In later years she told me that this was the hardest decision she had ever made and not attending my wedding was the greatest regret of her life. She wasn't involved in any of the planning but she told me that she followed it all in her head, trying to imagine what was going on. A neighbour told me later that she wept the entire day.

I was in floods of tears myself after that and wished it could be like Canada, where these things really didn't matter, but I was determined to marry Don. And, as a matter of fact, things could have been a lot worse. Some families would have had a permanent feud over this but the one silver lining was that Dad was determined this wouldn't happen.

'If you go ahead, you know we can't be there on principle,' he said. 'But everything will be fine afterwards. We will welcome your Don as part of the family and treat him as a son.'

And he was as good as his word.

Because Mum and Dad wouldn't attend, Dad's sister and her husband, Aunt May and Uncle Jim Menaul, who I was very close to anyway, helped me plan the wedding and choose my dress, and Uncle Jim gave me away during the ceremony. They didn't have the strong anti-Catholic feelings like my Dad. And, in all fairness, Dad didn't prevent my sister Lena, her husband Rupert and my brother Charles from being there.

Don and I were married on 28 April 1961 in a very moving ceremony by Father Hugh Murphy. We held the reception at Belfast's Wellington Park Hotel and given that most of my family were not present, there weren't that many older family members to keep the young 'uns under control so it was quite a boisterous occasion, as the guests let their hair down – a real party atmosphere. In a box of mementos my son Michael still has the invoice for the wedding feast, which was the princely sum of £34 for the whole lot. Many people since have asked me was I not totally heartbroken because my parents weren't there. But strangely enough, because I always knew how highly principled my dad was, in a way I understood it and we had a really joyous day.

Don and I planned to spend our honeymoon driving round Southern Ireland. We got into a car at the reception, adorned with traditional 'Just Married' signs and tethered cans and confetti and, ultimately, a troubling and fishy smell. After a while we opened the bonnet of the car – and found kippers tied to the engine baking inside. Nor did matters improve much when we finally got to Dublin's Gresham Hotel: we were just making ourselves at home when Reception rang up and said there were friends of ours in the lobby. We thought there must have been a mistake, but when we got downstairs, we found one of the soundmen, Morris, and his wife waiting for us. They'd had far too much to drink at the reception and had enjoyed the wedding so much that they'd followed us all the way to Dublin and then insisted on having dinner with us! Much as I liked them I couldn't wait to see the back of them.

When at last we'd got shot of them I informed Don that I was finally going to have my wicked way with him. And then I discovered there was definitely something to be said for waiting until you're actually married…

★ ★ ★

Marriage always causes a big upheaval, but in my case particularly so as the policy of the TV network was to forbid husbands and wives from working in the same department, and so I had to give up my job.

We settled into a little rented house in Cedar Avenue in Belfast and I attempted to get to grips with my new role as a housewife. It was not an easy time. I couldn't cook for toffee, producing inedible stews and lumpy custards and calling Don – who was a very accomplished cook – at work and demanding to be told how to make gravy. One Cornish pasty I'd spent all afternoon making went flying all over the floor as I presented it to my new husband, but to his credit I picked it up and he ate it all. To show you my knowledge of cooking, on another occasion I was mystified when trying to order bacon and pork in a kosher butcher's shop.

We soon moved again, to a house on Hollywood Road, and as well as coping with the deep snows of 1962 were quite thrilled when we discovered I was pregnant. But I didn't show it at all. I suffered from really severe morning sickness – in fact, all day sickness – and couldn't eat, so much so that I actually lost weight rather than gained it. I didn't even wear maternity clothes until my seventh month. In later years I heard about the terrible effects of thalidomide on expectant mothers at the time and briefly wondered if that's why I was so ill, but the GP reassured me I'd never touched the stuff.

The baby was clearly going to be a child in a rush. When I was not quite eight months' pregnant Don and I decided to have a quick break in London before our baby arrived and we were nearly at the point when I couldn't fly. I love the theatre, having been on stage myself from such a young age, and so we headed to the West End to take in a performance of *Oliver!* Ron Moody was doing his bit on stage when, halfway through the first act, I felt an overwhelming desire to go to the loo. I squeezed my way along the row of seats and had barely got to the ladies when my waters broke. I went into a state of shock, but somehow got back to Don and whispered, 'My waters have broken.'

'*Shh*,' said Don, with a preoccupied wave. He was totally absorbed in the show and hated being interrupted.

'My waters have broken!' I protested.

He did a triple take.

'What, *now*?'

For a moment we sat there in a frozen panic and then Don leaped up, panicked, and ushered me frantically into the foyer.

'Help,' he implored the staff. 'My wife's having a baby, I think…'

An ambulance was called and I was bundled in, feeling very scared. I was just twenty-two and while London was an exciting place to visit, it wasn't where I wanted to have my first baby – I wanted to be with my own mother, at home. And then it got worse: we got to Charing Cross Hospital, only to be turned away. There was no room at the inn.

I was badly shaken; this would never have happened in Northern Ireland. Don tried to make light of it:

'If it's a boy we'll have to call him Oliver,' he said.

Eventually we ended up at a maternity hospital in Fulham. It was well past 11pm before I was settled and comfortable. I can't remember much about it – I was dosed up to the nines on a drug called pethidine and was apparently babbling away about how marvellous *Oliver!* had been and how lovely it was to have a tea party in the middle of the night.

'You may as well come back in the morning, first babies take hours,' the staff told Don.

Men were not encouraged to be in the delivery room, back then anyway.

In the event, of course, my first child popped out less than two hours later, on 5 October 1962, and Don barely made it back in time. But while she might have been five weeks premature, she was perfect in every way, with an exquisite rosebud mouth. I decided to name her Caron, after my favourite movie star Leslie Caron – I had originally thought of Karen but 'Karen Keating' just sounded too harsh. We gave her the middle name Louisa, although I'm not sure why – perhaps the other mothers had been talking about it while I was doped up on the ward!

Caron was so small she was popped into an incubator for a while, but thank God she was in a good state and I went from the shock and surprise of being in a strange city to the profound feeling that nothing else mattered at all. Of course I believed she was the most beautiful girl ever to be born and I still do. I remember when my father saw her for the first time he just said, 'She has the most perfect rosebud mouth I've ever seen in my life.' And that summed it up.

I think the first time I truly appreciated my parents was the moment Caron was born. I remember writing to them from hospital, saying, 'If Don and I can be anything like you as parents, then we'll be very complete.' In fact, I found this letter among my mother's things after she died.

And the moment Caron was born I could see why my parents had been protective. I knew why they hadn't wanted me to do certain things. I knew why they had lavished so much love on me and I knew how it felt to have the treasure of a child and to feel that total emotion and responsibility.

★ ★ ★

There was a great deal of camaraderie on the maternity ward, but I missed my mother and the rest of the family. But travel was not so easy in those days. Don stayed for a bit but there was no such thing as paternity leave back then so he had to return to Ireland for work. So it was just Caron and me, staying with a couple of friends of Don's, Fen and Harry, who had initially just been expecting to put us up for a couple of days, and now had to convert their sitting room into a nursery. I didn't want to fly with Caron too soon because she was premature and I felt I needed to recover myself: right after the birth I weighed under seven stone – the last time I ever weighed so little – and when I look at the pictures now I seem to be all eyes in an emaciated frame.

I was able to breastfeed Caron; I had lots of milk and she was a little gulper, but she guzzled so fast, she often projectile vomited. I was mortified when she was sick over Fen and Harry's furniture and was terrified of staining something. In the end I put towels across the settee and bed and covered the floor; if they took a hit, I would wash them myself so my kind hosts would never know.

We were alone together in a strange city, without my family or husband, and so were locked into each other from the start. I got to know her baby nuances, the little expressions and noises that meant she was thirsty, hot or bored. Because I was breastfeeding I couldn't leave her with someone else to give her a bottle; she had my complete attention, with no one else to divert it, and although I was frightened and tired, I look back on it as a very special period of my life that was completely suspended in time. In fact, many years later, when Caron was battling her cancer we talked about how perhaps that period, just the two of us, was the beginning of our incredibly close bond.

A soon as he could, Don took some time off and came back for us. It had only been a couple of weeks but it felt much longer. We decided to go to Manchester first to see his family – I remember feeling so proud as we headed north to Don's parents, as I hadn't spent much time with them before. They were fantastic. Don's sister-in-law Mary had given birth to her daughter, Janette, shortly beforehand, so we had a lot in common and it was very exciting being with the two little girls.

I don't remember who did but it was suggested we should have a joint christening service when we were there, so Caron was baptised into the Catholic Church with her cousin. And when we got back to Northern Ireland we had her baptised a second time, this time into the Church of Ireland, in St Mark's, Portadown. Caron was always amused by the fact that she was baptised into both the Protestant and Catholic Churches! My parents and Lena were the godparents, so any lingering unhappiness about my Catholic wedding was totally washed away.

Now that there were three of us Don and I decided to save for a home of our own, although money was a bit tight and rows would erupt over the silliest things. Once I spent five shillings on a waste paper basket, which thoroughly upset him:

'We didn't need that!' he complained. 'Five shillings for a bloody bin!'

Men!

But I hated not having my own money: after all, I'd been earning all my life. I was determined that I would never have to justify buying a pair of shoes to Don or anyone else, and so I became an Avon lady, which at that time was a whole new concept. Ding dong! I'd put Caron in the pram, settle cosmetics all around her and push her around, visiting friends and people around the neighbourhood. But it was only a bit of pin money, as they used to say.

At the same time we were searching for our first house to buy and one day visited a show house in Marnabrae Park in Lisburn, about 10 miles from Belfast, where a developer was constructing American-style bungalows. You stepped into a small hallway that took you into one central living area, where you stepped down into the sunken lounge and up into the dining area. It was totally different from anything I'd seen before – it even had a sunken bath.

Now this is style, this is Hollywood, I thought to myself.

It now seems incredible to us that it cost £2,800, with £300 extra for heating, and on a 30-year mortgage it came in at just over £29 a month, just within our budget (how could that have been?).

We watched it being built and finished it off with rough hessian on the lounge walls, very much in vogue at the time. We stretched it right across the top of our 'stylish' stone fireplace. It was very expensive, but we bought a bale of it cheap from a sacking company, with six of us needed to handle the whole sticky mess of putting it up. I remember Mum came to help me make the curtains and paused at the natural brick wall.

'Lovely, darling,' she said. 'Once you get this wall plastered it will look wonderful.'

When we finally moved in we had almost no furniture: just a cot for Caron, a bed we'd bought for £10 and a couple of chairs borrowed from my sister, along with a couple of mats scattered on the floor. I spent so much time on my hands and knees polishing the new raw floorboards with button polish. My joy was unconfined a few months later when we put underlay down, never mind an actual carpet.

'Listen, Don, we can't hear our feet any more!' I cried.

We had some very happy years in that house. Our neighbours included Anne Thompson and her husband Billy, who would become the youngest ever gynaecologist and Obstetrics professor in Northern Ireland. Anne became one of my closest friends and not only did we both have daughters of the same age, we fell pregnant with our second child at the same time, too. They were carefree days, walking together the two miles to the clinic each week to pick up our babies' milk and buying fish and chips to dig into, surreptitiously, on the way back. We would hide them under the pram covers – gosh, life was so sophisticated then.

★ ★ ★

Caron was just nine months old when I found out I was pregnant again. My Granny Hunniford died just before my due date, which not only upset me greatly but meant I couldn't attend the funeral. Mindful of what had happened the first time around, Don was extremely reluctant to go on his own without me.

'I'm not going unless you're admitted to hospital,' he said.

So I gave in and he settled me on the ward, but as he was leaving he turned around and said:

'Remember Frank Sinatra – just take it nice and easy.'

I could have thrown something at him and, sure enough, the contractions began soon after. My mother once told me that, 'births and deaths often come together', and coincidentally the next day was her own birthday, 10 June, which she hoped she would share with her grandson.

And so Paul rushed into the world almost as quickly as his older sister had done and, like her, he was perfect.

Don returned from the funeral just in time to hear the news. He ran to the baby ward and asked the nurse to hold his baby up to the glass. The nurse picked up baby Paul and when Don saw his ginger hair he looked puzzled.

'No, no, the name is Keating,' he insisted.

The nurse nodded and pointed to Paul.

'No, *Keating*,' said Don before it finally sank in that this lovely little red-haired boy was his own son.

We were a happy and devoted little family and I loved motherhood with a passion. But still I hankered for something else. After all I'd been working and singing all my life and had had exciting jobs, both in Northern Ireland and in Canada. Deep down I didn't think I was destined to be a full-time housewife. And I was right.

CHAPTER 4

BOMBS, BULLETS AND BARRICADES

As a wife and mother of two young children, I was very fulfilled and happy but the deep-rooted work ethic that stems back to my earliest days as a child performer meant that I wanted to do something else, as well. And so, at the age of twenty-four, I found my way back to Ulster Television, on the same shows that I'd worked on previously, but in a totally different capacity. In fact, in some ways I was returning to my earliest experiences in television in Canada, because now I was beginning to appear in front of the camera.

It was another request show called *Tea Time with Tommy* and, as previously, the audience would write in with their requests. These tended to be numbers like 'Strangers In The Night' and I was accompanied by the pianist Tommy James, who was rather like Len Goodman in appearance but well known back then for a party trick in which he tickled the ivories with two oranges. It could only happen in Ireland!

And just as I had done in Canada, I began to branch out, not least to Radio Telefís Eireann, the official broadcasting station in Dublin. It was a much more productive station at that time with bigger budgets and producing more entertainment programmes. In a way it really felt like the 'big time'. By this stage in 1964 the cabaret scene was beginning in Northern Ireland, with sophisticated nightclubs including the Abercorn, Tito's and the Talk of the Town. My favourite cabaret place I performed at was the Half Door Club in Bangor, which was attached to the Royal Hotel right on the seafront. It was a round trip of 50 miles and I did it three times a week for £4 a night – which believe it or not at the time seemed like a rather good fee. And I was moving up in the world. Rather than just being accompanied by a pianist, now I had a quartet, or sometimes even a quintet or sextet, playing in the background, often headed by Marie Murphy, who had once been the pianist for Ruby Murray, the only woman to have had more hits in the Top 20 at any one time over The Beatles.

My more sophisticated cabaret called for an upgrade in the wardrobe department, and so it was back to Auntie Myrtle and her trusty sewing machine. She created a memorable silver lamé mini-dress, which was more like a belt than anything else, and which I teamed with a pair of white go-go boots that came in very handy when I sang Nancy Sinatra's 'These Boots Are Made For Walking'. Years later I teased Danny La Rue by saying that I'd copied a few of his ideas, including a stunning cloak trimmed with feather boas. I couldn't afford proper boas, so I used a double frilling of the material from my dress, something Danny found hysterical. Meanwhile I would be zipping around the country in a green Mini that I'd bought from my friend and neighbour, Anne Thompson, for £338.

Dad might not have wanted his wife to have a career, but he was increasingly proud of his daughter's, and Don was happy to do his bit too, babysitting the children when I was out at night.

But this was the 1960s and trouble was in the wings. Despite a period of relative calm and prosperity for the rest of Northern Ireland, the nationalists were feeling more and more marginalised, penalised and demonised. The loyalists, on the other side of the political and religious divide, felt their way of life was under threat. Cautious distance was gradually being replaced by suspicion and agitation. Tension, which had just about been kept under control by the B-Specials on the border, that I'd been so afraid of as a child, was rising. Catholic pubs and homes were attacked and burnt to the ground and there had been numerous murders, so by the end of the 1960s the precarious status quo was hanging in the balance. The IRA decided it was time to mobilise again and so did the British Army, who moved in to Northern Ireland.

I had been singing as a cabaret artist for about five years when the Troubles proper broke out in 1969 and things began to fall apart. Driving home at night I'd often run straight into a street riot and, finding myself in the middle of a harrowing scenario, I'd have to turn the car around and find another way home. There was one particularly nasty incident on the Holywood Road in Belfast: I became increasingly panicked when I couldn't turn the car round and get out as all around me cars were being overturned and set on fire, and bricks and bottles were being thrown everywhere. Sometimes I would arrive at a club only to find out it had been blown up the night before. On one occasion my car conked out on the M1 motorway and I flagged passing motorists for help but no one would stop because these really were increasingly dangerous times. Eventually the police approached and circled me three times before stopping, fearing I might be a terrorist decoy. That was an especially terrifying time for me, on my own, left hanging in the dark on the hard shoulder of a very busy road. Eventually, very much to my relief, I was driven home in a police car to a very worried Don.

★ ★ ★

By contrast, my professional life was flourishing. On TV I was now appearing on *In Town With Tommy* (without the oranges), featuring increasingly full-blown production numbers, overseen by the entertainment producer Rob Harding, who was brought over from London to produce them, teach me a bit of choreography and make my wardrobe even more glamorous.

Once I was joined by the comedian and songwriter Alan Hawkshaw and he approached me with a unique opportunity; he had a song that had originally been written for Lulu for that year's Eurovision Song Contest, but as it hadn't been chosen by the public, he thought it might be right for me.

'Why don't you record it and we'll release it as a single in Ireland?' he asked.

The song was called 'Are You Ready For Love?' and the orchestral backing track had already been recorded. Now all that singing into the wireless really was paying off – and my very own song would soon be transmitted out of the Bakelite radio, still in its pride of place in Mum and Dad's home.

I was flown to London which in itself was thrilling, and the excitement mounted as I was taken to a proper recording studio. As I walked in I saw none other than Sacha Distel, the Parisian pop star who had just finished making his latest album. *Wow!* I thought.

I made my way into the tiny recording cubicle and could hardly believe it as I heard the playback of my voice over the backing track that had been recorded for Lulu. It was one of the most extraordinary days of my life and rounded off when my old friend Mike Kent, who was by now living in England, took me for a spectacular dinner at the Carlton Tower Hotel and then put me on the plane back to Belfast, woozy with excitement.

And so a new world opened up as I set about plugging my record. It was played a lot on the radio and I couldn't believe it when 'Are You Ready For Love?', which had been released on the Tangerine Label, got to No.8 in the Ulster charts.

I was featured as 'Local Lisburn Housewife Top Of The Charts' and appeared on all three television networks. But what turned out to be life-changing was when the Northern Ireland equivalent of London's *Today* programme, *Good Morning, Ulster*, got in touch to ask for an interview.

'How does it feel to be an overnight sensation? How are you coping with your sudden notoriety? How do you balance career, home and family?'

It was intimidating but thrilling all the same, though nothing could have prepared me for what came next. The morning after the interview the producer, Dan Gilbert, came on the phone.

'I was very impressed with the way you handled yourself yesterday – not short of a word or two,' he told me. 'Have you ever thought of becoming a broadcaster?'

A what? Of course I hadn't – I was a cabaret singer on the verge of a major recording career.

'Mr Gilbert,' I began, 'I'm flattered, but I really don't think–'

'Listen, I'm desperate for a female interviewer,' Dan interrupted. 'I'm losing two of my best people: Diane Harron is going to the newsroom; the other, Pat Lindsey, has left to become a producer. What I need is someone to do the voice pieces and some interviewing.'

You have to remember at that time there were very few women in broadcasting either in front of or behind the camera; men totally ruled the roost and Dan was years ahead of his time. But still, I wanted to be a singer…

'Why don't you drop by and see me for a chat,' he persisted.

These days I can't believe how blasé I was about the whole thing but then again, *he* was sounding *me* out, not the other way around. Mum and I were spending the day shopping in Belfast anyway, so I loftily informed him I would try to fit it in. On the day itself, I pulled up outside the impressive Broadcasting House in my little green Mini, parked at the door and said to my mum, 'I won't be long, I'm just nipping in to see this producer. He's asked me to be an interviewer. Can you believe it?'

Once inside Dan and I had a pleasant chat and then he said, 'Look, I've got a tape recorder here,' he said, pulling it out. 'I'd like you to do a test interview.'

I was almost – almost – too stunned for words when I realised he'd set me up to do an audition and I hadn't had a moment to prepare. After all, he had asked me to come in not the other way round. But before I could speak, a woman walked in whom I recognised as Cicely Mathews of *Children's Hour*. Now here was another odd coincidence: I had auditioned for Cicely Mathews for my very first singing job in broadcasting, but hadn't got it as they wanted someone to sing classical pieces, while I preferred popular hits. Now, it turned out, Cicely was retiring and I was interviewing her. What with the combination of circumstances, I certainly didn't feel I'd made a very good job of it.

'That's the end of that little episode,' I snapped at Mum as we drove away. I felt very affronted. 'How dare he give me an interview on the spot! I didn't even ask for the bloody job.'

Nonetheless I was curiously disappointed that I'd clearly blown it and was brooding on it all the way home.

But when I got home that night, the phone was already ringing.

'Terrific, Gloria,' said Dan. 'When can you start?'

'How about tomorrow?' I asked.

The truth is that I had grown tired of those dangerous late-night drives, but I had no idea that as a news reporter I was going to be confronted with considerably worse because right from the start – as this was the time of the Troubles – it was clear that I was going to be in the midst of it all.

Dan took me straight into the newsroom the next day.

'What do you see?'

'A lot of men thumping on typewriters,' I replied.

'Don't think you are coming in to do women's things like fashion, knitting and recipes,' said Dan. 'Remember you are as good as any bloke sitting in this room, and you will take your place alongside them. You'll be out there on the streets covering current events just like the guys. Do I make myself clear?'

He was ahead of his time really, but from day one, I've never felt the brunt of sexism or felt inferior to men and that advice has stayed with me throughout my entire career. I have always felt that I'm as good as the next bloke, simply because Dan told me so. It's extraordinary how certain pieces of advice stick with you.

* * *

I quickly realised that I had made the right move. I loved my new job and although I was still singing, it began to be a greater focus of my life.

But there was an almost immediate complication for just three months in I discovered I was pregnant and while I was naturally delighted I was also rather sad to think that I might have to give up my new career. But Dan wasn't having any of it. When I told him the news, certain that that was it and I'd have to go, he looked me straight in the eye and said, 'Listen, as long as you can fit behind the microphone, you'll be there, even if we have to cut a lump out of the bloody table!' Yet again he was proving himself to be years ahead of his time.

With this type of programme at breakfast time we were mostly freelancers and we were very much expected to go out and find our own stories or at least suggest them. And it was around that time that Cliff Richard came to perform a gospel concert in Lisburn, where I was living at the time. At that point very few big stars were coming to Northern Ireland because of the Troubles so it was a very big deal indeed that Cliff was arriving and I decided that I would see if I could get an interview. When I mentioned this in the office, everyone laughed me down.

'We've tried every conceivable way of getting an interview with him! You haven't a chance.'

I never take no for an answer and I had a trump card up my

sleeve because socially I knew the vicar of the church where Cliff was performing, and I also knew that he was staying at the manse. So I approached the vicar.

'Do you think Cliff would do an interview with me?' I asked.

'Well, I'll talk to him when he gets back from performing,' he said. 'Bring your recording machine with you just in case.'

So I lugged my old Uher reel-to-reel recording machine around with me and that night at about 9.30pm, the phone rang.

'Cliff said yes to the interview,' the vicar said. 'Can you come now before supper?'

I dropped everything, left the kids with Don, picked up the machine, jumped into my green Mini and was round there in about five minutes.

As I walked in to the sitting room, heavily pregnant, glad to see a very welcoming Cliff Richard, the vicar introduced me as 'Miss' Hunniford. Looking back it seems utterly stupid and ridiculous but for some strange reason, knowing that Cliff was a very religious person, I set out to make sure he knew I wasn't an unmarried mother.

'I've left my husband at home to look after the children.' I quickly remarked – not that it would have occurred to Cliff that anything else might have been the case. But they were different times back then. We've had many a good laugh about that since.

And so I got the scoop with Cliff. My boss Dan was most impressed and that earned me a lot of brownie points with the BBC.

In fact, I've always felt that I owe quite a bit of my initial success in broadcasting to Cliff: he helped my career to take off. Ultimately he became a regular interviewee of mine, whatever programme I was working on, and later, when I was at Radio 2, he invited me round to his place for tea and tennis. A great friendship formed, which today is stronger than ever, but more of that later.

* * *

With Dan's blessing I worked right up until the day before the baby was born and as the due date was close to Christmas my doctor suggested that I could have the baby induced in time for the holidays. I wouldn't normally have done this but I was being looked after by my best friend Anne's husband Billy, now firmly regarded as one of the best gynaecologists in Northern Ireland, so I knew I would be fine.

However, as soon as I got to the Royal Victoria Hospital in Belfast, I began to regret my decision. Caron and Paul had popped out easily, but the latest little one appeared to be wanting to take his time. I endured hours of pain before I was taken to the delivery room and the comforting sight of Billy. And then all the pain and anxiety evaporated when I welcomed my third child, Michael, into the world at 5.30pm on 16 December 1970.

When I took him home to meet the family, Caron, now eight years old, took an immediate and maternal interest in him. Her fascination with dolls transferred to Michael and from then on she behaved like a little mother to him, even when she had children of her own.

On reflection, it seems utterly ridiculous that I only took two weeks off after Michael was born. But my friend Flick's sister-in-law was a former nurse, so she was perfect to help me look after my beautiful new baby. Despite Dan's reassuring words, Ireland was still very much a man's world, especially at work, and I wanted to prove I could hold my own in the workplace. At the same time I was determined that no one could accuse me of neglecting my children and so I managed to fit work in and around family life. I'd get the older children off to school and perhaps ask Anne or my sister Lena to babysit, and on occasions I would bundle Michael up and take him into the studio with me. No one objected. In that respect at least Northern Ireland was very accommodating – I don't think I would have got away with that in London.

Don was very much a new man, too. As well as his own job in television he encouraged me in my career, did his share of making dinner and shared the school run – although on one memorable occasion, that I was to be reminded of for years afterwards, I managed to leave Paul waiting at school to be picked up until 6pm.

Sometimes the children would all accompany me into the studio, where they would play cricket in the corridors or eat the canteen's delicious fish and chips. I made sure that I never missed important occasions like sports days or school concerts, and they soon realised there was an upside to having a working mother, too. I'd take them on interesting assignments and so they saw, for example, the birth of a baby bear at the zoo and a ship being dredged up from the seabed. I'd sometimes be given tickets to pop concerts, to see stars like Elton John and Rod Stewart, at which point I'd become the most popular mother in the world.

And my journalistic skills were blossoming under Dan's expert tutelage. The first interview I had to do for *Good Morning, Ulster* was about a meteorite and what I knew about that subject you could write on my thumb nail. I sat up practically all night studying and by morning I had a most informed list of questions, which I was very proud of.

As I went in to the 'live' studio, Dan asked me, 'What's that list?', taking it from me, looking at it briefly and immediately tearing it to threads. My heart almost stopped: this was a 'live' round table discussion and now my finely honed questions had all been taken away. But it was a blessing in disguise – Dan was responsible for teaching me to listen and not to depend on a pre-planned list of questions. He would always say that if an unexpected answer comes, then a list is useless. It was incredibly good advice and, although I do write down bullet points and reminders for any interview, I do believe I am a better listener for it.

* * *

As the Troubles worsened, the daily beat grew more fraught. I worked on a semi-freelance basis and I cannot count how many times I had to turn off the hob, get in the car and drive to report on the atrocity of the day. The call would come in: 'There's been an explosion in Belfast. Get down there and cover it.' And so I did.

Once, when Caron was poorly and off school, I was asked to go to Londonderry to do an army programme and I was so used to the bizarre circumstances of my job that I simply bundled her into the car and set off. It was the worst decision I'd ever made: when we got to Derry and were being transferred from our car to one of the army's Saracen vehicles, we got caught up in a street riot, with bricks and bottles hurled everywhere. We were totally surrounded and poor Caron was terrified, as was I. It suddenly came to me that what I had been taking as normal, everyday life was nothing of the sort.

And when I saw it through the eyes of a child I realised how awful it had all become. I never took my children out to work with me again.

I saw some terrible things during that time. The worst disaster was the Abercorn restaurant bombing in March 1972. At only 2lb, it was a relatively small explosive – nothing like the more common bombs and at worst a 500lb bomb on top of a petrol tanker – but it had been planted under a seat in a very crowded restaurant space in Belfast's Corn Market, which made it a particularly impacting and a totally horrible incident. By the time I arrived at the scene, all the sirens were blazing with scores of people littered over the floor, screaming in pain, terror and confusion. A fire had broken out too and many were terribly badly burnt over their entire bodies. Police and medical staff were trying to impose order amid the dazed onlookers, the overturned tables and debris from the walls and windows and I shuddered when I heard two young women had been killed, with 139 maimed or seriously injured.

By a terrible twist of fate, one of the girls was the daughter of the surgeon who'd been called in to administer emergency aid.

Many of the injured lost their legs or arms; others lost their sight when they were hit in the face by shards of glass. One television reporter was so overcome that he broke down on camera, trying to cover it up by saying that he was out of breath from running up the stairs.

The full impact of what had happened hit me the next day. London's *Today* programme asked for a story on the lost property office set up to return victims' belongings and I ended up doing it. It was to be my first national broadcast.

I walked into the grim hallway and saw all the ravaged

belongings set out, among them a single shoe, a pair of tights with a leg blown off, a charred teddy and a leather handbag flattened and ripped apart by the blast. But worst of all was the driving licence of one of the girls who was killed, singed around the edges. The sight of that brought it home to me: a young life had been wiped away in a single, searing second. It took me years to recover from that. In fact, it's one of my most vivid and disturbing images from the Troubles. And the restaurant was frequented by people from both sides which made the motive even harder to understand.

I was close to one bomb, too. It was by now the mid-seventies and I was just about to go on air for a programme called *What's West* when we were told a car bomb had been placed at the base of the BBC studio wall and was set to go off in minutes. The building had already been evacuated, except for a small group of us involved in getting the show on the air. We were given the option to stay or leave and I chose the former on the grounds that Broadcasting House was a very strong building, made of stone and so pretty impregnable, but the sense of nervousness was overwhelming. In the end there were only three people left in the building – the overall transmission controller, my engineer and me.

Quite suddenly, the blast erupted, a deep sonic boom as the car bomb exploded and the solid building shook like jelly. The whole place rocked to its foundations from the force of it; dust was pouring out of the walls and all the windows were blown out over the entire studio block. The air was so thick that I couldn't see across the room; it was almost impossible to see or breathe. But we were 'live' on air and I had no choice but to describe what was happening to the aghast listeners. I have no idea what I said, I just remember the dust and the

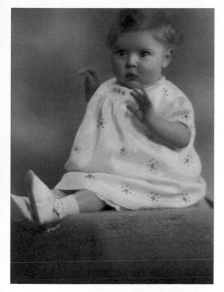

Above left: Me as a baby – love those chubby cheeks.

Above right: Me in my mum's arms on my christening day.

Below left: Me being held by Granny Hunniford along with my parents when I was only a few months old.

Below right: Lena and I on Newcastle beach in those infamous knitted swimsuits. In those days we were forced out onto the sand whatever the weather.

Above left: Looking very pleased with myself in buttons and bows…

Above right: Charles, Lena and I. Charles would have been only two at the time and Lena was sixteen.

Below left: I'd just started singing on stage at the age of seven. Those sequins were the only ones we could afford at the time.

Below right: Hay-stacking on my grandmother's farm. Those are such happy memories…

Top left: My granny and grandad Hunniford with Aunt May and Myrtle who designed all my dresses. She was so good, she really could have cut it in the Parisian couture houses.

Top right: My mum with Aunt Ina, Uncle Joe and Grandad Hunniford. He was always so proud marching with his war medals.

Middle left: My parents and Lena, with Great Uncle Jim. He had such an influence on me as a child and it was because of him that I became obsessed with going to Canada.

Bottom left: Dad with his pigeons outside the coop. He loved pigeon racing but it's only now that I realise just how important his hobby was.

Bottom right: Dad with his magic box. That special box smuggled so much food over the border during the times of rationing.

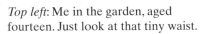

Top left: Me in the garden, aged fourteen. Just look at that tiny waist.

Top right: My new bicycle, which dad made me repay at a rate of two shillings and sixpence each week.

Below left: That's me onstage in the wig playing my part in 'Trial by Jury' – I'm lucky I didn't cause permanent damage.

Below right: At sixteen singing at the City Hall in Belfast. It was a magnificent building and my biggest gig to date. I was paid £16 – a fortune at the time.

Above left: I'm sixteen here and on a boat on Lough Erne, where we later spent such happy times as a family.

Above right: I'd arrived in Canada at eighteen and my world completely changed. Here's me sitting in the chair that The Queen used when she came to visit Old Fort Henry.

Below left: That's me – the cheerleader – at the top of the pyramid. I really was an all-Canadian girl.

Below right: The train from Portadown to Belfast that I took when I was working at Ulster Television. Not sure about that perm!

Top left: On my wedding day with Don. Although my parents didn't come, it was a fantastic day.

Top centre: Our receipt for the wedding breakfast – it seems unbelievable that it only cost £34!

Top right: Don with his best men, John Scholz-Conway and Mike Kent from UTV.

Middle left: Don and I with beautiful baby Caron.

Bottom left: Three years later, Caron was joined by baby Paul. They were such innocent and happy times.

Bottom right: Caron in the arms of my father. He absolutely adored her.

Above left: Paul and Caron playing together.

Above right: Caron loved playing with her dolls, and I'd bring one back for her every time I went away. I stayed up till 3am making that dolly dress.

Below left: Caron and Michael – she really was like a second mother to him and they shared an exceptionally close bond.

Below right: I adore this shot of me holding new-born Michael in December 1970 – the best Christmas present ever.

Left: On stage performing a musical number at the Arts Theatre. It was all feather boas and show tunes.

Right: I loved being a mum but missed my career. Here's a promotional picture for my single 'Are You Ready for Love?', which was a top ten hit and led me into broadcasting.

strange quiet that followed the blast. The whole building was rocking and shuddering around us as people were coming back in, looking dazed but determined. I still remember the sight of the producers rushing outside to plough through the rubble to rescue valuable tapes that had been blasted out onto the street representing months of work. As I was still broadcasting 'live' our controller, Ronnie Mason, came round with a bottle of brandy and insisted I took a shot. By the end of the programme not only was I relieved to have completed it, but my face was flushed with alcohol and adrenalin.

★ ★ ★

The first time I was told my name had appeared on an IRA death list it's a wonder I didn't reconsider my career, but the truth is that I didn't. Not for a second.

In 1969 my fellow broadcaster Sean Rafferty and I started to record a show together for the British Forces Broadcasting Service (BFBS) called *Ulster Calling*, with a view to keeping families on the military bases in Germany, the Rear Party, in touch with soldiers in Northern Ireland. I was to do this for eleven years.

The soldiers' tours would last five months, and it was a gruelling separation for everyone concerned so we tried to keep the families in touch with one another via the radio. We sometimes went out to Germany to visit the families and the rear party too. It was there we learned first-hand how much that Sunday programme meant to them. It really was their only way of hearing how their loved ones were getting on in Northern Ireland and they seemed to enjoy the guys talking about their cramped military bases, the local tea-runs and hearing all the gossip.

I had an officially sanctioned letter from the top military brass allowing me to go into any army base in Ulster to make recordings. Fairly early on I visited a camp not too far from where I lived, which was sheathed with barbed wire fences and lookout posts, so much so that it reminded me of a Nazi concentration camp. I asked the soldiers what it was and they said, 'Can't tell you. Top security'. Much later, I realised that this was the construction of the notorious Long Kesh Prison, which later became known as the Maze.

So much of Northern Ireland was in upheaval, with large empty houses, factories, old buildings and much else turned into army bases. They were often miserable old warehouses with no electricity, heating or running water and hundreds of steps to climb up and down every day. One exception to this was the Grand Central Hotel in Belfast, which must have been the only army base with en-suite bathrooms.

Sometimes there could be an element of farce to the proceedings. I did a lot of interviews at the army bases and on one occasion I was confronted by a soldier with his leg encased in plaster, all the way from his ankle to his hip. I was a little worried about approaching him: what on earth had happened? Had he been wounded by shrapnel? Hurt in a bomb blast? There was nothing for it but to grit my teeth and come out with it.

'What happened to your leg?' I asked.

The soldier's eyes filled with tears at the recollection of the pain.

'It was terrible,' he replied. 'I was at a disco the other night and I fell off my platform shoes.'

You had to laugh.

When Sean and I took our first trip to Germany to visit

the rear parties and families, we didn't know quite what to expect. We were flown there on a military plane, sitting at the front with the colonels and generals, and to make a good impression I had worn a full-length black Cossack coat and fox-fur hat to create a bit of elegance under siege. But quite suddenly, as I sat there chatting to the top brass, the plane dipped sharply and I felt my stomach turn. As the flight got rougher, I became increasingly dizzy, flushed and panicky; off came the hat, the coat was ripped open and I sat there in a sweaty mess. By the time we landed I was an interesting shade of green and could barely stand up. So much for the glamour of broadcasting and trying to make a good impression.

The trips to those camps were an eye-opener. The commanding officers' wives were in charge of morale and a lot of the families included teenage girls, away from home for the first time, not knowing what was happening to their fathers and husbands in Northern Ireland, and often with young children and not speaking the language. It was difficult for everyone to cope.

After a while, it was deemed too dangerous for us to go to the camps in Northern Ireland and so the soldiers were brought into the studio instead. Most of the messages were heartfelt and straightforward: 'I'm fine. Hope you and the kids are OK.' 'Miss you, love. Look forward to coming home soon.' The most ambitious one we had heard was, 'Don't change the sheets, love – I'm coming in with me boots on.'

But the British squaddie sense of humour soon changed all of that because one even more ambitious message came through. 'Well, love, it's not long now but it will be when I get home!' one soldier cheerily assured his wife, prompting Sean and me to laugh so much we couldn't even introduce the next record and had to get our lusty young guest to do so instead.

And then it happened. Once, when we were on our way back to the airport after visiting the families back in Germany, we were called to the brigadier's home for coffee. After the pleasantries he stunned us by explaining that we'd both been placed on an IRA death list. We looked blankly at each other, neither of us knowing what to say. The brigadier then told us we could stop the programme whenever we wanted as he didn't want either of us to be subject to danger. I was a mother of three, after all, and certainly didn't want to deprive my children of a parent, but as we'd been doing it for years, Sean and I decided there was no point in stopping now. The damage, as such, had already been done.

The second time I was allegedly put on a hit list was a few years later, by which time I had moved to London and was presenting my own show on Radio 2. On 20 July 1982, two catastrophic bombs ripped through Hyde Park and Regent's Park, killing 11 people and 4 horses. Again I was 'live' on air and like anyone in broadcasting that day we were linking in to the horrific hourly news bulletins, with little else under discussion that day. However, unknown to me, complaints had started coming in, with threats along the lines of, 'Get that Irish bitch off the air or someone else will.'

I closed the microphone and finished the programme, at which point I realised that the control room had filled with very serious-looking men in suits, who I assumed were doing a tour of the BBC. But no, they came into the studio and told me that a death threat had been made against me. They were taking it extremely seriously and I was to be secreted out of another entrance and taken home by car. I was a bit shaken up at the time as, after all, I'd only recently moved to England and it was a different ball game. From then on, for the rest of the time that I was at Radio 2, I was allowed to drive right up to the back of the building and park my car safely out of sight. So it did me a favour in the long run.

Ironically, the only other bomb I was frighteningly close to was also in London, in the run-up to Christmas, in 1983. I had taken Michael, by now thirteen years old, to Harrods, and as there was a specific game he was after, I let him explore the toy room while I went to the china department. The IRA had warned that there would be a pre-Christmas bombing campaign but, as in Belfast, Londoners simply got on with their lives. As it turned out, on the day itself, the shop received a coded message just after 11am that a bomb would go off and I registered that a voice on the Tannoy asked all the department heads to report to head office. At the time I remember thinking, *If I was in Northern Ireland, I would say that that's a bomb scare.* But I put any concerns down to all those years dodging bombs in Belfast and, anyway, bomb threats didn't mean there was an actual bomb anywhere. The staff were sent to look for anything suspicious, but when nothing was found, decided not to evacuate.

That decision probably saved many lives. At 1.30pm, a car bomb exploded in a nearby side street, killing 3 officers on their way to investigate it, 3 civilians and injuring 90 more. Inside Harrods itself we certainly felt the vibration of the bomb going off and its impact followed by that eerie silence. Everyone was instructed to file out via a certain exit and I was hysterical, not knowing where Michael was but had no choice but to comply – I just had to hope that he was doing the same and that he was all right. Outside, the scene was chaotic: some of the injured were staggering around, with rumours rife that there was another bomb elsewhere and this was a decoy to send us into its path. The scene got more frightening as offices nearby were also evacuated but all I could do was struggle back to my car, which I had parked nearby, and pray that Michael would come and find me there. It was as if time stood still, except my heart was racing with panic. Thank God he turned up minutes later, although to me if felt like hours.

I thought that I was pretty battle hardy after all those years in Belfast, but nothing can prepare you for the terror of waiting for your child to reappear in a situation like that. It is one thing worrying about yourself but, as I came to learn in later years, it is a far worse torture when you are in fear for your child.

But London and the hard-hit areas of Northern Ireland both had to learn to sweep up the glass and get on with their lives.

And although there are hundreds of very serious moments about experiences within the Troubles, there are always of course those black humour moments that bring much-needed laughter. One of these involved a very famous film cameraman in Northern Ireland, called Patsy Hill. He was always in demand because of the extent of the Troubles, and because he was such a brilliant cameraman on those on-the-hoof occasions. Whether it was buses being overturned and burned up the Falls Road, or riots and explosions in many parts of the city, Patsy was always in the midst of it all. He lived on the Antrim Coast road on the east side of Northern Ireland, which would have involved, before the motorways were improved, a 2 ½ hour journey home and his wife, naturally, wanted him to come home every night. So if he'd been out late, and maybe had a drink, the security men at the

BBC would say, 'Patsy, have a rest before you drive and I'll wake you up in an hour or so and bring you a cup of tea'. So, on this occasion, he had a nap followed by a strong cup of tea, drove the journey home, did the proverbial of slowly putting the key in the door, went in as gently as he could, crept up the stairs and was just in the process of taking his trousers off when his wife woke up, looked at the clock and said, 'My God, Patsy, they're not calling you out at 20 past 4 are they?'. 'They bloody are', he replied, and he promptly pulled up his trousers, put on the rest of his clothes and sped back to Belfast.

And if ever there was a symbol of Northern Irish resilience, it had to be the Europa Hotel in Belfast. The Great Northern Railway Station was rebuilt as a hotel during the city's post-war heyday, with tourism boom and optimism at an all-time high. But as well as attracting tourists, the hotel became a mecca for international journalists and when the Troubles took hold, the tourists moved out altogether, leaving only the press. The Europa became the place to live, eat, drink and get vital information about the quagmire of infighting and splinter groups within the paramilitary groups on both sides. Everyone from John Suchet to Sir Trevor McDonald, Simon Hoggart to Anne Robinson cut their teeth in Northern Ireland, and the rule of thumb was to book a room above the fifth floor and never one overlooking Great Victoria Street. There were at least 36 very good reasons for this.

'The most bombed hotel in Europe,' as it came to be known (another moniker was 'the Hardboard Hotel') was bombed at least 36 times after it opened in 1971 and, every time, the brooms came out, the boards went up and within minutes it was business as usual. In fact, under the deft touch of its then manager, Harper Brown, it became a symbol of the people's resilience, warmth, hospitality and endurance. Apart from a three-month period in 1975, the hotel never closed its doors. As other businesses in Belfast staggered to a halt, as strikes cut off the power supply and the city centre shut up shop, only the glaziers in the city centre thrived. Urban legend had it that as soon as they had replaced the windows, they would return to their factories to cut glass for the next time.

Eventually, the hotel was damaged so badly in 1993 that it was sold off to the Hastings Group and closed for a refurbishment. It subsequently reopened in February 1994, a world-class hotel in the world-class city that Belfast has become, with the Hastings family still at the helm.

It is incredible to me to think back to what we all became accustomed to living through, patiently queuing up to be searched, never knowing who or what was in the line. I got so used to being searched and having the contents of my bag rummaged through that when I first moved to London, I automatically opened my handbag under the nose of a rather surprised doorman at any department store I was visiting. We had so many bomb scares at Broadcasting House in Belfast that we'd simply get the warning, step out of the office, grab a coffee, go shopping and then come back when we were told the coast was clear. Of course we were affected by it all, but we had to suppress our feelings. If you let the fear get to you then life would simply close down. Ulster's endurance was simply extraordinary, with the people showing a level of resilience it is hard to overestimate to this day. Of course, with all the terrorist action in Britain recently it takes me once again to an attitude of, you can't let the terrorists win. You have to get on with your life and can't let it psychologically affect you.

CHAPTER 5

A TASTE OF
HUNNI

Northern Ireland in the 1970s could be a pretty grim place with nothing to report but bad news and so, to counteract that, BBC Northern Ireland decided to experiment with a new format. When *Good Morning, Ulster* went off the air for the summer in 1972 the producers decided to try out a considerably lighter format, with guest interviews, records and chat.

I must say it was a relief to be able to talk about day-to-day things and not hard news; it was probably the first of what we now call free-flow broadcasting. Up until then things were mostly scripted but this new format was cheery and personality led. I was approached to front it alongside another journalist called Helen Madden, and we took turns hosting, one week in, one week out. It was an immediate success. People were clearly sick of hearing constant depressing news and wanted something a little cheerier. And that is what they got.

As a result of that, the BBC decided to continue the programme and fortunately asked me to stay on as sole presenter, renaming the show *A Taste of Hunni* (boom, boom), a two-and-a-half hour programme that went out mid-morning on Radio Ulster five days a week. I had a reputation as 'a girl never short of a word', now I was really having to prove that.

It actually could not have come along at a better time. Don had been promoted from a cameraman to a director/producer and the children were growing up. And now, instead of dashing all over the country at the drop of a hat, I could work within school hours – to begin with, at least. Caron and Paul often came into the office with me where they would play cricket in the halls or listen to the latest pop records and in a small, friendly working environment like that, no one had a word of criticism.

My career was going from strength to strength. The new job meant I had to wear any number of hats: disc jockey, reporter, interviewer, game show host, even auctioneer. We talked about everything from the ongoing bombs and barricades, to the shortage of public loos in Belfast. We ran a second-hand shop on air, where people swapped their goods, held phone-in competitions and Funny Photo contests – and this was radio, remember, not TV. Sometimes the pictures on the radio are the best. For example, we had a karate expert on the show who cracked open his head when he was trying to break a pile of bricks – ridiculous. But who would really know the full impact on radio?

Then there was an illusionist sawing me in half with a chainsaw and for all the audience knew we could have been using sound effects, but no one ever complained. We also hosted community service projects, including one to establish a guide dog fund. Listeners sent in several thousand pounds worth of Green Shield stamps, which was enough to train seven dogs. One day I said to a blind person ringing up, 'How's your blind dog today?'

'Oh,' she exclaimed, 'Gloria, it's not my dog who's blind, but me.'

I never made that slip-up again!

Guests on the show came from hugely varied backgrounds. We had doctors, artists and educators, bottle collectors, herbalists and even my personal hairdresser. And for the first time, I branched out into the world of interviewing celebrities: Andy Williams, Telly Savalas (then famous as Kojak), US President Carter's mother, Miz Lillian, and the world renowned flautist James Galway, of whom more anon.

Alongside the daily show, *A Taste of Hunni Irish-style* gave me worldwide success when it went to the BBC World Service and as I sat in the Belfast studio it always amused me to think of people in the depths of darkest Africa listening to this mish-mash of Irish jigs and reels. I got letters from all over the world, but one from India stood out: 'Madam, you'll always be assured of a bed in Bombay.' Mind you, I haven't taken him up on it yet!

We had many extraordinary people on the show, but one I remember in particular is Willie McElroy. Aged seventy-four, Willie was a labourer who came from a very remote area of Ireland, County Fermanagh, and who possessed an extraordinary talent for singing and dancing authentic Irish jigs. He had been performing in pubs and halls for fifty years when the folk singer Bobbie Hanvey discovered him and decided to record him. But Willie came from such an isolated area that he had never had electricity, he'd never seen a television and had only been to Belfast once before – in 1918 on a horse and buggy.

When Willie entered the BBC studios, he looked as if he'd entered the set of a sci-fi film, not that he had ever seen such a thing. He'd never been in a lift and looked nonplussed as the great oak doors opened; in the canteen he ate everything in sight and proclaimed, 'This is some grand hotel you've got here.' He was a charmer and a terrible flirt, and after I interviewed him, he joined Barry Cowan on the 'live' evening television show *Scene Around Six*. We recorded it for him especially and so were able to replay it immediately, with Willie given a chair in front of the television screen in the green room. The look of utter exhilaration and stunned wonderment on his face as he came up on screen was a wonder to behold. He leaped out of his seat, examining himself on screen from every angle. It was a wonderful moment – and at seventy-four Willie had embarked on a brand-new career.

I remember another interesting experience from around this time. It was decided that Belfast would have its first ashram. We were all very intrigued about how this yoga business would work out so a few of us traipsed right across town. Personally I thought it was marvellous and very relaxing but it came to a very sharp end because it wasn't practical with the Troubles going on all over the city. However, during that period, I interviewed the swami from the centre and he came in to the studio to talk about how good this would be for the stresses and strains of the political situation in Northern Ireland. So, in advance I practiced his name over and over again for the 'live' programme: *Swami Satyumurty, Swami Satyumurty, Swami Satyumurty*. All the time I made sure to say his name as often as possible and was so pleased that I got through the interview. But when I closed the mic, the swami turned to me and said, 'To tell you the truth, Gloria I'm just Johnny Smith from The Falls Road'! They were certainly interesting times.

It was during *A Taste of Hunni* that I also made a very embarrassing gaffe on air. Rushing to the studio with an armful of records, I slipped on the kerb and tore several ligaments in my leg so for a while I had to hobble around on a crutch. In the studio itself I used to store the records I had chosen on the floor to the left and on one particular occasion I laid my crutch on top of the pile. And then, caught up in the excitement of announcing a major contest winner, I crowed, 'Congratulations Mrs Jones, you've just won £50, isn't that fantastic! The only problem is, you should see my poor producer grovelling under my crotch looking for the next record.'

Behind the glass my engineer burst out laughing just as I realised what I'd said.

'Oh no, I meant my crutch. Crutch! C-R-U-T-C-H!' But it was too late: I had compounded it.

We really did have a laugh on the show; it was a wonderful few years.

* * *

There was movement on the domestic front, too: we had outgrown Marnabrae Park in Lisburn. After Michael was born, Caron and Paul had had to share a room, which was much too small for them, and they constantly squabbled and argued. One day I smelled burning, raced to their room and discovered that a T-shirt had been thrown over the lamp and caught fire. Fortunately only the T-shirt and lampshade were damaged, but it was another sign that it was time to move on. That home held many happy memories, though: of the children romping around on the nearby farm, playing in the hay shed, collecting freshly laid eggs, feeding the chickens and milking the cows. It felt so much like where I'd grown up. Paul used to play his trumpet out through a back bedroom window, which the cows must have appreciated as they would gather round in the fields outside to listen. He still says it was his best audience ever!

The house was also the scene of the first advertisement I had ever done, in which Caron was perched in the high-chair and I was the supposedly exhausted mother gasping for a cup of tea. Lyons green label tea, with the famous slogan being 'A proper cup of tea'. Recently on holiday, Caron's sons Gabriel and Charlie looked the ad up on Google. I hadn't seen it for over fifty years and it was so funny, as the boys watched their mum in the high-chair, eighteen months old. As you can imagine, they played it over and over again. Oh the joy of it.

The children were involved in other ads as well – one had Paul in a supermarket trolley when he was about a year old, which made Caron jealous as the trolley was filled with toys. However I didn't rope them in when I did an ad for sherry. Actually it was the only time my children saw me totally tipsy because by the time I'd done 35 takes I'm not at all sure I was aware where I was, let alone anything else.

And so, as the family grew we were looking forward to more space. We moved to Hillsborough, near the Queen's Northern Irish residence, Hillsborough Castle (my second close encounter with the Monarch), a lovely Georgian village surrounded by lush green fields and about fifteen minutes' drive from Belfast. We had a new four-bedroom bungalow standing in about three quarters of an acre on the edge of the village. Back in those days, despite the wider turmoil, no one locked their doors and the children took full advantage of that, as did Che, our Labrador. He was a treasured member of the family at that time. Che would leave the house in the morning, call in at the pottery to pick up his girlfriend, then the pair of them would cross the road to the butcher's, get a bone each before walking round the lake at the top of the village and then he would come home when he felt like it. What a charmed life!

On one occasion the owner of a local antiques shop took a client up to inspect a four-poster bed and found Che fast asleep on it, snoring away on the beautiful bed that was now splattered with mud. Fortunately the owner forgave me and Che.

In later years, when we moved to Sevenoaks, Che thought he could pursue the same carefree lifestyle – indeed, I naively thought the same. He was constantly escaping our fenceless garden, which meant that for the first six months I was either in the police station or apologising to my neighbour Mary Day. Che took a particular interest in her bins and indeed her rose beds... Obviously Mary forgave me as well because to this day she is still my secretary.

But we all quickly settled into life in Hillsborough, with its beautiful village and castle. In years to come, when Sir Harry Secombe came to record an episode of his programme *Highway* at Hillsborough Castle, I had the pleasure of singing a song on it called 'In The Gloaming'. It has a rather poignant relevance because the story goes that the English composer Annie Fortescue Harrison wrote the song when visiting the village. Apparently Annie and Sir Arthur, who gave his name to the village, fell madly in love, but as his wife was quite ill at the time sensibility prevailed, hence the line: 'It was best to leave you thus dear/Best for you and best for me'. The story continues that many years later Sir Arthur heard the song, enquired who wrote it and was reunited with Annie. At that point his wife had died and he was free to marry, and so the two lived happily ever after.

Ironically, in 2016 I also hosted an evening to announce that at long last Hillsborough Castle would be open to the public, who will be able to relish not only the Queen's home but the magnificent lake and surrounding gardens. On that evening Historic Royal Palaces managed to find the original TV programme with Sir Harry when I sang 'In The Gloaming' and it was a rather gorgeous moment to watch the video in the room where it had originally been recorded. My boys in particular couldn't wait to get a copy of the video – if only for the big retro hairstyle and the *Dynasty*-style fashion at the time! Well, it *was* the eighties.

I remember other slightly less propitious times up at the castle – Jeanette Charles, who found fame as a lookalike for the Queen, was a guest on *Good Evening, Ulster*, of which more anon, and Stanley Matchett, a photographer with the *Daily Mirror*, thought it would be fun to take a picture of her at Government House. We asked the secretary, who was the custodian of the house when the Queen wasn't there, to greet her and to our amazement he agreed. He even consented to say, 'Ma'am, so pleased you could make it. Please come inside.' We took photographs from the driveway and it all seemed to go very well until he rang us later, having been on the receiving end of a furious tirade from his wife. She was furious he'd taken part in such a tasteless stunt. So the pictures were pulled and Stanley lost his exclusive.

* * *

I have such happy memories of that time in Hillsborough in the seventies. Christmases were a particularly pleasurable time in a small village. We established a routine where on Christmas Eve we'd go to the midnight service in our local church and then the neighbours would come to our house for hot toddies and mince pies. Christmas morning, we'd go neighbour-hopping from house to house and after the family would all sit down for Christmas dinner. In Hillsborough, Boxing Day was an active rugby day and as we knew everyone in the area we usually ended up in the Hillside pub afterwards, telling jokes and stories, with a sing-song and long chats around the fire. In the early days of my marriage, Christmas dinner was traditionally held at my parents' house in their immaculate two-up two-down where I was born. As the family grew, how my mum ever managed to cook for and seat my sister Lena, her husband Rupert, their three children Lawrence, Nigel and Pamela, my brother Charles, his wife Libby and their two children, Michael and Kerry, Don and me with Caron, Paul and Michael, and of course Mum and Dad. *Woah*, sixteen people around two tables in a very small space! But my children remember those Christmases so vividly and with such lovely memories. I still treasure getting all the family together at Christmas and New Year.

I was now working full-time on *A Taste of Hunni* during the week and spending the weekends at home. Don would go out to play golf and my long-term friends Anne Thompson and Patsy England would come round on Sunday mornings to catch up over coffee or I would go to their houses and we would chat about the week's gossip. On Saturdays the kids and I would go out to the shops in the morning and often come back with a Swiss chocolate cake oozing with cream from the local bakery: we'd brew a pot of tea and settle down in front of the television and a roaring fire to watch the old movies of my childhood: *Breakfast at Tiffany's*, *An Affair to Remember* or *From Here to Eternity*. Many years later Caron told me these were some of her happiest memories. All the while, Don played his precious golf – yes, I was a golf widow on weekends.

Then weekends changed when we rented a cottage on Lord Erne's Crom estate, in County Fermanagh, which was about an hour and half away on the West coast of Northern Ireland. These cottages had previously been known as the 'piggeries' and housed Lord Erne's staff, but he had rehoused them in newly converted apartments in the stable yard, complete with all the mod cons, and he rented the cottages out, mainly to people who lived in the city who really thought they were city-slickers. He only charged a peppercorn rent of a paltry £135 a year, the idea being that the renters would make a few improvements during their stay.

Our 'cottage' was actually an immense stone double-fronted house on the edge of Lough Erne, which was a perfect spot for fishing – the locals said it was 29 feet deep, 27 feet of which were fish and 2 of which were water. There were many other local legends, for example, that the lough should be avoided at Easter, as it would inevitably claim lives. And indeed, there did often seem to be a boating accident at Easter. There was also a fable that a leprechaun lived on the estate and was the custodian of the castle.

Lord Erne, like many of the Irish, went along with this mysterious leprechaun tale. Apparently the original castle burnt down and had to be re-sited but the day after rebuilding began, the workmen discovered that it had been mysteriously flattened again. So the building was re-sited again, at which point a story about the silver disappearing from the castle took on a new meaning. It had always been pointed out that if anyone tried to dig for the silver then someone would die, and indeed, when a workman did try to retrieve the booty from where he thought it was, his dog keeled over on the spot. So it remains a mystery. The silver was never found and no ever took a chance to look for it.

To this day some Irish people treat leprechauns with a healthy respect. When they dig for turf, they always leave a mound of dirt for the fairies, and no one would dream of cutting down blackthorn trees, which is where they are said to alight. If a proposed roadway was found to have a blackthorn tree in the middle of it, the developers would plan a detour. And the Irish are very superstitious in other ways: my mother would never have had green carpets in the house or green clothes, and she'd never put new shoes on a table. A picture falling off a wall for no reason was supposed to herald a death, as did the cry of a banshee – the cloaked women, something I was terrified of as a child and I would imagine I could hear at night. You may be very sceptical, but...

Mum had another odd one: 'Saturday flit, short sit'. This meant that you should never move house on a Saturday or you'd only have a short time there, but she took it to much further extremes. When she went into hospital once for an operation, she was due to be discharged on a Saturday and point blank refused to go. When we finally persuaded her – 'Mum, this is silly' – she ended up back in hospital the following Tuesday with complications of phlebitis, so we learned our lesson. I myself can't help but retain some of these superstitions: I never cross anybody on the stairs and if I drop a glove I won't pick it up myself. If someone else does, I won't say thank you. And don't get me started on Friday the 13th…

Superstition aside, our country cottage was perfect for the children growing up and gave them opportunities they couldn't otherwise have had, with 1,800 acres to roam around. Paul had a second-hand mini and, aged just thirteen, learned to drive around the estate. Lord Erne's daughter, Lady Cleone, was then also getting too big for her pony, Brandy, so we bought it for Caron, along with a year's grazing rights, at the ridiculous sum of £50.

In total we had the cottage for five years. Sometimes if Lord Erne was away he would allow us in to the castle to swim in the pool contained in his huge conservatory. At other times we would fish in the lake, hold communal barbecues, and on a Saturday night it was routine for Jamesie, the head gardener, to take us all in an old smuggler's rowing boat up the river to Belturbet, which was across the border. He called it 'going to town' but looking back it was quite irresponsible because when we were all in, the boat was barely an inch out of the water. But we all piled in merrily nonetheless. It seems mad looking back now, as no one had lifejackets and some of us couldn't swim (including me) but we paid no heed to the dangers back then.

And this was particularly odd, because I was terrified of water and still am. I'd never had proper swimming lessons as a child and our local swimming pool at school was a nasty, icy factory pond which I hated. The only time we had anywhere decent to swim as a child was on the annual Sunday school trip to Bangor, an occasion of great excitement. Mum would curl my hair the night before we went, by setting it in rags or fashioning ringlets from curling tongs heated over a gas flame; we were also given five shillings in spending money, a fortune back then. One year I was standing at the edge of the Pickie Pool, when someone pushed me in. I was absolutely petrified. People talk about going down for the third time and I was on the verge of believing that was going to happen to me, because a lot of the bystanders thought I was just larking around, but fortunately someone realised I wasn't and pulled me out. I spent the rest of the day soaking wet, with bedraggled hair, in a state of shock, with my mother's painstaking curls gone.

After that, when we went to Newcastle on holidays, I avoided the water at all costs. I've never really got over that fear of water although I made sure my children learned to swim, but even then I wouldn't let them go into the deep end and I wouldn't let them dive.

'You can learn to swim but stay in the shallow end. You can swim just as well in three feet as you can in six,' I'd say.

And actually, my fears were realised on one occasion. When he was still a young child, Paul was playing by the steps in the shallow end of the pool whilst on holiday when I looked up to see him floating head-down in the water. I screamed for help and dragged him out with the help of a passer-by. We thumped him on the back and forced the water out of his lungs and, perhaps unsurprisingly, Paul too developed a fear of water after that, although as an adult he did eventually learn how to swim.

★ ★ ★

Like every working mother, I felt a certain amount of guilt, and so when we weren't at the cottage at the weekends, I'd take the children on cultural excursions. Caron would have been around fifteen, Paul thirteen and Michael a mere six years old. Whether they liked it or not, I thought they should see plays and films, and visit museums or galleries. I just wanted to expose them to all forms of culture, even though some of it was so boring to them. There would also be short beach holidays, although the Irish climate invariably meant we'd be at the centre of a gale. Fighting against the elements, Don and I would determinedly encourage the children to build sandcastles, while being lashed by the rain.

'Go on, dig, it's only a bit of liquid sunshine,' we'd say.

Although life was getting increasingly busy, being freelance I managed to fit my work schedule around family life. When I was away I'd always bring back a doll back for Caron (as much for me as for her) so she had shelves and shelves of them. Often, I'd sit up until the small hours sewing or knitting new outfits for them so that when she opened her eyes in the morning she'd awake to a newly dressed doll. But we also had our fair share of unhappy incidents: once, when I was at work, her school rang to say that Caron had cut her face. I leaped into my car and drove straight there, tears streaming down my face and wondering if she'd be scarred for life. It turned out she'd been peering over some railings, her foot had slipped off the concrete plinth and she had become impaled on a railing spike. Just a fraction of an inch to the right and it would have gone through her jugular vein. An inch to the left and she could have been blinded, the doctor said. By the time I arrived at the hospital she'd been stitched up by an emergency doctor and in fact it was done so brilliantly she only had a fairly small u-shaped scar under her chin for the rest of her life.

Paul was an excellent sportsman, first as a runner and then as a rugby player. The latter, in fact, inspired one of the very few episodes when I was forced to use extreme discipline. I'm not normally violent, but he failed to turn up to a match on one occasion and when I found out from his sports teacher, I was incensed. When he came home I said, 'How was the rugby match?'

'Great,' he said. 'We won.'

Well, that was it. He was not only letting the team down but also telling lies. I've always believed if you commit to something then you should turn up so I confronted him over the washing up that night.

'I know you're telling lies – why didn't you turn up? Where were you? How dare you do this?'

Paul tried to defend himself, just making me angrier and angrier with his excuses, until I finally hurled the cup I'd been drying at him. He of course ducked, and the cup smashed against a wall.

'Now look what you've done to my good cup!'

Incensed even further I promptly went after him brandishing a breadboard with a handle, chasing him all over the house and hurling abuse at him. We all came to laugh about it in later years; it was just one of the stories often told around the family table. Imagine me today on *Rip Off Britain* chasing a dodgy builder down the street with a breadboard!

This was a lot later but I remember the worst incident involving Michael. He went off on a mountaineering trip after we had moved from Ireland and were living in Kent. One day Michael came home from school and announced that he was going on an expedition to Greenland with the army and the Royal Geographical Society for seven uncontactable weeks. I gazed at him with my jaw almost to the ground as he is not particularly known for his sporting enthusiasm; after all he was the one driven to and from school every day.

However, he always had a very smooth tongue and had clearly talked his way onto the expedition. And so the instructions arrived from school with a long list of equipment he needed, including special hiking boots. I did suggest that he should break them in and make time for a few long walks around the Sevenoaks area, so one day he walked four miles to a friend's house in the country. But then I got the phone call: would I come and pick him up? And that was the extent of his training.

However, the trip turned out to be a total life-changing time because the last phone call came from Iceland before they were dropped in Greenland. I know I got panicked because no Irish mother wants her child uncontactable for seven weeks, so I warned Michael that if he saw a helicopter land one day it would be me. The leader had told me that the walk to base camp would take fourteen hours and so I went to bed, got up, had breakfast, went to work and thought, *He's still walking!* But when Michael came home, he told me their fitness had improved so much that they skipped that journey back in just 6 hours.

Michael also said that on that long trek they rewarded themselves with very restricted treats: a raisin here, a nut there and one square of chocolate. He said he would never look at a bag of fruit and nuts in the same way again. When he finally arrived home with his hair having grown inches and blonder than me, I placed a trail of goodies, including chocolates, sweets and shower gel from the front door, up the stairs and to his room. It turned out he was a changed boy because he said that after walking to hell and back on those walks, he could tackle anything. In fact, one of the first things he did was to organise and visit universities of his choice; ordinarily I would probably have tried to do it for him but he insisted he would do it himself. However, he couldn't go back to school with his long, scraggly sun-bleached hair, so I packed him off to the hairdresser. But of all the worries you can have concerning a child, that one was quite mild.

There were other memorable occasions. We were still living through a grim period in Northern Ireland's history and one prank did not go down so well in the neighbourhood. By now Paul was about thirteen and had made friends with a neighbour's son, Michael Shields, who lived across the road in a place that sat on about eight acres, including a lake. On one dark rainy night, his mother, Diane, was driving up the long lane that led to the house when suddenly a man dropped out of the trees on to the bonnet of her car. She was absolutely terrified, but it soon turned out that the man was in fact a Guy Fawkes dummy, made by Paul and Michael and dressed in their dad's clothes. They had been hiding in the bushes ready to launch it at the right moment. It took a long time before anyone saw the funny side of that.

★ ★ ★

By the late 1970s, the children were growing up quickly. Caron was in her late teens and got a Saturday job behind the bar at a local pub, the Hillside, and also acquired her first boyfriend, Shaun McIlrath, who she first met at school when she was ten-years old. As time went on I often had to spend the day working in Belfast, so Caron acted as 'Mum' to Michael, bringing him home from school and very much acting as his second mum, as she had done from the moment he was born.

Because the Troubles went on for decades, I very quickly learned how fragile life could be and how it could be snatched away from you in a split second so, as a parent, we always had to know where our children were because of the unpredictability of the Troubles. That in a way was an advantage with teenagers. However, I discovered years' later from Caron's friends after she died, that when I thought she was safely at the Arts theatre or the cinema in Belfast she was likely to be visiting 'shebeens' on the Falls Road. Shebeens were illicit drinking dens and the Falls Road was one of the most notorious areas in the city, and a Republican stronghold. Perhaps it was just as well that I didn't know what she was up to at the time. Oh, those big innocent eyes!

If I had known, perhaps I would have coped with Caron's first stint away from home a little better, because at least I'd have known she was out of harm's way. But in 1979, when she was seventeen in the summer before she headed to university, she went off for a stint in France to work as an au pair. The night before she left we were both in tears. I had a dreadful pang as I saw her get on the plane to London and all of a sudden I realised how Mum must have felt all those years previously, when I'd set off to go to Canada at Caron's age. It's only when you have your own children that you understand what your parents went through and, looking back, I'm actually very grateful to Mum that she never let me know how she really felt and how worried she was.

But I missed Caron so much that I had an overwhelming

urge to be close to her. Completely on impulse I put Michael in the car, shot off to Dover, got on a ferry and drove as close to Paris as I could. I finally turned back but not before telephoning Caron and telling her, 'I just want you to know we're close. You're not alone. We're thinking about you.' She later told me she thought that was brilliant; it just shows how close we were.

As it turned out, Caron couldn't stand the job and only lasted for three weeks so she packed it in, went to Paris and had a whale of a time. So much for me worrying about her being homesick! And at any rate, she would soon be crossing the Irish Sea to study at Bristol University, one of a number of seismic changes that the family would undergo a few years hence.

Life had changed in other ways, too. In 1970 I'd got a call from Mum to tell me that Dad had had a stroke: 'It's a bad one, Gloria.' I went straight round to the hospital in Belfast, where my sister Lena had already joined Mum, and where the prognosis was not good. He was semi-paralysed down one side after a deep bleed to the brain and was only semi-conscious. The doctors told us to expect the worst. He was in a cot with rails to keep him from falling out and gave me such a blank look, I realised he didn't recognise me. It was frightening, knowing that this was my gorgeous, talented and clever dad and that he might never be the same again.

But deep down that fighting spirit was still there – men like him were a 'tough wee nut' to use the phrase prevalent in Northern Ireland. When the nurse came in to feed him, he'd stubbornly push her away – clearly furious with himself that he wasn't able to manage on his own – something he did more and more forcefully as the days wore on until he was finally able to feed himself. After a while, he managed to sit up, insisted that the side of the bed was kept down and finally, after ten days, he started to recognise us once more. After that he began to recover properly, although he was never again the big, strong Dad I had when I was growing up. In some ways it was really sad because in order to try and show you he was still strong he would lift you up, which sometimes was a bit irritating but we just went along with it, only too relieved he was alive.

Eventually, he was even able to go home, and managed to regain some strength in his limbs and power of speech, though he still slurred badly and often made no sense. He would say things like, 'It's a hot moon today,' and I could tell how bitterly frustrated he was not to be able to make himself understood. He became extremely demanding, probably as a result of the fright he felt at the loss of his strength, demanding dinner right there and then when he wanted it and not waiting for anything or anyone. He also became extremely emotional.

It is so painful to watch the parent you have known and loved deteriorate to such an extent and I found it very difficult. But with sheer determination, Dad went on to have a good quality of life and despite suffering a few small strokes he lived ten years more. On his seventieth birthday in the late seventies we managed to give him a wonderful surprise: Lena invited him round to help her choose the colour of her new carpets. Unbeknownst to him we were all waiting, hidden in the sitting room. When he arrived we sprang out at him with a birthday cake and candles; you could tell how thrilled he was from the look in his eyes with all his loved ones around him.

His last Christmas was to be in 1980. By that time my

brother Charles was living in Staffordshire, where he was working in computer graphics, and so I got him to fly over to Portadown with his wife Libby and their two children, Kerry and Michael. I hid them in the car outside my parents' house and went in to prepare Dad in advance.

'Now, Dad, just sit down here, I've got this big box I'm going to bring in for you.'

Charles and the family burst in to the room and again the expression on Dad's face was a sight to behold. I kissed Dad goodnight that night, with a feeling that somehow I had tied up the loose ends.

The following year he died peacefully in his sleep.

We were all devastated of course but it was particularly hard for Mum and, for a time, Lena moved in with her in Portadown to help. But after only a month or so Mum told her, 'This is silly. You can't go on like this, you've got your own family.' She hated being alone but she put a brave face on it. Lena lived nearby and I was only a 45-minute car drive away so we made a particular effort to see her and would especially go round on Saturdays. Dad had been buried on a Saturday and we wanted to lift her spirits by getting her out of the house. More often than not we'd find her in tears baking his favourite bread. But over time she grew stronger and managed and learned to live on her own.

As we gradually cleared out Dad's things, at long last I was able to have a proper rummage through his magic cupboard without fear of being found out. I felt myself becoming a little girl again as I went through his tricks, and yearned to feel him once more lifting me on to the stage, holding my little hand in his big one as we both took our bows. Finally it came home to me how much I am my father's daughter. Lena, Charles and I all had our favourite possessions of his, and mine is his treasured book of magic tricks, like the one he gave me to record my childhood singing performances in.

My only regret about Dad is that he never lived to see me achieve the national broadcasting success on television, which was to come so soon after his death. But it was the path that he had started me out on, even without my realising it and a part of me thinks, wherever he is – he knows.

★ ★ ★

My big break into television was just around the corner, but again, somewhat unwittingly, I was laying down the foundation of something I could not ever have dreamed would come my way.

I had recorded an album towards the end of the 1970s called, inevitably, *A Taste Of Hunni*, and decided to see if I could get it some airplay. And so I did what you never do and went straight to the top: naively I just phoned up the big bosses in London and got a meeting with Charles McClelland and David Hatch, who were the BBC London controllers at the time.

'You don't know me but I work for BBC Northern Ireland. I'm coming to London soon; is there any chance I could come in and see you for a cup of coffee?'

Well, I walked into the room with half a dozen albums under my arm, hoping for nothing more than a little airplay on Radio 2.

I already had my next move lined up in Northern Ireland – of which much more in the next chapter – and so I wasn't that worried about sticking to the party line. In fact, I was definitely more unguarded than I would otherwise have been. When you're not looking for a job, you get very brave.

'Look, I'm in the process of leaving the BBC,' I told them. 'I don't know if I'm doing the right thing, but I'm going to work on Ulster Television. So I'm not here looking for a job.'

Without even mentioning my album, they straight away asked me about Radio 2 and what might be wrong with it. So I launched in and told them, 'There is a huge void in your network because there are no women. You may think it's only women who are at home listening, but men have car radios and listen at work. Retired men tune in at home, then there are the unemployed and women might like to listen to another woman.'

'You're absolutely right,' they said 'By the way, do you know anything about music?'

I quickly whipped out a copy of *A Taste of Hunni*.

'Why don't I leave this with you along with my details and maybe sometime something might crop up?'

Truly, the most I was hoping for was that they would actually listen to the record and perhaps get me some air play. Instead, something quite different happened and it was to lead to the biggest break of my career.

CHAPTER 6

MOVING THE BIG PIECES

Shortly before that conversation in London, there had been some pretty big upheavals back home in Northern Ireland, too. By 1978 *A Taste of Hunni* had been going on for years, but it was around this time that Ulster Television got in touch. They had decided to do a complete overhaul of their six o'clock nightly news programme, *Good Evening, Ulster*. Until then they had concentrated solely on hard news, but Brian Waddell, who was Head of Programming at the time, decided that the viewers must be getting sick and tired of such unremitting grimness, with violence and destruction on the screen night after night, and they were going to try an altogether softer format instead. It was the first time that an ITV region had extended their local news to one hour which by any standard is a lot of daily television.

The news would still get the amount of time it deserved, so if it had been a heavy news day, it would get, say, 35 minutes of the programme. But on a quieter day, if it only merited 10 minutes then that's what it got. The rest of the time would be filled with magazine-type pieces, celebrity profiles, community events and perhaps even competitions. And they wanted me to front the show.

A whole new chapter of my life was opening up. I was a bit nervous about leaving the BBC, but the opportunity was just too big to pass up. I had become well accepted for my radio work, but this was something different all together. Just before the programme launched, I organised a trip to London to visit as many publicity people, agents and record companies as I could, asking them to consider us for celebrity guests. Bearing in mind that the Troubles were still raging, this was not a time that many celebrities wanted to visit Northern Ireland, but it was a useful trip for contacts and of course to do a bit of clothes shopping!

It was a hugely formative time in my working life; not only was I presenting the show at UTV, but I was also its assistant producer. This meant that along with the main editor, Alan Wright, I had to come up with the items, research the stories and then go out in the mornings to film them.

Back in the office I'd have to edit the film myself, write the script and prepare for the rest of the programme, leaving room for the news part of the show which was put together by the extremely efficient news room. Then there were other considerations like hair, make-up and clothes to worry about. I'd leave the house first thing in the morning and often not be back until eight or nine at night.

Somehow, we established a rollicking pace on the show and kept it up. And we were getting great feedback too; people were glad of the light relief from all the hard news, as hoped.

The show was an immediate success and if we didn't get all five programmes in the weekly Top 10 ratings we wanted to know why.

The BBC in Northern Ireland couldn't hide their disdain at what we were trying to do. 'It'll never work,' they said. 'Imagine all this devastation going on and they're going to come out of the news and talk to some pop star.' But it soon became apparent that the BBC was going to have to eat its words. The audience wanted something to take its mind off the Troubles, not constantly harp on about one atrocity after another and, anyway, there were other things going on in the province and they wanted to hear about it.

Of course, this all meant a lot of changes at home. For a start, this put me in competition with Don, who was directing a rival BBC news programme – which made for some lively table talk – but again he was very supportive. He left work earlier than me, while I was still on air, and did his bit to look after the children, as did Caron with her two younger brothers. Sometimes she would pick Michael up from school and at other times Michael would go straight to the UTV studio, where he remembers doing his homework in my dressing room – 'I knew all the make-up girls – they were like family,' he recalled as an adult. On one rather hilarious occasion Michael came actually into the studio when I was 'live' on air to ask a question about his homework: a hand shot out from one of the production staff and he was yanked out of sight behind the weather board until the advertisement break, when he was set free to come across and talk to me.

We also depended on our elderly babysitter Gilly and her husband Tom, a former bank manager, who lived not too far from Belfast and on my way home. The children even called Tom 'Papa' and they were both almost like honorary grandparents to the kids. I have very fond memories of picking Michael up from Gilly's house when I finished work. There he would be sitting on Papa's knee being told stories by a roaring fire. On the side would be a beautifully laid trolley, set with the best china and dainty sandwiches and cakes. 'Darling,' she said, 'you must never let your standards drop.' It is a valuable lesson to this day. And certainly Michael knows how to set a table!

It was still far less common for women to have a career and work fulltime back then as it is now and so a few eyebrows were raised. I did feel a bit guilty at times. But now it's widely accepted that a fulfilled mother is a better mother and, anyway, when I asked the children if they would rather have had a stay-at-home mother, they assured me they would not. Family was and always has been at the centre of my world; Paul often reminds me that I was ready to drop everything if there was a crisis or drama, but I wanted to work, too.

Anyway, there were a fair few compensations in having a mother who worked with the stars. Of course I'd interviewed big names in the past, but not that many of the internationally famous ones. Now, these were the people we were managing to get on the show. Many remained reluctant to visit because of the Troubles, but we went all out to get the really famous stars of the day. We were also happy to talk to any of them at any time, having binned the previous policy of only running interviews with a big name when they had a show or a book to plug. And they quickly started to appear. Jean-Michel Jarre, Charlotte Rampling, Bob Geldof, Billy Connolly and Des O'Connor all came on the show. My son Michael was particularly impressed when the singer Hazel O'Connor came on; he was also very excited when he got to meet Rod Stewart and Elton John. After Rod's appearance, in his trademark leopard-print pants, we all rushed off to see him in concert (a particular benefit of having a mum who worked in television). Caron was especially thrilled when we got up close to Rod Stewart – she used to pretend, on days when I was able to drive her to school, that I was Rod and she was the interviewer asking me all about my next record or concert tour. After all I was blonde and partial to a bit of leopard print! Those were such innocent times.

Elton John took some wooing. He was coming to Belfast for a concert and we tried every conceivable avenue to get to him: his promoters, agents and personal assistants. Now, as you probably know by now, I rarely take 'no' for an answer so I sent flowers to his hotel room and even got the manager of the hotel, whom I knew, to put in a good word. But for days and days, despite even sending a bellboy to deliver a rather begging note to his room, there was nothing. Then, at around 5pm one day, we got a call out of the blue.

'If you come round to the hotel at 6.30, we'll do the interview,' Elton said.

The minor problem there was that we were actually on air at 6.30, but I was determined to get round it somehow.

So I did the programme 'live' until 6.20pm, at which point I just announced, 'I've got to leave now as I'm off to do an interview with Elton John, which we'll have for you tomorrow night.'

It was unprecedented back then, but I immediately packed up all my things and left the studio, with my co-presenter Gerry Kelly, who went on to become one of Ireland's biggest celebrities, left running the show. I remember running so fast to make sure I wasn't late to meet Elton at the much-bombed Europa Hotel.

'I'm very sorry we didn't get into the studio,' Elton said, after we'd finished the interview.

My ears pricked up at this: he was clearly in an accommodating mood.

'Well look, we've done this great piece now, why don't we do a really big special and have you "live" in the studio tomorrow night so you can take phone calls from people?'

'Yeah, I'd like that,' said Elton. 'It'd be nice to talk to the young people of Northern Ireland.'

What a coup!

And so the next night, we completely surprised the viewers by telling them that after the ad break, Elton would be 'live' in the studio to take their calls. The switchboard practically melted from the numbers that immediately rang in. It was fantastic! Elton thoroughly enjoyed himself and was fabulous at talking to his fans. But what we hadn't reckoned on was that his fans, alerted to his presence, would mob him as he left. The crowd was so strong that one of the windows of his car caved in and a visibly shaken Elton, covered in glass, was driven away. This would have been unnerving anywhere but particularly in Belfast at the time of the Troubles. However, I gave Elton top marks for bringing a lot of pleasure to the viewers at that tough time.

Another notable interviewee, although this was considerably less successful, was Van Morrison. On this occasion we got the news that he was coming back to his native Belfast to do a concert which had sold out in 10 minutes. Satellite links weren't all that common for us then, but we used it to do an interview with him from London, where he was sitting in a chair with his feet up on a table, dunking biscuits in his tea. He proceeded to slurp his tea and pick bits of cracker from his teeth, while his answers to questions didn't go much beyond 'yeahs' and 'yups' throughout. For years afterwards people would talk about how incredibly rude he was during that interview. But I still adore Van Morrison and go to his concerts whenever I can. Once he even signed a record and picture for my brother Charles, who is Van the Man's ultimate fan. I know that treasured memorabilia is still up on his wall.

A considerably happier experience came when I got a call from John Howson from Polydor Records.

'How would you like to do an interview with Donny and Marie Osmond?' he asked. This was when The Osmonds were at the absolute height of their fame and so I flew to London to record the interview on a Saturday, which was to be aired the following Monday. They always have been, and always will be a delight to interview, and the audience absolutely loved every minute of it. Little did I think that many years later Donny would stand in for me presenting *Open House* on Channel 5 – but that's another story.

Luckily, UTV were very understanding about me being a working mum because all three children were constantly pleading to come to the station or to be allowed into my dressing room. As an adult, Caron remembered that all her friends at school would be green with envy when she told them all how she'd met David Essex, Elton John or whoever the pop star of the moment was.

Paul was equally pleased – he's always been an extreme U2 fan and on one occasion in the early nineties, when we were travelling through Nice airport back to London, he had gone slightly ahead of me and through Passport control. I was carrying two smallish paintings under my arm, plus a handbag and along came this familiar chap in a fedora and dark glasses, and he said, 'How are you, Gloria? D'you remember me? I'm Bono, and you did my very first interview with U2 on Ulster Television.' Well of course I remembered, and he in a gentlemanly way offered to carry my paintings. And as we went towards Passport control all I could see was Paul pressed up against the glass pointing and mouthing, 'It's Bono, it's Bono' as if I didn't know. He was beside himself and was thrilled to meet him.

Later, because we were sitting separately on the plane, one of the stewardesses was chatting to Paul and said:

'You'll never guess who's onboard today?'

'Oh I know, I know,' he replied, presuming she was going to say Bono.

But instead, he always revels in what she said:

'Gloria Hunniford'!

★ ★ ★

Even my own mother got a bit carried away by all the star names. The one that meant most to her was the world snooker champion Dennis Taylor. She adored snooker, especially if Dennis was playing, and once, during a final of the world championship, the match was so close that I couldn't bear it. I had to hide out in the hall, asking Mum for play-by-play reports, something I told Dennis about and got roundly teased for. [Ultimately, after moving to London, I was actually able to introduce him to Mum when he came on *Sunday, Sunday*. She was thrilled and I still have the photograph of the occasion.]

But of all the people I met and interviewed back then, the

one that most stands out was my encounter with the big band leader James Last. He was performing in Dublin in 1980 and we went to the Mirabeau restaurant to record the interview; it was just outside Dublin and was owned by Sean Kinsella who had been a chef on the *QE2* and the *Canberra*, and was Ireland's first celebrity chef. There were no prices on the menu and Sean would also choose the wine for you, with prices varying depending on whether you were on a corporate jolly or paying for it yourself.

James Last had a reputation of being a true gourmet, as well as someone who looked after his 70-strong band of musicians very well. But when the crew and I walked into the restaurant, I saw a banquet the likes of which I had never encountered before. Tables were piled high with Dublin Bay prawns, smoked salmon, seafood and Sean's speciality boneless duck in a delicious sauce. All of this was washed down with Salmanazars of champagne, buckets of Chablis and three crates of Chateau Margaux that Sean had bought for £124 a bottle. Per bottle? I'd never heard of such a thing. The bill that night – and this was 1980 – came to £17,500! James said that that was why no one ever left his orchestra, because he looked after them so well – and on a subsequent trip to Belfast, he insisted that Sean came on the bus to feed them en route.

In total, I was on *Good Evening, Ulster* for two and a half years, and during that time my life was beginning to change massively. For a start, now that I was on television every night rather than the radio, the public recognition increased. Our format was a very relaxed, easy-going one, and so people had no qualms approaching me on the street for a chat: they would ask for the answer to the previous night's trivia question, or compliment me on my dress or what was so-and-so like. Sometimes they'd say, 'Oh, Gloria, you look just like yourself'. Given that I'd been performing since I was a child, this didn't faze me in the slightest, although the kids teased me about the fact that in supermarkets I had to stop every two minutes to chat. It took a very long time to shop and still does! Michael still hates going to Tesco with me. They told me later that they'd walk behind me to listen to what people were saying about me, good and bad. They'd talk about my clothes and hair, and some women would even go into the hairdresser's and ask for a Gloria cut. Caron once said, 'It was frightening – she was becoming an institution.'

Mercifully, the kids were never bullied or teased about who their mother was and, while there might have been the odd bit of sniggering, I was on the whole viewed as the mum who not only interviewed pop stars, but probably knew more about them than did the younger generation. When music came on television, other parents would say, 'Turn that rubbish off,' I'd say, 'Turn it up!'

But change was on its way.

* * *

Throughout my whole life I've had the feeling that someone, somewhere, was moving the big pieces around. I had all but forgotten about that meeting a few years earlier in London with Charles McClelland and David Hatch, but it seems that they had not forgotten about it. Nor had they forgotten the fact that I said that men still dominated the airwaves and they needed a few women to counteract that. Given that the debate is still raging today, I was somewhat ahead of my time.

I was in London in 1981 filming an interview for *Good Evening, Ulster*, when my secretary, Ann Black, rang.

'You've had a call from *The Jimmy Young Show* on Radio 2,' she said. 'They want to know, can you do two weeks' holiday relief during your summer break in July?'

I honestly thought someone was having a laugh. Jimmy Young was one of the biggest presenters on radio back then, with the top political programme in the country. Why on earth would Radio 2 want me?

'C'mon Ann, someone's pulling your leg,' I said. 'If BBC London were going to ask me to present a programme, they'd want to talk to me, audition me, find out what it is I do, if I'm even qualified. They wouldn't just offer it out of the blue.'

'Well,' she said, 'don't shoot the messenger. Here's the number and the name. I really think you should call back.'

Much against my better judgement I did so, and to my great astonishment found out that it was true. It turned out that David Hatch was the man behind it. He was offering me the chance of a lifetime to go on network radio. In fact, there was a meeting to confirm it, rather oddly in Barclays Bank across the road from the BBC. The Jimmy Young team was on its way to Japan to do some programmes and as they were picking up their Yen from the bank that was to be our clandestine meeting place, as apparently Jimmy was a bit suspicious about stand-ins.

It was made clear to me almost immediately that the job was mine. At first I felt sheer euphoria, mixed with sadness that Dad wasn't around to hear about it, but Mum, Don and the kids were bound to be thrilled. I couldn't wait to tell them – until quite suddenly a chill ran down my spine. And that chill took the form of another of the biggest names in broadcasting, Sir Terry Wogan. I suddenly felt quite apprehensive.

I already knew Terry – I had interviewed him in Ulster

and knew him to have a rapier wit. Should he choose to do so, he could wipe you out with a single barb and one of the few people who could stand up to him was Jimmy Young. I knew that, the rest of the country knew that, heck, even the Queen knew that, because it was said that she was a listener to that regular slot, which was the handover between Terry who did the breakfast programme, to Jimmy who had the mid-morning slot. They would swap banter for five minutes about who was going to be on *The Jimmy Young Show* and the gossip of the day. The thought of having to do likewise scared me half to death.

Even so, there was no way I was going to let this opportunity slip away from me – this was moving from regional into national broadcasting, and I was determined to give it a go and do my best. So, during the summer break at UTV I came to London a couple of days early to familiarise myself with the place, meet the team and to swot up on national politics. This was the early part of the Thatcher decade, and I wanted to make sure I knew my stuff.

But it was that interchange that was keeping me awake at night, as I lay in bed wondering how on earth I was going to manage to hold my own. I started ringing around all my contacts to find out what Terry was up to, how his golf was going, anything, really, that could be used as ammunition. And finally I settled on my strategy. I was going to have to go on the defensive and get my retaliation in first.

When the day came, taking my chair in the broadcast booth at Radio 2, I was so focused on escaping the jaws of Wogan that I didn't have time to brood about the fact that I was setting myself up for an almighty fall. The show had 8 million listeners and if I made a mess in front of all of them, that would be that. Terry looked as if he was enjoying himself:

'Next up we have Grievous Bodily Hunniford,' he announced. 'Gosh I can see her now behind the glass, wearing those slinky fishnet stockings and high heels.'

'I'm so disappointed,' I sighed in return. 'My grandmother's been talking about you for years. I expected some handsome man in a sharp suit and here you are sitting there unshaven with egg stains down your dressing gown. Look at you. You're a disgrace!'

It worked. In fact, it not only worked, it made a sensation. Little Miss Nobody daring to cheek the great Wogan went down a storm and that was the way I was introduced to the listening public. It made all the difference right from the start. And Terry, bless him, let me get away with it and treated me wonderfully from then on in, for which I remained eternally grateful.

There was real banter between us too, with Terry calling me everything from Honey Gloriford, Hot Lips Hunniford, GBH, Gus Honeybun and many more. Michael told me that he thought the reason for my success was that I came across as both a working mother and a bit naïve, which many people could relate to. Whatever the reason, it worked and I really think it was the banter that led me to greater things with Radio 2.

Once the ordeal of handing over was done with, I could actually get on with enjoying the job. I had been used to local news until then – although, saying that, Northern Ireland featured pretty heavily in the national news back then – but now I had to shift my focus to a global perspective. I had to do my homework. Don was back home with the kids and when

I rang and told him that I'd have to talk about the Lebanon, he was greatly amused: 'What do you know about the Middle East?' *Not much*, I thought.

In Ireland I had avoided sticking to a list of prepared questions, but now I let myself be guided by John Gurnett, who was the senior producer on Jimmy's show. He was a mine of information and it worked. 'You sounded so knowledgeable!' the research team teased me afterwards – it was only thanks to them and their fantastic research.

★ ★ ★

I loved it, and I loved living in London; the two weeks sped by. It was extremely hard work, but as I was away from home I could really concentrate on the programme and the news.

On the Friday at the end of my second week, David Hatch called me into his office – I was very proud of the way it had gone but I wasn't expecting anything more than a cup of tea and a pat on the back. If I was really lucky, I hoped they might ask me back for a second stint some time.

'Look,' said David. 'We're very impressed with the job you've done. How would you like your own programme?'

Well, that floored me. I looked at him in amazement. Here was the opportunity of a lifetime, not least because I'd be the first female presenter to be offered a daily programme on Radio 2. But I couldn't just drop my life in Northern Ireland and the thought of moving from being a big fish in a small pond to a minnow in a giant one was unnerving.

Thrilled though I was at the offer, I wasn't so sure I could take it up. My husband and children were settled in Ulster and I couldn't just make them up and leave everything they

134

knew. But again, it was as if someone was moving the pieces of my life...

When I got back to Hillsborough, I told Don about the offer and it turned out that he had also had an approach of his own – to go to South Africa for a prestigious producing and directing job that was to begin in January, and he was keen on taking it. As for the children, Caron was at Bristol University reading English and Drama, while Paul was just about to go to college in Guildford to study Stage Management at the Yvonne Arnaud Theatre. That would leave Michael, just ten, and me in Hillsborough. Perhaps the timing was right for a change?

That summer we took a family holiday to Florida and I asked everyone's opinion

'I say, just go for it, Mum,' said Caron.

'It's a fabulous opportunity. Take it,' said Paul.

Michael was really excited about the thought of moving to London too but I wouldn't have gone if Don hadn't encouraged me.

'We don't want to hold you back,' he said. 'If you didn't take the job, you'd always look back and say, "What if?" You'd always wonder. I don't want there to be any regrets. It's a marvellous opportunity, once in a lifetime. If you want to do it we're all behind you.'

'Anyway,' added Don, 'you know how you like a challenge and if you don't take it you'll be hell to live with.'

So I picked up the phone to David Hatch.

'Is the offer still open?' I asked.

★ ★ ★

We decided that I would do a three-month trial starting the following January, which suited everyone as it meant that I could fulfil my UTV contract and we could have Christmas in Ireland together before Don went to South Africa and we moved to London. But it was a daunting prospect. It wasn't the job per se – I was a very experienced presenter by now, accustomed to everything from celebrity chat to hard news. What was unnerving was the idea of scale. I was moving from regional broadcasting to national. And if I failed, what then?

There was another totally unexpected and oddly upsetting aspect to it as well. While my bosses at Ulster Television understood exactly what kind of opportunity awaited me, the public at large did not; there was a perception that by moving from television back into radio, I was taking a step back. I had built up a relationship with viewers and realising that some felt I was letting them down was hard. Even the *Belfast Telegraph* piled in, publishing a cartoon with the caption, 'Snot Funny, Losing Our Hunni, Must Be The Munni'.

But one person delights in telling me how thrilled he was that I left, and that's my good friend Eamonn Holmes. It's always flattering listening to him talk about how much he learned from watching *Good Evening, Ulster*: it was an ambitious way to make a programme and involved a steep learning curve. At that time, Eamonn had been working on *Farming Ulster* and was the obvious choice to get the job as my replacement: he was young, good-looking and perfect for a presenting job. I often tease him that I knew him for six years in short trousers, but if truth be told he has the same Ulster work ethic that I do: he might have six projects on the table but he'll always be worried about the next. And look what's happened to him since!

Back on the home front there were practicalities to consider: we decided to leave the house in Hillsborough as it was and

Top left: Behind the microphone, in the *Good Morning Ulster* studio.

Top right: A bit of a coup on *Good Evening Ulster*, when we had the first DeLorean off the production line. I now wish I'd bought one and kept it.

(© *Ulster Television*)

Centre: With Jimmy Galway – he's become a true friend, and even played the flute at my wedding to Stephen.

(© *Ulster Television*)

Right: Val Doonican on my show *Good Evening Ulster* – he was such a big part of my career. (© *Ulster Television*)

Above: When I went to London, he returned the favour by inviting me on his Saturday night show. Here we are singing 'Mysterious People'.

Below left: With Jimmy Young – my opportunity to stand in for him set my career on a path that I never could have imagined at that time.

Below right: In the BBC Radio 2 studio lining up the next record. Listeners didn't realise that it was all self-operated. Such wonderful times.   © *BBC*

Left: My dad, before he became ill. He was a dapper chap.

Right: I love this photo, taken at my dad's 70th birthday party, with Caron beside him, Lena to my left and Don cheering from behind.

Left: I had such support from all my family, particularly my mum. Here we are at her house in Portadown where I was born and raised.

Right: A Mother's Day special on *The Des O'Connor Show* alongside Russell Harty and Michael Parkinson's mums. Mum was a local star in Portadown after that. *(© ITV)*

Right: I couldn't believe my luck when I interviewed the Duke of Edinburgh on *Good Evening Ulster*.

Left: I was thrilled when I was asked to perform on the *Royal Variety Performance*. This is me meeting The Queen Mother, beside Esther Rantzen and Jan Leeming (after our show-stopping cowboy routine!) in 1982.

Right: I was also lucky to present the *Royal Variety Performance* a number of times and met some incredible people. In 1983, The Queen was the royal guest of honour and it was a privilege to meet her.

Left: At a charity event with Princess Diana. As we ceremoniously cut the cake, I cheekily said to her, 'I think this means we're married now.'

Left: There will never be such a legendary broadcaster as Terry Wogan. Here we are on the phone lines for Children in Need in the late eighties.   *(© BBC)*

Below: Terry and I dressed as Sonny and Cher for BBC's Children in Need – I can't believe Su Pollard didn't even recognise me.   *(© BBC)*

Left: I'll miss the fun and banter that we had together. He was such a good man to talk to and became a great friend.

Top left: Michael and his grandmother, when she came over to visit us in Sevenoaks. They had such a lovely relationship.

Top right: Mum meeting her hero, world champion snooker player Dennis Taylor. She couldn't contain her excitement.

Middle: With my brother Charles and sister Lena. Look at the size of my hair.

Bottom right: Caron and I on Clearwater Beach, Florida. Thank goodness this bathing suit wasn't knitted!

Above left: Caron when she first started at *Blue Peter* in 1986. Look at that smile and what radiance she had.

(© *BBC*)

Above right: Caron with the famous *Blue Peter* dog. Landing that job was transformational for Caron.

(© *BBC*)

Below: Michael, Caron and Paul in 1991. Whilst Caron worked on the BBC1 programme *Summer Scene*, we rented this sweet Welsh cottage, which was surrounded by fields and sheep.

My gorgeous mum, with her delicious award-winning wheaten bread.

rent it out, just in case things didn't work out. I had to break the news to Mum too, who was delighted for me but also torn: 'London, why it's a million miles away! I'll never get to see you again!' Irish mothers take it hard if they think their children are leaving them and I had to promise Mum over and over that I would visit frequently, starting soon.

I found it hardest to say goodbye to Don, though. We were both setting off to pastures new but at that time we'd been married for twenty years and had never spent any more than twelve days apart. Now, not only were we going to be separated for months, we were going to be on the opposite sides of the world. But there was no going back now. What was done was done and despite my reservations I was excited.

One of the first and most urgent priorities was to find a school for Michael. I hadn't a clue how to go about that, so I rang the BBC education advisor to ask for advice. She told me she'd just moved to be near an excellent school in Sevenoaks and when I pointed out that Michael had been offered a place there, she said, 'Look no further.'

The problem about where to live had essentially been solved for me: we were going to settle in Sevenoaks, although I hadn't a clue how to get from there to Broadcasting House. But someone moved a piece again, because right across from the school was a place to rent called Courtyard Cottage. And so that became our new home. By pure coincidence my old boss at UTV had also recommended Sevenoaks as a good place to live – half an hour on the train to London but out in the country – and I love it so much that I am still there to this day.

Saying goodbye to friends, family and colleagues represented an even bigger upheaval, though. I remember standing looking at Broadcasting House in London, thinking to myself, *Do I have to go into that building, open my mouth and actually say something?* We had been huge radio buffs as a family, listening to the likes of *Children's Hour*, *Workers' Playtime*, *Two-Way Family Favourites* and the *Billy Cotton Band Show* – was I really up to the job of following in those hallowed steps? And then I started belatedly fretting about my accent. The Troubles had spilled over to the mainland and sometimes the high-profile Irish, whatever their own thoughts about the turmoil, were the subject of negative comment. Even in the early days Terry had been on the receiving end of that. At the time though, there were quite a few Irish presenters on the airwaves and we called ourselves the Irish Murphia. If people said, 'What makes the Irish good broadcasters?', I would tell them it was the Guinness!

I didn't really know London either, just places from the Monopoly board, Piccadilly Circus, Trafalgar Square and Oxford Street, so I had to learn my way around my new city. I also quickly discovered that Sevenoaks is not near the heart of London: it's a couple of hours' drive away in Kent. So I went from a fourteen-and-a-half minute commute in Northern Ireland to a two-hour drive every day, in and out of a bustling metropolis. I had to do a dummy run with a map in my lap, just to make sure that I could find my way to the BBC. Remember, it was long before the days of Sat Nav.

* * *

On my first day I nervously made my way to Studio E, where the producer Colin Martin had been teaching me to operate the control desk. It was all self-op and I learned that a TV crew from Northern Ireland had been sent over to film my first day on the job, which was incredibly daunting but I was determined to make them proud.

I remember my first record on my very first programme was 'Afternoon Delight' and for some strange reason I decided to sing along to it in the intro – *doodily doo doo doo doodily doo doo doo*... Why did I do that? Was it in order to show everyone how relaxed I was? Inside, of course, I was a complete bag of nerves.

My first guest was Lord Lichfield, the famous photographer and cousin of the Queen who I personally chose on the grounds that he was something of a good luck charm for me. He had been on my first show on UTV and later he was also to be one of my first guests on *Sunday, Sunday*. He was married to Leonora, daughter of the Duke of Westminster, who had a family seat in Northern Ireland, and it meant that he knew both the mainland and Northern Ireland and was himself well-known in both. He was a wonderful raconteur and I knew I could count on him to tell a few good stories, while I concentrated on learning how to use all this new technical equipment. And after a few hours, I was soon driving the desk by myself and loving it all.

During that first week I also had the infamous actress Diana Dors on the show and I remember thinking to myself, *I'm sitting here with this legendary bombshell and getting paid to do it*. I truly couldn't believe my luck. And so it went on from then on in, this new life making my way on national radio in a new city, meeting some of the most famous people of the day and reaching out to millions of viewers. I remember one day in particular, when I was sitting spinning the records, reading the news and I looked through the glass and thought to myself, *Dustin Hoffman is sitting out there, drinking out of a BBC polystyrene cup and waiting to talk to me.* It was that unreal feeling, but incredibly thrilling and exciting at the same time, and it was happening every day.

But everything comes with a price. I was enjoying success that I dreamed of as a child, and meeting so many of my heroes from the golden period of Hollywood. My children were all settled in England as well, and seemed happy. But that was no longer the case between Don and me. Had I stayed in Ireland I doubt things would have turned out the way they did, but life clearly had other plans.

CHAPTER 7

BREAKING THE BOUNDARIES

It didn't take long to find my feet at Radio 2 and I was loving every minute of it. Sevenoaks became a real home, Michael settled into school and while he remembers the move as being a big upheaval, he was perfectly happy, as were Caron in Bristol and Paul in Guildford. I got used to that two-hour commute to London, which I would use to go over interviews, mentally write scripts and listen to tapes. It was actually often extremely useful when preparing for some of the guests who could be a little complicated: for example, the great Barry Humphries appeared on the show as Dame Edna Everage, Sir Les Patterson and as himself, so I'd have to prepare, depending on which version of him was appearing. I'd also use the time to rehearse if I was going to be singing at a charity event, or on a television programme. I'd put on the backing tape and sing to my heart's content. Mind you, I did get some funny looks when I was stuck in traffic.

I was brought up in Ireland where complete strangers will greet each other with warmth and affection, and I had been warned that on the mainland the English were very different. London, in particular, had a reputation for being a cold and somewhat unfriendly place. I soon found that out when I was walking down the lengthy corridors of the BBC and saw a man in the distance. It seemed to take hours before our paths finally crossed but when they finally did, I said, 'Good morning, how are you?'

He peered at me. 'Oh, do I know you?' he asked.

'Not really, I just thought I'd say "good morning,"' I said.

'Oh, how jolly nice,' he said as he kept on walking.

From that moment onwards any time I met him he treated me like a long-lost friend, asking after me and how it was all going. I realised that sometimes you just need a bit of Irish warmth to take on English reserve.

In fact, sometimes I forget just how endearing the Irish sense of honour can be – not that long ago, Stephen and I were staying in a Dublin hotel where there was a very nice doorman called John, whom we got to know rather well. As we were going out one morning he said, 'Sure now, it's a fantastic day for a walk. Do ya know? If I had a dog I'd go for one.' Or the time when the American in the Gaelic-speaking area of Donegal asked one of the locals, 'Say, bud, d'you have a word in the Irish language that's the equivalent of *mañana*?' The Irishman scratched his head and said, 'Do ya know something. I don't believe we have a word with that degree of urgency about it at all'.

If you ever go to an Irish pub, you will never sit on your own because everybody talks to you. One night in Dublin, Stephen and I were in one waiting for some friends to come from the North and we were chatting to a local fisherman, Seamus. After talking about fishing and so on, I said to him, 'Are you married, Seamus? 'Not at all', was his reply. Cheekily I said, 'Now, a good-looking man like you must have a girlfriend.'

'Oh I have, I have, I'm engaged to her.'

'How long have you been engaged?'

'Well now,' he thought, 'must be twenty-odd years.'

'For goodness sake, why wouldn't you marry her?'

And he leant towards me and said, 'To tell you the truth, Gloria, she's so ugly even the tide wouldn't take her out.'

If you'd ever been to any of Peter Ustinov's one-man talks, he would always bring up his passion for Ireland and one of his favourite recollections was when he arrived at his favourite hotel and the doorman said to him, 'Ah now, Mr Ustinov, sure it's great to say hello to ya, because I never got to say goodbye to ya the last time you were here'. Which brings me to the movie *The Old Curiosity Shop*, which Peter Ustinov was starring in and filming at Ardmore Studios near Dublin in 1994. I was there to do a radio documentary about film-making and as I got to know the director quite well, I said to him, 'D'you think I could have a small part in this? It would add so much to my documentary.' He said, 'OK, I'll make you a flower seller'. Then I cheekily said, 'D'you think I might have a few words of dialogue as well?'. So he said, 'Alright then, be in Make-up at 6 o'clock tomorrow morning, sharp'. Having made me as ugly as they could, I joined the set at the point where Peter Ustinov, in character, was looking for Little Nell. I was supposed to do my line in a Cockney accent but that I couldn't manage, so I did it in a very broad Dublin accent.

'Ah now, sir, sir, would ya ever be buying a flower now for the little girl?'

It probably was a terrible Dublin accent as well but when I saw the director later he said, 'I have spent millions turning this set into a Dickensian scene, and what do I get but this strong Dublin accent searing through'. Though I discovered much later that the scene actually stayed in!

★ ★ ★

As I became better known through Radio 2, though, I started to discover that people have a certain perception of the way those in the public eye should behave. Occasionally, rather than driving in, I would take the train. Once, having a bit of time to spare at Charing Cross station, I went to have a quick snack and had settled down with my paper when a woman sitting nearby asked, 'What are you doing here?'

Totally taken aback, I said, 'I'm having a cup of coffee and waiting for the train.'

'That's ridiculous,' she sniffed.

'Why?' I protested.

'My dear, you would never see Terry Wogan or Jimmy Young waiting for a train! They all have chauffeurs to take them to and from work.' That told me.

I know the Internet has made things a lot different nowadays but some things will never change; people really do think that those of us who appear on radio or television don't have to do the shopping or the housework or clean the toilet. If only they knew!

I actually don't use the train any more but that's only because I always seem to be carrying such a lot of stuff around; scripts, clothes or what have you. But recently I was meeting

Michael in London and he suggested I use the train so I went to the station, got on the train and twenty-two minutes later we were at Charing Cross. I began to think this could change my life! We had a nice few hours with a friend from Australia, then Michael walked me back to Charing Cross. He was taking the Tube, so he pointed to the departures board and said, 'There you go, Mum, platform 4 in three minutes,' so I promptly got on a packed commuter train and sat down.

The next thing I knew, a hand was vigorously shaking my shoulder.

'Luv, luv, you've got to wake up,' said a voice. 'Wake up, wake up. We're at the end of the line in Sidcup.' I had my face turned to the window and as I turned round, she said, 'Oh my gawd, it's you!'

Blinking, all I could think of was those endless commuters who got off the train and had left me fast asleep at the end of the line, and this lady was now clearing up all the rubbish they'd left behind. From that moment on I was prize exhibit number one: there were endless questions from everyone in the station as they asked me about *Loose Women* and *Rip Off Britain* and then introduced me to every employee at the station. She was a very helpful lady though and explained that I had to go back six stops to get the train to Sevenoaks. Having said my goodbyes and thanks, I got on a train again then got off where she told me and at that point I saw a train going to Orpington. *I know where that is*, I thought, so I rang my husband Stephen. 'Don't ask any questions, just pick me up at Orpington station,' I told him. The journey that should have taken twenty minutes had by now taken two-and-a-half hours!

However, this is where one of those chance-in-a-million

coincidences crops up. The next day Stephen was in central London for an appointment and jumped into a black cab.

'Where to, mate?' asked the cabbie.

'Charing Cross,' said Stephen. 'I'm going to Sevenoaks.'

'Going for a holiday then?'

'No,' said Stephen, 'I live there.'

'Oh,' said the cabbie, sounding interested. 'Gloria Hunniford lives there you know.'

'Does she?' asked Stephen, suppressing a smile.

'Yes and you'll never believe it, mate, but my wife had to wake her up on the train yesterday to tell her how to get back to Sevenoaks.'

'Really?' said Stephen. 'What's she like?'

'Oh, my wife said she's a very nice lady,' asserted the cabbie. 'Well-spoken and very well-dressed.'

Well that's something, at least!

I do seem to get myself into odd situations at times. Quite recently, we had a new branch of Lidl open in Sevenoaks and I decided to check it out. It's a rather long and narrow building and as I walked down I seemed to talk to everybody in sight, either about *Loose Women* or the weather or a *Rip Off Britain* scam they wanted to tell me about. I finally made it down to the cheese counter right at the bottom of the store and I felt two fingers tapping me on the shoulder. This very nice lady said, 'I hope you don't mind me bothering you, but you have something stuck to the back of your coat'. I turned around and to my horror, I had two shoulder pads magnificently stuck to my backside. Although I'm no Kim Kardashian, there's enough there already! I am rather partial to my shoulder pads, but certainly not on my bottom! What had happened was I'd laid them out on my bed and put the double-sided tape on ready to put them in my jacket and then, to my peril, had sat down on the bed to put on my shoes without realising – not a good look!

* * *

Back on the work front in the early eighties, everything was steaming ahead. I was initially hired on a three-month trial run at Radio 2 but my contract was quickly extended and it became clear that there was no question of my going back. England was my new home.

It seems very behind the times that in 1982 I was the first woman to have her own daily programme on Radio 2 but it was regularly brought home to me that it was still a man's world.

Radio 2 moved to a new building, which was all very well, except that it turned out no one had thought to install a women's loo – there was a brand-new men's facility but us women had to go to another floor. There was eventually a rebellion among the women, who insisted that one of the male loos should be declared unisex. I must say, I had some good chats in there with the blokes, particularly Steve Wright, who was then broadcasting on Radio 1. We would meet in there every day before we went on air on our respective stations, and have a lively chat about who we were both interviewing that day. Then, as we were leaving, he would say loudly, 'Gloria, I'll see you in the loo tomorrow, same time, same place.' People would gawp at us, a bit mystified, but it's a happy memory – I was actually quite sorry when a ladies' loo was finally installed in 1992.

We were enjoying some ground-breaking moments on the show though. We had Esther Rantzen on, who had just been on the receiving end of a lot of stick in the press for breastfeeding her baby in public at a literary lunch – this was just not done back then. She had actually gone into an ante room but there had still been a lot of fuss, so she asked me not to mention on air that she'd brought her baby with her that day. However, the interview was on at lunchtime and Esther had to breastfeed.

As soon as I turned on the microphone, the studio was filled with sounds of suckling, clearly audible to everyone tuning in. I had to say something – it would have been impossible to pretend that nothing was going on – so I took a deep breath and said, 'In case you're wondering what the sucking noises are, there's nothing weird going on with my producer but I have to point out it's Esther breastfeeding her baby at the moment!' The studio promptly went into meltdown with everyone, including Esther in hysterics. We dined off that story for years; for us it was another newspaper headline.

These were the days when you could do proper half-hour interviews in some depth and we certainly had our share of fun with them. One of those was with Gene Wilder, who was his wonderfully funny self, so totally engaging and great company. After he left the studio, I could see through the glass as he went next door to the control room and quite suddenly the place erupted into hysterical laughter. The technicians were leaning on the glass they were laughing so hard, and Gene himself was on the floor, waving his legs in complete hysterics.

'What's going on?' I asked.

I had played a track from *Willy Wonka & the Chocolate Factory* when the interview with Gene finished and, back on air, I apparently announced, 'Wasn't Gene Wilder fabulous and of course that was a track from Willy <u>Wanker</u> & the Chocolate Factory.'

People were actually calling in to the station commenting, 'Did she say what we thought she said…?'

'Just blame it on my Ulster accent,' I replied

There were some truly incredible moments during that time at Radio 2. I'd only been on air a matter of weeks when the legendary Dame Barbara Cartland came in to be interviewed, traditionally dressed in pink and pearls. In between records she said to me, 'Darling, I know you're new over here but I must tell you, never wear grey or beige because, if you do, you will look grey or beige.' Bearing in mind I was sitting in a grey dress, that didn't go down too well but maybe she had a point. She also said, 'It is my belief that after the age of forty you have to decide whether you want a face or a figure because, quite frankly, you can't have both'. She then topped it off with, 'If you ever want to interview me, you'll always find me at Claridge's every Wednesday with my toyboy'. She was at that time nearly ninety; I did enquire how old the toyboy was. She replied, 'He's eighty-two and gorgeous'.

One of my favourite guests was Howard Keel, who I had seen many times in films when I was growing up in classics like *Annie Get Your Gun* and *Seven Brides for Seven Brothers*. On one occasion, my first guest on the programme was the world-famous tenor Plácido Domingo, with Howard coming on second. As soon as I trailed the line-up to the audience, Plácido's ears pricked up. After I closed down the 'live' mic he asked, excitedly, 'Is Howard Keel actually here "live"? Would you mind if I stayed because I styled myself on Howard Keel when I was growing up?'

And so, I introduced the two of them ('live' on air) and Plácido told me that it was one of the best moments of his life. They stayed in touch after that actually and became great friends, always meeting up for dinner when they were in the same city.

* * *

Over the course of the next few months, more doors began to open as well – I was the new kid on the block and the opportunities just kept rolling in. My *Taste of Hunni Irish-style* show continued on the BBC World Service and I also got offered a monthly chat show for Ulster TV, which kept that Northern Ireland connection open and also gave me a chance to see my mum. Star names like Val Doonican and Des O'Connor appeared, so when I came back to England to do the radio show they returned the favour and I was invited on *The Saturday Night Val Doonican Show* to sing. Amazingly, this led to a six-week prime-time summer series, *Saturday Live From Pebble Mill* alongside Simon Bates. At times I had to pinch myself; this really was a big glossy opportunity for me and we had major stars coming on the show, including John Hurt, several of the *Dallas* crowd and none other than Mr Spock himself – Leonard Nimoy of *Star Trek*, who obligingly brought on nine pairs of Vulcan ears.

There was huge excitement as we heard that Sylvester Stallone, who was at the height of his *Rocky* fame, had agreed to appear on the show. He pulled up outside the studios with a huge entourage in six black limousines, but when he got out of the car I remember being amazed by how much smaller he was in real life! We'd also booked a real-life boxing hero,

Henry Cooper, for the show that night and I remember that when we brought him to the dressing room to meet Stallone, you could see Sly pushing out his chest, nearly popping the buttons on his cream silk shirt, as he tried to stand as tall as Henry. It was very funny but I managed not to laugh. And it was a defining moment.

Someone else who appeared quite a few times was the Spanish singer Julio Iglesias, who was wildly popular in the UK at that time in 1982. His first British hit was that year with, 'Begin the Begin'. His popularity was such that when he first appeared on the show, he was joined by a fourteen-strong entourage, which is what American performers usually surrounded themselves with. He was clad in a long mink coat, with sparkling white teeth and a handsome tanned face. Now, I had never seen a man wearing a fur coat, never mind a mink, but he waltzed into the studio and, with a grand gesture, swept the mink coat off his shoulders where it slid to the floor. I assumed that one of his entourage would pick it up, as I'm sure he did too. But to my horror no one moved. And we waited. And waited... Eventually, Julio was forced to pick it up himself, but he caught my eye as he bent down and we both burst out laughing.

I remember that his English was so appalling that we had to pre-record the interview and then edit it so he could actually be understood. But every time he came back, his English would have markedly improved and in later years he would tease me, 'I can have a lot of fun in English now.'

Julio has actually become a great friend. Towards the end of the 1980s he appeared on the show again and, as we generally chatted between records, he asked, 'What are you doing over Christmas?'

'We're going to Los Angeles and then spending the New Year in Las Vegas.'

Julio looked interested.

'Ah! It just so happens I'm in Vegas over the New Year. You must come and see me. Listen, I'll give you the number of my assistant. Call her and she will set everything up.'

'You'll regret that,' I said. 'There are six of us in the party.'

But Julio was as good as his word and everything was duly arranged. It turned out he was singing at an exclusive party in Caesars Palace and we were given amazing seats; it felt wonderful to be a part of it. Once the cabaret was over he told us, 'I'm having a party in my suite. You all must come up.'

So we made our way up to the executive suite, expecting a cast of thousands, and instead discovered an elegant soirée with just fourteen of us invited. Sadly, Julio had to head off early but there was no question that we'd have to leave with him.

'Stay as long as you like,' he told us. 'There's plenty of food and drink. Feel free to use the suite.'

And with that he flew off home to Miami on his private jet, leaving us to party the night away.

That night was the first time I met his now wife Miranda Rijnsburger. She was so beautiful and I remember that we all kept looking at her, wondering who she was. It's funny to think of that now because we all have a great relationship! Julio has since invited us out to his homes in Miami and in the Dominican Republic – such luxurious surroundings, different to anything we had experienced before. Every conceivable luxury was on offer: meals were served by the ocean in a specially constructed gazebo, even the eggs were flown in specially from Julio's place in Spain, and the whole complex is so vast you have to go around in a golf cart. Before dinner every night, we'd meet in the most enormous sitting room I've ever seen, lit by hundreds of vanilla candles.

The children had one nanny each, there was even a schoolroom for his then young children, who had a private tutor. It was such a whirlwind to be around. Many years later, when his fifteen-year-old twin girls were about to spend a period of time at a boarding school near Bath – Miranda thought it would be so educational for them to experience a spell at an English school – she rang me to see if I would be a local guardian, on hand if needed. Of course I was delighted to do that and met them in Bath as they arrived. However, the girls absolutely hated it; they just couldn't adapt to the cold, damp weather in England compared with their extremely luxurious life and the warm weather in Miami and the Dominican Republic, so they begged to go back home and that was that experience. Just as well they had a private jet on hand to take them home!

* * *

Back to that first year in London, it just could not have been more eventful; one particular highlight was in October 1982 when the director and choreographer Norman Maen got in touch after my programme one day.

'How would you like to be on the *Royal Variety Performance*?' he asked.

Would I? I could hardly believe my ears. Along with most of the rest of the country I had been glued to it on the television for years and it had been one of my dad's annual TV highlights. Now I was being asked to take part! It took me all of two seconds to say yes.

The *Royal Variety Performance* has the capacity to unnerve even the most seasoned entertainer though, and so by the time the big night arrived, I was just hoping to get by without making an idiot of myself in front of the Queen. I was performing with Esther Rantzen and Jan Leeming singing 'Anything You Can Do, I Can Do Better' from *Annie Get Your Gun*. The three of us were dressed in suede cowgirl costumes made up of fringed skirts, boots, hats and holsters, but there was very little rehearsal time due to our busy and conflicting schedules and even when we did, we could only find small rooms to practice in. When we saw the vast stage of the Theatre Royal, Drury Lane, we were aghast: 'What are we going to do?' we asked the choreographer Norman Maen. 'How can we adapt the moves to such a large space?' I kept reminding myself I'd been on stage many times before, but it was hard; this was quite a complex number, with intricate choreography, too. Norman had worked hard with us but it still didn't come particularly easy.

It just so happened that one of the other performers that night was Howard Keel himself, who by then was becoming known to a new generation in his role as Clayton Farlow in *Dallas*. I went and nabbed him backstage.

'C'mon, you've got to give us support here,' I said. 'How do we do it?'

We had to start out with our backs to the audience, turning around one by one to identify ourselves and Howard could not have been more helpful. He stood in the wings, calling out, 'Turn! Turn! Turn!' Somehow the three of us managed to end the number at the same time and were rewarded by warm congratulations from Howard and the audience. The whole thing was surreal. *I'm being coached by Howard Keel,*

I thought to myself. My dad adored him and he would have loved it; I thought a lot about my parents that night and how proud they would have been seeing the three of us being presented to the Queen Mother in the line-up on stage after the show.

Life kept moving at an almighty pace and I wouldn't have thought that it could get much better, but it did.

★ ★ ★

In January 1983, with me just trying to keep up with myself, I was doing the radio show as usual, this time interviewing Stan Stennett, then star of *Coronation Street*. We were chatting away and taking calls from the listeners who were curious to learn more about their favourite soap, when suddenly the producer said, 'Take a mystery caller.' Somewhat taken aback, I did so and a voice said, 'Hi, this is Eamonn Andrews.'

Eamonn was one of the most famous television presenters of the day, especially known for *This Is Your Life*, the show that took well-known people back through their lives, with mystery guests and the help of a big red book. The subject of the show was never warned in advance; it was always a complete surprise.

I couldn't believe that *the* Eamonn Andrews was tuning in to my show.

'Hello Eamonn. What brings you on the line today?'

'I just wanted to ask Stan how he felt last week when he was hit with *This Is Your Life*.'

I was just so delighted and flattered that Eamonn had called into the show that I hadn't noticed a camera crew had entered the studio from the back and Eamonn himself was actually walking towards me. Even when I realised he was really there in person, I still didn't get it – despite the fact he was holding a big red book. I couldn't work it out because Stan had been on *This IS Your Life* last week, so who was it for? It really never occurred to me that I was about to be honoured in this way. After all, I'd only been in London for a year.

And then Eamonn said it:

'Gloria Hunniford, this is your life!'

I was so stunned that my first thought was that this must be a practical joke. I didn't know what to do: should I play another record? I somehow managed to introduce the news but then Eamonn said, 'We've got a broadcast van waiting downstairs. Let's go.'

Of course everything had been arranged beforehand and a newsreader took over as I was bustled away from the studio; all I could think was that the news would soon be over, and there was still another half hour to fill which I had to continue to broadcast 'live'. I was so taken aback that I couldn't think straight. And to my utter astonishment, I could see people waving at the van as it passed, with cabbies shouting congratulations and more amazingly still, crowds – actual crowds – were beginning to form. 'Good on you, Glo!' they called. People were even running behind the van; it felt like I was part of an incredible parade. All the while, I was trying to interview Eamonn about doing *This Is Your Life* or anything else that came into my scrambled brain. It was completely surreal.

I felt a surge of emotion and excitement and couldn't quite believe that this was happening to me; it remains one of the most privileged and mystifying moments of my life.

It was only when we got to the theatre where the show was filmed that I began to realise the amount of planning and preparation that went into it. The night before I had been working at London Weekend Television and rang home to make sure everything was all right. Caron, then aged twenty, was babysitting Michael, who was then twelve, and I told her I'd ring again when I finished filming later that night.

'Oh, we'll probably be in bed,' she said. 'We're going to turn in early tonight.'

I subsequently discovered that the two of them had left Sevenoaks, nipped up to London, had dinner with all the family and crew, went through a rehearsal and nipped back again. By the time I got home both of them had been in bed fast asleep and I was oblivious to it all!

Of course, Paul had been in on it too:

'All the family had been put up in the White House Hotel and the get-together the night before the programme was fabulous,' he remembers. 'It was quite ironic the way we managed to pull it off without Mum being any the wiser but afterwards she was a bit miffed about missing out on our family reunion.'

So all the kids had been in on it and none of them had so much as breathed a hint as to what was going to happen – it was quite an impressive feat, actually! On the morning in question, Michael had gone to school as usual but actually had been hidden in the pub nearby. Caron was supposed to be coming into work with me, but had to find a way to get out of it. 'I'll take the next train, Mum. You better get going.' It turns out there was actually a car stashed away around the corner, containing people armed with walkie-talkies (this was well before the days of the mobile phone) tracking my every move. As soon as they saw 'the subject' leaving the house, they put Michael in the car, collected Caron (who had packed a change of clothes for me to wear on the programme) and set off.

MY LIFE - GLORIA HUNNIFORD

It was a wonderful day. The programme was jammed with happy incidents, memories and surprises all along the way. The whole family was there, including my lovely mum, who was clearly adoring every minute of it. There were all manner of figures from my past – thank goodness I recognised and remembered all of them: there was my first voice coach and pianist, Gail Sheridan, friends from Portadown including my old school friends (now gold medallist athlete) Mary Peters, Pat Farrell and Anne Downey. Even my old neighbour Anne Thompson and her daughter, Christine, were there. As for the rest of Portadown, I was later told the streets were practically deserted that night as everyone was at home watching the show.

People had come from all over the world. Henry Knotek, my great friend from Old Fort Henry in Canada had flown in, as had Gerry Kelly and Dan Gilbert, my broadcasting colleagues from Northern Ireland. Terry Wogan, Jimmy Young, Jan Leeming, Esther Rantzen and Val Doonican were all there, too.

'And now, Gloria,' said Eamonn, 'we're going to Hollywood for our next guest.'

Hollywood? I thought, in confusion. What on earth was he talking about? I didn't know anyone in Hollywood. What on earth was he talking about? But at that moment, the satellite went 'live' to the set of *Dallas*, and there was my new friend Howard Keel, who gave a moving and lovely tribute.

Caron later recalled the whole evening as one of our family triumphs: 'It was truly one of the highlights in Mum's career. I remember calling up all my friends and telling some of them, "You've got to watch television tonight, we're all going to be on!" Being on *This Is Your Life* was a sign that you'd really arrived.'

In the years that followed, I would watch the tape of the show, and it was always very endearing to see Michael as a little twelve-year old dressed in his Sunday best grey suit. And, after my mum died, it was very comforting to look back and see her enjoying herself and to remember how she dined out on it for months afterwards, even being invited to speak to the Mothers' Union in Portadown about it. She had become a local star and it certainly brought a lump to my throat.

Strangely, I can't watch it these days because my treasured daughter Caron was so instrumental to the programme and I still can't bring myself to sit down and watch her alive, laughing and having such a joyous time. I'm sure I will take great comfort from it eventually but it's a bittersweet memory to me as so many of my family and friends who appeared on the show have passed on: my mum, sister Lena, former husband Don, Caron, not to mention Terry Wogan, and even Eamonn Andrews himself.

★ ★ ★

I often think that if I had stayed in Ireland my marriage to Don would have lasted. He had been my only great love and although, like most couples, we had our moments, there were no fundamental flaws in our marriage. But my new life in London meant that we started to drift apart.

Not that Don didn't make an effort. When his stint in South Africa was up and it became clear how much I was relishing my career in London, he found a job directing the BBC current affairs programme *Nationwide*. But he just couldn't settle. He hated the job, he hated London, he hated the commute and he wanted to go back to Northern Ireland where he could be with his mates and play golf. Of course, by this stage I didn't want to go back. Not only was I loving my new life but the kids were all based in England now and I wanted to be in the same country as them. Sure, Michael was still only young and could have come back to Northern Ireland with me but Caron and Paul were now firmly settled.

I wanted to try and resolve things, though, so that Christmas I went home to Northern Ireland. But it was a miserable time. I knew that everything between us had changed for ever. I have never subscribed to the theory that absence makes the heart go fonder; we had sadly just grown apart.

So, without making too much of a fuss about it, we separated in late 1983, though we remained as amicable as we possibly could. Don would come to London to visit the kids and I would occasionally go to Hillsborough, where he still lived in our family home; it was a very bittersweet experience indeed. We actually remained separated for a long time before we finally got divorced in 1988. When it finally happened, I remember my lawyer Monty Raphael saying to me, 'Remember you can't put a lid on twenty-one years – there will always be births, deaths and marriages to deal with. Keep the communication line open.' And so we did.

The kids stayed very close to their father. I recall Michael worrying about his dad being lonely, as children will, but all the kids were aware that we had simply drifted too far apart for it to work any more. Caron was particularly close to Don and in those early years of our separation, she had got a job working in television back in Northern Ireland so she stayed with him at the family home. Because Michael was living with me 24/7 in Sevenoaks I always made sure he went back to Hillsborough for Christmas too but I have heart-breaking memories of watching him go down the ramp onto the plane. To this day, when I hear the Christmas carol, 'Have Yourself A Merry Little Christmas' and the line, 'One day soon we all will be together if the fates allow/until then we have to get along somehow' I still get a lump in my throat. Thank God Paul was with me over those Christmas periods.

* * *

At that time I worked hard getting on with my life and, over time, Don met someone else, a very nice woman called Moira. It was Michael who, a few years later in 1989, told me they were going to have a baby, who is now a lovely lad called Patrick. I was perfectly happy about it but it did feel odd in one respect as I thought, *Oh my goodness, my children are going to have a brother that I have nothing to do with*. But it has actually all turned out brilliantly. When Patrick was born he was a dead ringer for Don, and Caron always kept me in touch with what was going on, something Michael has taken over in more recent years. The two of them are now very close and Patrick runs a very highly-regarded design and creative studio called PSK.

Don sadly passed away in 1997 – he was only sixty-one when he had a massive heart attack. Our old neighbour from Hillsborough, Michael Shields, found him: he had gone round to visit him after another neighbour, who had arranged to meet him for a drink, had rung and said Don hadn't turned up. When there was no answer at the door, Michael went round to the back of the house and peered through the kitchen window. He saw Don sitting upright at the table: the television was on, there was a half drunk-glass of wine beside him and a plate with his dinner. At first he thought Don was asleep, but then he began to suspect it was something more than that, so he smashed a window and got in. Don's death was terrible because it was so fast, so sudden.

Totally coincidentally, I happened to be in Northern Ireland at the time: I was taking part in a Friday night 'live' television chat show with Val Doonican and a host of other big names. What I didn't know was that just before we went on air, the producers were told what had happened by Caron's husband Russ and there was a big discussion about whether they should let me know. They consulted the boys and Caron, who took the decision that telling me before the show wouldn't change anything and so they should wait until afterwards. As soon as the show finished, I quickly realised something strange had happened because no one came over to talk to me about how it had gone, as they would normally.

It was eerie; there was no talk about the programme or the guests – was it good, not so good, anything! Then I was just side-tracked into a dressing room, where my sister Lena and Stephen, who was my boyfriend then and is now my husband, were waiting for me. They broke the sad news; it was a terrible shock. By that stage Don and I had been divorced for years but we'd still been married for two decades, so it was incredibly sad and I also felt the loss very deeply for our children, who were bereft at the news.

By this time Caron was married to Russ. They already had one child, Charlie, and she was eight and a half months' pregnant with her second son, Gabriel. She was really too late on in the pregnancy to fly but when Don died she just instinctively got on a plane, hiding her large bump under an oversized Crombie coat and threw caution to the wind in her despair.

MOVING THE BIG PIECES

In Ireland the tradition is to hold the funeral very soon after the death and of course Caron was adamant that she had to be there.

Looking back, I think why on earth didn't we just postpone it until Caron had had her baby and was in a better condition to attend? At the time, though, we were all in a huge state of shock and did what we thought was right. Caron wanted to go back to London to have her baby induced and she asked me to be with her at the birth, as I had with Charlie. I was so concerned about her emotional state on top of having to give birth. My heart was breaking for her and I wanted to be with her every step. Caron gave birth to another beautiful baby boy, and named him Gabriel Don. Russ and I cut the cord together, which was such a privilege, and I always tease both Charlie and Gabriel that I have known them from the second they were born. Most times, they've heard it so often they finish the sentence for me! Caron, in a way, didn't know whether to laugh or cry; there was so much turmoil going on in her mind. Then she had to face the journey back to Hillsborough so she could attend Don's funeral. I'll never forget watching her in the church going down the aisle carrying this tiny baby swaddled in blankets. Her brothers were deeply concerned about her physical state and her state of mind, but Caron was exceptionally strong-minded and that was that. She was determined to be with her dad to the end.

In Ireland, though, there always seem to be moments of dark humour. Michael and Caron had gone to the local M&S to buy Don a new shirt to be buried in. A sprightly young assistant came over and asked, 'Can I help you with anything?' She looked more closely at Michael. 'Is this shirt for you?'

163

'No it's for my dead father,' he replied.

Gallows humour indeed.

Don's cousin, Liam Owen, lived in Dublin with his wife Norah who was, at the time, the Minister for Defence in Southern Ireland, and both were determined to come to the funeral to pay their respects. Bearing in mind the 'political atmosphere' at that point, you've never seen so much panic among the local police in Hillsborough in that they would have to manage this visit from a high-profile political minister from Dublin – there were helicopters overhead and police on every corner. Funnily enough I ran into Norah on a television programme recently and we had a good old reminisce about it all.

Don's brother, also called Liam, came from Manchester for the funeral. In Ireland, tradition has it that most coffins remain open and at home. The two brothers hadn't seen each other for a while at the time of Don's passing and when Liam looked into the coffin to pay his respects to his brother, he observed, 'Doesn't he look well?'

I also met Patrick for the first time at the funeral and he was a very sad little boy, only eight at the time. And there were further complications because, while the service was held locally, Don couldn't be buried there because there were no graves available. So he had to be taken to a Catholic church much further away to be laid at rest overlooking Strangeford Lough, a favourite spot of his – so his resting place turned out to be perfect.

Don's early passing made for a bad period; it was a very rough time. All the children were deeply upset obviously, but Caron was particularly close to her dad, and having to have her baby induced and attend a funeral within a matter of days of each other was very tough. It took some time to come to terms with all of that and in the event Caron ended up suffering from a bout of depression, which was very painful to watch. She didn't get the full joy of her baby's birth or the full sadness of her dad's death.

You always want the quick fix for your children – when they're small and they hurt themselves you're so used to saying: 'There, there, I'll kiss it better' – but this time it was so different. When your children are older and they are faced with grief it's very hard. Your natural instinct as a parent is to take on their pain, to take away their hurt. But unfortunately it gets to the stage where you can't and that's a hard lesson to learn. You can only be there for them and pray and listen when they want to talk. And everybody grieves at a different pace, and has different thoughts. You think you're in control as a mother – but there comes a time when you have to let go.

CHAPTER 8

STARDUST MEMORIES

L ittle did I think, when I was going to the 'pictures' in Portadown, that one day I would be kicking sand with the big star I wanted to be – Doris Day. I had lost my young self in movies like *Annie Get Your Gun*, *Move Over, Darling* and *Pillow Talk*, revelling in the glamorous clothes Doris wore and the romantic leading men she played opposite.

The year was 1993 and the way it came around was a phone call from a good pal of mine, Jackie Gill, who is in the record/PR business and she said, 'How would you like to interview Doris Day?'

'Yeah, yeah', I replied, very sceptically.

'No, it's true', she assured me. 'Her son has found a lost album and they're willing to talk about it.'

Well, I was on the plane to LA the next day!

When we got to her hotel, the Cypress Inn in Carmel, her son greeted us by saying, 'If my mum's original make-up artist doesn't make the journey from Hollywood by tomorrow morning she won't do the show.' So I went to bed thinking, *I've come all this way to meet my childhood idol, to interview her for* Pebble Mill *and Radio 2, and now she may not turn up.* Thank God, the next morning, she was there spot on time – the same blonde hairstyle, the trademark white polo-neck sweater and, apart from being not as svelte as she was in the movies, she was exactly the same.

Doris hadn't given an interview since 1969, when her husband Marty died, and apart from speaking at a tribute to Rock Hudson she hadn't really been seen in the media, so this was a one-off at that time. As we talked, Doris reflected on her career, her past marriages – even talking about the domestic violence she'd suffered at the hands of her first husband – and her great friendships with the likes of Rock Hudson and James Stewart.

Doris was regarded as somewhat reclusive and at that stage in her life, any publicity revolved around the number of dogs she had. We weren't allowed to film them but I did establish she had twenty-one at the time, and the dogs had a specially designated kitchen and cook, and were fed off red gingham placemats on the floor. After the interview, for a bit of extra filming, it was decided that we would go on to the beach, along with her grandson. I had gone to LA in my black straight skirt, tights and high-heeled shoes and did feel a bit stupid kicking sand with Doris in my stockinged feet. In some ways I wanted to pinch myself: here was I, a girl from the provinces in Northern Ireland, interviewing one of the greatest stars of the twentieth century and we were like two old friends strolling along the beach. Just what had got me to this place?

During those magical, in a way naïve, years after I moved to London, one door after another just kept opening. I received a call from David Bell and Alan Boyd, Head of Entertainment, with an idea for a chat show. Me! With my own chat show? I was immediately overexcited.

'What time is it slotted for?'

'Sunday afternoon at five o'clock.'

'Oh.'

Suddenly the sheen wore off a little.

Throughout my broadcasting career to date I was lucky enough to be on air at the peak times, either in the morning or evening. Who was going to watch television at that time on a Sunday afternoon?

Plenty of people, it turned out. *Sunday, Sunday* debuted in October 1982. People were relaxing at home after Sunday lunch, more often than not with it raining outside, so viewers in their millions were only too happy to tune in and see the cream of Hollywood, old and new, paraded before their eyes. I was in utter awe of the production team working under the first editor Charles Brand – I didn't know how they had managed to do it, but every big name under the sun seemed to appear on that show, which was to run for nine series and usually featured four guests per episode. All those big-name movie stars I had seen as a girl growing up in Portadown came on the show – Kirk Douglas, Charlton Heston, Howard Keel (again) and so many more. I never dreamed I'd meet so many of them. Audrey Hepburn, Leslie Caron, Doris Day, Burt Lancaster, James Stewart, June Allyson, the entire cast of *Dallas* – and I got to interview all of them. For that first year I was so busy trying to keep up with the pace that the full unbelievability of what I was doing and who I was meeting didn't fully register. Although, when it finally did, the impact was huge. In fact, if I could relive a period in broadcasting, it would be that.

* * *

One of the reasons *Sunday, Sunday* did so well and we managed to attract so many huge names was a young Scottish chap called Graham Stuart. He has become a huge force in broadcasting, setting up a company with Graham Norton (So Television), not only producing such a successful show as *The Graham Norton Show* but many others as well. It's a truly international company these days. On *Sunday, Sunday* he started out as a researcher and I always know whether a researcher's going to go far or not by the quality of their work. I knew from the start he would do well, not least because he always made sure everyone was properly looked after, but as he rose up the ladder – researcher to assistant producer to producer to editor – he insisted on hiring a researcher for each guest and that concentrated, deep research unearthed anecdotes we hadn't heard before. That of course led to a very fresh interview with a well-established star. What a difference for me from Ulster Television days when I had to do it all myself. And boy, what guests did we get...

As I said before, one of the films that I dragged my mother to was *The Glenn Miller Story*, when we were forced to sit at the front row of the picture house, staring up at the screen. My mother hated it but I loved it, and it starred James Stewart and June Allyson, both of whom came on the show. In fact, James Stewart became quite a regular on the programme – 'I'll always remember your name because my wife is called Gloria,' he told me when we were introduced, and he told me to call him Jimmy. At the beginning of Jimmy's career his father had owned a general grocery store in Indiana, Pennsylvania, where he grew up. He never took Jimmy's career seriously, though, constantly telling him to stop day- dreaming and get a proper job. Finally, in 1940, Jimmy won his first Oscar, for Best Actor in *The Philadelphia Story* and took it home to his parents. For the first time ever, his father showed an interest in his career. 'The next time I went back, Gloria,' he told me, 'I saw the Oscar sitting on the bacon slicer. I finally knew that as far as my father was concerned, I had arrived.'

But Jimmy was one of many and I have so many incredible memories of these years. Most technical teams – the cameramen and soundmen and their like – have seen and done it all in TV but the day Bette Davis was on the show I had never experienced such studio silence. I had seen all her films and could hardly believe that such a Hollywood legend was appearing on the programme, and it turned out that it was to be one of the last interviews she did before she died. I remember, she was dressed all in black and wearing a stylish hat. Unusually for the time the show had been pre-recorded, because she was quite frail; normally, when you introduce a guest on television, you walk forward and there's naturally some 'kissy kissy', but on this occasion I had been told not to touch her and to put my arms out towards her in case she needed help. I felt like a right prat, standing there with my arm stuck out at an angle, but she didn't take it and we made our way safely over to a small table, where we both sat down.

I had never seen anything like it before. Her assistant had set the side table with Bette's new autobiography at the back, with the title well displayed. Next to it was a beautiful little black patent handbag out of which was draped a lacy white handkerchief. In front of that was a silver goblet of water and a long cigarette holder (in the days when you could smoke on TV), so that Bette knew where everything was and could reach out to have a sip of water whenever she wanted without turning away from me. Bette sat there, with exactly the attitude you would expect. You could have heard a pin drop on the set; the cameramen were in total awe of her.

Then suddenly, in the middle of the interview, she said:

'Are you ever going to talk about the goddamn book? That is the reason I am here.' She certainly got straight to the point – like so many other American stars.

Another totally memorable guest on the show was Audrey Hepburn. I could hardly contain my excitement because *Breakfast at Tiffany's* has been one of my favourite films of all time and although I now know that when she came on she was already suffering from cancer, you would never have guessed it at the time. She was as graceful as ever, her long swanlike elegant neck still there for all to see. Much of her conversation was about Unicef, which she was so passionate about and the work they do worldwide for children. However, all the time my mind was going back to *Breakfast at Tiffany's* and that scene with George Peppard when they were gazing at all the exquisite jewellery in Tiffany's. It's so pathetic but the first time I went to New York I had to re-enact so many scenes from that film and see it all for myself.

Another icon was Leslie Caron. I had seen her in *Gigi* on the ship when I sailed to Canada and like any seventeen- or eighteen-year old at the time, I wanted to be Gigi. In fact when I was on *Desert Island Discs* in 2006, one of my choices was the overture from the soundtrack of the film because it took me right back to the first time I was ever on the high seas, plus of course the spelling of my daughter's name was after Leslie. (It ran in the family that we were named after film stars – I am Gloria after Gloria Swanson as my dad was in love with her.) I actually first met Leslie when we were both appearing on the *Royal Variety Performance* and there were so many people and so few dressing rooms that we all had to share. I looked at the list and saw I was sharing with Leslie, and thought, *Oh, fantastic! All my Christmases have come at once!*

It got off to a rather disappointing start, though. When I pushed open the door of the dressing room, there was Leslie, but she was sitting in her vest and doing her make-up, which is not really the way you want to encounter one of your idols for the first time. But matters improved greatly. After the performance, she asked if I had a car to go to the after-show party:

'Yes,' I said, not sure of what she was implying.

'Would you mind if I came with you?' she asked.

'Of course not,' I said, and wondered what my seventeen-year-old self would have thought if she'd known she'd be giving a lift to Gigi. Leslie subsequently came on *Sunday, Sunday*, where it emerged that she'd just bought a village in France and had also turned her talent to architecture and design!

Rod Steiger was another wonderful guest, but despite his tough guy reputation, he was reduced to tears twice on the programme. The first time he wept with tears of pride when he revealed that his daughter had become an opera singer, and he had been to Covent Garden to hear her perform. You can imagine the enormous fatherly pride and emotion on that occasion. He also talked about how his wife had helped him off the booze. That time the tough guy was in tears as he talked about the support and compassion she had shown, and the joy she eventually led him to.

Richard Harris was always a welcome and vibrant guest, too. As an Irishman, he was never short of a few good stories. As usual, I went forward to kiss him when he appeared on the set. About halfway through the interview he started to tell me about a severe accident he'd suffered that had necessitated a skin graft on his face, before revealing where the skin had been taken from. 'So when you kissed my cheek,' he said, 'you were actually kissing my arse.'

He also told me a great story about Pierce Brosnan who has a home in Dalkey, south of Dublin. He was so happy to be back there; he could just relax and nobody really bothered him. So he was in his local pub with a pint of Guinness, reading the *Irish Times*, when two nicotined fingers came over the top of the paper, pulling it down. 'How are you, Pierce? Now I know you're just relaxing but I simply want to shake your hand because that's as close as I'll ever get to Halle Berry's ass.'

Oh we definitely had fun!

Joan Collins was another regular on *Sunday, Sunday*. It can be quite daunting interviewing extremely beautiful women. And Joan Collins, even now in her eighties, is still looking magnificent. She has that Hollywood studio attitude of looking glamorous at all times. You do think, *Oh my God, what am I going to wear?* and there's no point in trying to compete. So, with Joan Collins, I decided to go for classical elegance. I had a really lovely black dress by David Emanuel and I felt very comfortable about it because it was innocuous, but it was very beautifully designed and slimming and I loved it. But then somebody in advance, doing some trailers for the programme, said, 'How are you going to dress to match Joan?'

'Well, I'm not,' I said. 'I'm going to dress down because I can't compete.' And when she came on the programme, me feeling good in my lovely David Emanuel black dress, she said, 'Oh I'm so glad you dressed down.' I thought it was very funny and Joan is always a very witty guest. It hit the right note from the start. Recently she was also on *Loose Women* talking about her make-up range. As I was sitting *very* close to her I immediately thought, *if she looks like that with her own make-up brand, that's for me*. But she really is always a welcome interviewee. There's a perception of her that she's very much a man's woman – she's not, she's a girly girl as well.

She's also very good friends with mutual pals of mine in the South of France, the famous lyricist Leslie Bricusse and his wife Evie, and I've met with her a couple of times at their house. There was one occasion when she arrived in a sort of gypsy skirt and a beautiful off-the-shoulder cotton top with her hair in a very casual style, *au natural*. She had a waspie belt on, but came in, gesticulated and said, 'Look at that stomach! But I'll get rid of that in two weeks by the time I have to go on stage again.' Joan can be very endearing and I really like her because you can have a good chat with her as well – plus we always have grandchildren in common as a topic.

In fact, thinking about this reminds me of another story with Joan and our mutual friends Leslie and Evie Bricusse, who are marvellous hosts, but never more so than on the special day of the Queen's Diamond Jubilee in June 2012. They have a magnificently placed apartment on the river at Battersea which was perfect to watch, totally uninterrupted, the spectacular flotilla and pageant on the Thames. There were hundreds of small craft from all over the world as well as a specially converted royal barge from which Her Majesty the Queen and Duke of Edinburgh and the royal party waved to thousands of onlookers.

The major problem was that the rain pelted down all day; with the excessive crowds it was so difficult to get through to the apartment itself. We always knew it was going to be a day with a difference when Michael Caine opened the door and took our sopping wet coats. Leslie, who knows and has worked with every big name you can think of, had a very impressive guest-list, including Joan Collins, Roger Moore, Cliff Richard, Susan George and, of course, 'my name is Michael Caine'.

The outlook from their extensive balcony allowed us the best view of the flotilla and the relentless rain didn't dampen the spirits of thousands of people who wanted to get a glimpse of this extraordinary spectacle, except for trying to get a taxi home afterwards. It proved impossible, so Michael suggested he would try yet again to get a cab and that we should go into a nearby café to shelter from the rain. With us were Cliff and Bill Wyman from The Rolling Stones, and you should've seen the reactions from the customers as we slurped our cups of tea. In the event, there was no option but shanks' mare. We nearly got blown off the bridge as we walked across to the other side of the river and when we got there, again no option but to take a bus down the King's Road. The sight of Cliff Richard travelling on a red bus inevitably led to everybody singing, 'We're all going on a summer holiday'. It was hilarious but in keeping with the celebratory atmosphere of the day.

Anyways, where was I?... Another beautiful woman who came on *Sunday, Sunday* was Sophia Loren, although my favourite anecdote about her comes from the film director Michael Winner, who I interviewed for *Cash in the Celebrity Attic*. Much to my surprise, Michael allowed us to go into his amazing house, full of artwork and magnificent antiques, which now actually belongs to Robbie Williams. It's got a wonderful garden that has everything you don't expect a townhouse to have.

We turned up on the day of filming with our very hard-working crew, who were usually used to people asking, 'Would you like a wee cup of tea?' Or, 'Can I get you anything?'

But as we walked in Michael completely ignored us. Instead he said to his assistant, 'Diana, do you remember I told you that I would never like any more than three of an effing crew in here? Will you tell the rest of this crew to get out of my house?' The crew looked rather shell-shocked and were forced to troop out, but I already knew Michael well, so wasn't overtly concerned. The director, the cameraman and I stayed but, friends or not, we were all booted out at one minute to one o'clock because he was going to have lunch. (I remember it as it was the only time when the *Cash in the Attic* budget allowed for a restaurant for lunch! The rest of the time it was sandwiches or a bowl of soup.) And then we weren't allowed back in again until five past two exactly. As you might imagine though, Michael was a fascinating interviewee. We did most of the filming in the cinema in his house, which was fantastic, like any plush small cinema. On the floor of the cinema, he had boxes and boxes and boxes of photographs of major stars with whom he had worked with, everybody you can think off.

When I asked him did he have a favourite, he said, 'I was always very fond of Sophia Loren. I was filming with her in France once and I said to her:

"Darling, where do you go when I don't need you on the set? I never see you around. Never in the Winnebago, you're never at the canteen. I never see you. Where do you go?"

"Oh, darling, I go to a little beach just along the coastline and I sunbathe or I read or I just pass my time," she replied.

"I hope you're not doing it topless."

"Oh, darling, don't worry. It's a tiny little cove. Who's going to discover me in that tiny little beach?"

So anyway, six weeks later, she rings me up.

"Michael?"

"Oh, Sophia, how are you?"

"Do you take *Paris Match*?"

"No, Sophia. Why?"

"Darling, eight pages of me, topless, lying on the beach in France."

"How are your tits?"

"Marvellous," she said.

"Worry no more."'

★ ★ ★

I interviewed Raquel Welch first on the radio and then again on *Pebble Mill*. That second occasion showed that she knew exactly how to position matters to her advantage. At that time, there were different presenters on *Pebble Mill*, each doing two programmes a week. We would do one 'live' and then record one in the evening for another day and thankfully, in this case, it was a pre-record in the evening. First of all, she didn't want to walk-on, but the producer wanted her to do so, to see that wonderful figure of hers and admire her sashay. In the end she agreed.

So we gave her an enormous build-up, billed her as the big interview, and on she came looking magnificent. She sashayed down the set and as she sat down I fired the first question. But she just looked at me and said, 'Do you honestly think I'm going to sit here and do this interview in crap lighting like that?'

The whole audience gasped – and so did I.

'I'm going to leave the set now and I will only come back when you get me honeycomb lighting.'

So she got up and walked off. You've never seen so many electricians in so many cupboards looking for honeycomb lighting. And of course, they found it. In the end, she looked magnificent. I looked like rubbish because every light was on her, but let's face it – she was always going to look just sensational.

Charlton Heston is another of the great Hollywood actors who I call 'real men'. I had watched him endlessly in films such as *El Cid*, *The Ten Commandments* and *Ben-Hur*. On one occasion he brought his wife Lydia on with him and I said to them, 'You have one of the longest marriages in Hollywood.' It was something like 60 years at that point. 'Have you ever thought about divorce?' I asked brightly. Quick as a flash, Lydia answered, 'Divorce, never. Murder, often.'

As a singer I used to have Andy Williams' songs in my repertoire so it was such a joy when I heard he was to appear on *Sunday, Sunday*. He certainly didn't disappoint, and recalled his very successful TV show in the States and the time he introduced Michael Jackson as a little boy to join his older brothers on his first telly experience. At the end of his show, he would always pick a girl from the audience and dance with her to the song 'May Each Day', which became his signature song. I had actually recorded a version of the song on my album, so when he came on the show, the producers hired an orchestra at enormous expense. Andy put out his hand and asked, 'May I have this dance?' and off we went. What an end to a show!

★ ★ ★

We had many home-grown stars, too, including the comedian Freddie Starr, then at the peak of his career. I first encountered him on *Good Evening, Ulster*, when we pre-recorded the interview and it's just as well we did because Freddie, who was one of the most outrageous entertainers of his day, was such a wildcard. Things could and did often go wrong with him, and so it turned out on that occasion when Freddie sat down and immediately broke wind. With someone like that you simply can't be prissy or look embarrassed, so I made a joke of it.

'That was you, wasn't it?' I asked.

From then on, every time I asked him a question, he broke wind again and moved his chair closer to mine and so I did the same in return (not breaking wind, of course). By the end of the interview the chairs were so close that our knees were touching, at which point he took my face in his hands and kissed me full on the lips. A bit of a shock but it was too late.

'You're beautiful,' he said. 'Will you marry me?'

'What, you'd leave your wife for me, would you?' I responded cheekily.

People ask how I coped in situations like that, but it made for very good television in the end, as it did when Freddie appeared on *Sunday, Sunday*. I started doing the introduction, but instead of coming through the door like everyone else, he burst *through* the set, which had been specially constructed to allow him to do so, not that I knew that at the time. I almost had a heart attack, but, again, it made for great telly.

Freddie was also a very good singer and on that show he launched into an Elvis song. Thinking I was safe while he sang, I mentally went to the next item on the agenda. The next thing I knew, Freddie's crotch was in my face, gyrating like Elvis, and all I could do was put up my clipboard to hide my embarrassment. To this day it still crops up in those shows like *It'll Be Alright on the Night*! These really were the heady days of 'live' TV.

Breaking wind was obviously something Freddie thought was funny at the time. I'm from a Northern Irish background where we would never even have thought of cursing at home, let alone joke about bodily functions, but you had to take it in your stride. 'Do you know what the poor man's Jacuzzi is?' the comedian Frank Carson asked me on air. 'A fart in the bath.' That was the first time I'd ever heard that one and fart wasn't a word we used on air at that time. But, believe it or not, black cab drivers in London still recall that gag.

I've long been an ardent admirer of Michael Parkinson. Latterly, Parky has presented a show called *Masterclass* for Sky Arts, but watching him all those years ago back in Northern Ireland, I always felt that that was what his talk show was – a masterclass in how to interview someone. I remember watching him with total envy as he interviewed huge stars like Jack Lemmon or Walter Matthau. I learned a huge amount from him. We would regularly bump into one another around Soho in London – not the seedy end, but where the film previews are held. Big names always wanted the interviewer to see the movie in advance which was always good research. 'Who have you got on this week?' he would ask. One day I replied, 'Robert Mitchum.'

'Ooh, tricky! Do your homework,' he said.

I always did my homework, so I assumed I'd be fine, but I did some extra that time which was just as well for I soon understood what he was talking about. I'd ask Mitchum a question and he'd reply, 'Yup.' Or perhaps, 'Nope.' There would then be a silence, which was only a few seconds, but on air felt like hours. The temptation was to rush in with another question, but then I learned to zip my mouth and if I stayed silent and made him fill the space, he'd start to talk. Then he'd finally come up with what you wanted; marvellous stories about the films he had starred in and the co-stars he'd fallen in love with. It just took some nerve on the part of the interviewer at first, not to leap in.

Sunday, Sunday also featured a critic's slot, which would reveal some remarkable facts in itself. We would send people who were well-known in their own field to see a show or film and report back on it, which they always seemed to enjoy doing as it meant they weren't just talking about themselves. For example we sent the botanist David Bellamy to the ballet, and in reporting back he revealed for the first time that at one point in his childhood he had wanted to be a ballet dancer himself – strange that. Later, he was reported to have said that his greatest regret was never to have danced in *Ondine* with Margot Fonteyn.

I'll never forget interviewing David Essex too, because when Caron was growing up, he was her schoolgirl crush. It was David Essex posters on the wall, David Essex records,

David Essex this, David Essex that, and then when I met him, it turned out that he was a delightful interviewee because he's quirky and multi-talented; acting, singing and writing musicals.

I actually initially encountered him when I was working in Belfast and of course Caron was there, hiding behind the set and watching it all. When I came to England and appeared on the Val Doonican Saturday night show, Caron, who was a teenager at the time, heard that David Essex was on the same programme and was beside herself with excitement. Of course she wanted to come too. David was in Make-up when she arrived and when I'd been in there earlier, I said to him, 'Would you mind if I bring my daughter along as she is just out of her head with anticipation here about me appearing alongside you?'

'Not at all,' he replied.

I remember Caron was so thrilled to be meeting her all-time crush. And he was so lovely to her – when I left to go to the set to do my 'live' bit, David came along and said to Caron, 'Would you like me to take you to the studio to watch your mum perform?' And then, when he heard that Caron was at university in Bristol he said, 'Oh, I'll be going to Bristol soon. Give me your number and I'll ring you up and organise some tickets.'

Weeks went by and Caron had almost forgotten all about the concert and assumed he'd totally forgotten as well. Then, one day, when Caron was sitting on the toilet in the house she shared with five other students, somebody shouted, 'Caron, David Essex is on the phone.'

'Yeah, yeah! Tell me another one. And I suppose Donny Osmond is waiting outside.'

'No, no, no, honestly, he's on the phone.' And, sure enough, it was David, getting full marks for remembering to ring and offer her tickets. It was such a lovely gesture. Even later on, when we were going to see her in Australia for her fortieth birthday, he signed a copy of his autobiography for her and she just loved it.

When we started to have some events for Caron's Foundation, we had a big evening at the Odyssey in Belfast, with 8000 people attending, and David headlined that. He really has made some beautiful gestures towards Caron over the years, which pleased her mother more than I can tell you. Sometimes when big names do relatively small things like personally signing books or sending some tickets, it means so very much.

★ ★ ★

There were many surreal moments during these special and wonderful years. My son Michael was doing a bit of PR at the time and he rang me to see if I would be interested in interviewing the legend that is Deborah Kerr whom I had adored in *The King And I*. As if! So we flew to Switzerland to interview her at her home in Gstaad, high in the Alps. Her assistant brought in a tray of tea as we were waiting. And then Deborah herself appeared and started to serve the tea, just as I'd seen her do in so many films. I remember thinking to myself, *Deborah Kerr is serving us tea in her home. Can this really be happening?*

Then of course we threw the rule book away when it came to interviewing Sean Connery – our programme was an hour long and usually had four guests, but we gave the whole sixty minutes over to the original Bond. I loved Roger

I've been so fortunate to meet legends of stage and screen over the years – Sean Connery, Bette Davis, Charlton Heston, Audrey Hepburn and Robert Mitchum to name but a few…

(© Rex/Shutterstock/LWT)

Above: One of my favourite films as a child was *The Glenn Miller Story* and I was thrilled when I got to meet, and know, its stars, Jimmy Stewart and June Allyson. © *LWT*

Below: Meeting some big screen sirens. Raquel Welch, Sophia Loren and Joan Collins. © *LWT*

Top left: It was a dream come true to sing with Andy Williams.

Top right: Meeting my icon Leslie Caron, whom I named my daughter after.

Middle left: I've had great laughs with Dame Edna.

© *LWT*

Middle right: With the infamous Cynthia Payne. My children thought that this unlikely connection with 'Madam Cyn' was hilarious.

Bottom: With Gary Wilmot and the comedy genius Kenny Everett, whom I worked with and became great mates. He really died far too young.

© *LWT*

Above left and right: Don't ask why I'm sitting on Julio Iglesias' knee, but I definitely look like I'm enjoying it more than I should be. Seriously, he came on my Radio 2 show many times. We then became great family friends and are pictured here at his home in the Dominican Republic with Stephen and Julio's beautiful wife Miranda.

Below left and right: I love Neil Diamond and we have had some great laughs together. Such a kind, humble and talented man.

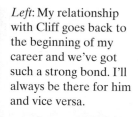

Left: My relationship with Cliff goes back to the beginning of my career and we've got such a strong bond. I'll always be there for him and vice versa.

Right: This is us jiving at Stringfellows. The headline the next day read 'Rocking around the crock'.

Left: Sir Cliff and I last year at the Hard Rock Pinktober event at the Dorchester hotel, which benefits The Caron Keating Foundation.

(© Jonathan Brady/PA Archive/PA Images)

Right: Cliff and I at his house in Barbados. We've had some wonderful times on the island together including my 70th birthday, when Cliff generously invited the whole family to stay.

Above left: With David Essex, who has been so kind to our family.

Above right: With Michael Ball – who'd have thought he'd go from being completely upstaged by my son Paul at college, to the huge performer he is today.

Centre: With Brian Conley and Kiki Dee. Brian is hilarious and sang for me when *Loose Women* did a second 'This Is Your Life' for me in 2017.

Right: Over the years I've loved working alongside Michael Crawford – a true talent.

Above: On the set of *The Old Curiosity Shop* with Peter Ustinov. I look like a proper old bag lady, complete with blacked-out tooth. Give us a kiss darlin'.

Below: As the Fairy Godmother in pantomime. Think how much my magician dad would have loved my magic wand.

Right: With Caron and Michael on the BBC 1 programme *Family Affairs*. Caron and I were the main hosts, though Michael made a few guest appearances. It was very special working with my children. © *BBC*

Left: *Open House* ran daily on Channel 5 for five years. I relish meeting up with the team, even now. Here I am with Graham Norton, Charlotte Church and Julie Andrews. © *Channel 5*

Right: With Ringo Starr and his wife, Barbara, at Ravi Shankar's 80th birthday party, in the grounds of George Harrison's house. It was a glorious night.

Moore of course and his humour in the Bond movies, but I still think Sean Connery was the best 007. There was a lot of excitement around the studio that day, particularly from the blokes. Forget about the girls: because Sean was much a macho figure, it was the guys who were particularly excited to have him around.

Barry Humphries, as I mentioned elsewhere, came on the radio show on a number of occasions, as well as various television shows, and because he had at least three different incarnations, it could get a bit confusing. When he was dressed as Dame Edna, then that is what you saw and he never came out of character. On one occasion I had to do a radio interview with Dame Edna, but Barry came into the studio dressed as Barry, which was rather off-putting. He realised I was having a problem, so he said, 'I'll help you out here' and took a big pair of silly glasses out of his pocket and put a trilby on. Visually, it gave me the hook. He was a blissful guest, though, and we were always glad to hear that either Barry Humphries or the outrageous Dame Edna or the even more outrageous Les Patterson would be on the show. From an interviewer's point of view, people like Barry are a dream because you know you're going to get a funny, interesting interview that makes TV gold, so I used to think, *Bring it on!*

I also got to know Michael Crawford very well when he was in the musical *Barnum* at the London Palladium, which I saw with Caron before I interviewed him, when his voice still had quite a high range. And then of course along came Andrew Lloyd Webber's *The Phantom of the Opera*. Michael went to a marvellous singing teacher called Ian Adam, who changed the timbre of his voice, completely bringing out those incredible vocals needed for the part. It was astonishing what he did with his voice.

At that time Michael lived quite close to where we had a house in London. I would stay there during the week when it wasn't practicable to get back to Sevenoaks and one night he rang me and asked, 'Are you in London?'

'Yes,' I replied.

'Would you like to come round for supper?' he asked.

It was actually rather unusual to be invited to his house, and when I got there it turned out that he wanted to play me the first cut of the duet that he did with Barbra Streisand, *The Music of the Night*. That was the kind of privilege that one had as a broadcaster – I got to see and hear things that I wouldn't ordinarily have witnessed and it was fascinating. At that time, because of various opening theatre nights and functions, I got to know Michael's two daughters as well and I always loved watching how supportive and close they were to their dad. Sadly I haven't seen him so much in recent years as he now lives mainly in New Zealand, but I also have very good memories of seeing him perform in EFX in Las Vegas – we did a special trip there for Radio 2 and of course it's always amazing to see someone you know up on those huge forty-foot lit-up boards outside the casino on the famous Las Vegas strip.

In my early days on the show, I was also sent to cover the Cannes Film Festival, which was quite an event for a girl from Northern Ireland. I interviewed Anthony Hopkins at the famous Hotel du Cap Eden-Roc, which should have been the epitome of glamour, but it actually rained solidly for five days. Although Anthony was already a very well-known actor at that point, he hadn't actually done proportionally that many interviews. He was strangely nervous, but of course came up with the goods. However, it was another lesson – fame does not necessarily bestow a person with confidence.

★ ★ ★

I've made some wonderful friends through the show. In 1982 I met Neil Diamond for the first time. He is one of the best songsmiths of his generation. In the early 1980s he was not that keen on doing interviews at all, but if he liked you and felt comfortable, he would relent. And so every time he came to Europe he'd do an interview for me and in turn I've been out to his LA studio, ArchAngel, to chat to him there.

There was one hilarious time when, in conversation with Neil in between records, I happened to mention that Cliff Richard was doing thirty-two consecutive concerts at the Albert Hall. Neil thought that was almost impossible as he was only doing four nights at Wembley. So I casually asked him if he'd like to see Cliff in concert and, much to my surprise, he said he would like to come on his night off. So it was arranged that Neil would arrive at a certain time when the lights were due to go down, and our man on the walkie-talkie talked to his man and then Neil slipped into a box with a good view of the stage. I had also arranged a private dinner in an executive suite at the Langham Hotel afterwards – there were only eight of us. When Cliff arrived after his concert was over, they got on so well. It was the first time they'd met and Neil told Cliff that when he was a fledgling songwriter with virtually no money, Cliff had recorded one of his songs which gave him the princely sum of $4000, a fortune at the time to Neil, and he lived off it for months.

After dinner, the singing started and didn't end until 4am, and as there were bedrooms next door to where we were,

Reception got a call to say, 'Would you stop those idiots singing away at this hour of the morning?!' If only they'd known the global award-winning stars who were doing the singing.

Whenever Neil is in London we go to his concerts and visit him backstage beforehand (never afterwards, as he always shoots back to this hotel). He even sent a huge bouquet of flowers on the day of my second wedding, which truly impressed the staff at Hever Castle where we got married.

★ ★ ★

I also got to know Billy Connolly (now Sir) through my fellow Northern Irishman, the songwriter Phil Coulter, who won the Eurovision Song Contest with songs like 'Puppet On A String' and 'Congratulations'. Phil invited Billy to Northern Ireland at the height of the Troubles, to Phil's hometown of Londonderry.

'Are you mad? I don't want to go to Derry. What about the Troubles?' Billy replied.

'It'll be all right,' Phil reassured him. 'It never affects entertainment. Don't be silly.'

So Billy went and of course there was a bomb scare: 'Get under the table or get out!' someone screamed.

Billy eventually crawled under the table on his hands and knees. 'I'm quaking,' he said. 'Coulter, where are you because when I get my hands on you I will kill you for bringing me to this place.'

Undeterred, a fan approached also on his hands and knees and, as the great man sought to recover his equilibrium said, 'Hey, Billy, could I have your autograph?' he asked. I wouldn't like to repeat his retort.

I've also known Sir James Galway, God bless his cotton socks, the most famous flautist in the world, since I was in Northern Ireland. James is from Belfast, near the shipyard, and grew up marching with the Orange Lodge Bands on the 12th of July. One of his tutors there realised that he had a very great and special talent and said to him, 'You know, you should consider going to music college in London.'

'Don't be ridiculous, I'd never get to music college,' said James.

But the tutor helped him get an interview for the Royal College of Music and that's where he studied. Jimmy often talks about the fact that that was such a huge jump, moving from Northern Ireland to London, as I discovered myself. And then in the course of time he was invited to audition for the Berlin Philharmonic Orchestra and, through no fault of his own, he arrived late and the auditions were over. The conductor was Herbert von Karajan, one of the most famous musicians of the twentieth century, but Jimmy was not put off. 'Look, I have travelled a long way to get here and it wasn't my fault that the plane was late. I demand an audition because this is what I've come to do.'

Von Karajan was not terribly pleased at this but I think felt obliged to give him the audition. Jimmy recalls that he threw at him some very tough and testing pieces but he rose to the occasion, impressed Von Karajan enormously and got the job immediately. So he became the principle flute at the Berlin Philharmonic but then astounded Von Karajan a few years later by saying that he wanted to leave and branch out into popular music as well. Everyone thought he was mad: 'Nobody ever leaves the Berlin Philharmonic, or Von Karajan. It's ridiculous that you're doing it.'

And he said, 'Well, I'm doing it and I'm leaving it. I'm going solo.' And then of course he recorded 'Annie's Song', which was a huge No. 1 hit all over the world...and the rest is history.

Because of the Northern Ireland connection, I've always known Jimmy and was sent to interview him when he had a really, really bad accident. He was walking back to his house in Switzerland and was mowed down by a motorcycle which broke both legs, leaving him in hospital for weeks, which is where I visited him. But even then he made me laugh – his young twins would be in the room with him and couldn't resist peeping under the sheet-covered framework around his legs when Jimmy had to use the hospital bottle. I have a great photograph of him sitting up in bed with his tin whistle and diamond-studded flute. And for the interview he played 'Flight of the Bumblebee', during which I always say he has to have circular breathing. By tradition, he always finished his classical concerts with the 'Londonderry Air' he is so proud of where he comes from.

When he married his third wife, Jeanne, the four of us became really great friends, and we've been over to Switzerland to visit them many times. Jeanne is a flute player herself and they play the flute together every morning before breakfast, sitting under the shadow of those wonderful Swiss mountains. When my second husband Stephen and I were getting married, we invited them obviously, but there was initially some doubt as to whether they could attend because James thought he would be in Japan or somewhere. In the event, he ended up being able to come, of which more later.

Terry Wogan, of course, was another great Irish friend. We were so deeply shocked when he sadly died in 2016. Shortly afterwards, we were all invited to a big dinner to celebrate his life, which many of the Irish people in the media attended, in the course of which his children were presented with a Waterford Crystal bowl. Jimmy and Jeanne were in town and we were supposed to have dinner anyway, so I said, 'Would you like to come to this event tonight?'

Jimmy was very enthusiastic – I've noticed that the older he gets, the more Irish he becomes. Jeanne rang and asked, 'Would you like him to bring the tin whistle?' Well of course, although I would never have suggested it myself.

At the dinner I was asked to say something about Terry, which I did. And then they asked me to introduce Jimmy. When he took to the floor, brought the tin whistle out of his pocket and played 'I'll Tell Me Ma When I Get Home' and various other Irish tunes, it brought the house down. Jimmy and Jeanne still travel the world performing and giving masterclasses. I never know whether they're in Japan, Australia or the USA, but somehow we always manage to keep in touch.

In 2017 I was fortunate enough to be the guest of honour at the same media event that was held at the Irish Embassy and hosted by the Irish Ambassador. It's quite astonishing how many high-flying media people are Irish. That night the guest list was controller of, head of entertainment, senior producer and so on. But as I was nervously coming back from the loo ready to make my speech, one of the top executives stopped me and told me a very heartwarming story. He and his family lived in one of the tough areas of Belfast during the bombs, bullets and barricades time. There were ten children in the family and he said it was mandatory that they all watched the nightly programme I presented, *Good Evening, Ulster*.

Because we had veered off the standard routine of news and current affairs, he said that even though he was so young he realised what television *could* be. Furthermore, he told me eight out of the ten children are now working in TV! It was a very encouraging story as I stepped up to the podium.

★ ★ ★

There are many other happy moments from that period of my life in the mid-eighties. In the early days of BBC Children in Need, Terry Wogan and I dressed up as Sonny and Cher: I had about ten pounds of eyelashes on, a long dark wig and when I bumped into Su Pollard backstage, who I knew well, she didn't even recognise me. But Tel and I had a great laugh doing it.

Another story involves the infamous Cynthia Payne, aka 'Madam Sin', who became notorious when she was found to be running a brothel in a Southwest London suburb. One detail that stood out was that the men paid for the services of her girls with luncheon vouchers, which were prevalent in the UK in the 1970s and 80s. We had her on Radio 2, which made for a different type of interview, and when her autobiography came out we were invited to the press launch. My son Michael and I headed off to The Savoy and as we walked in, the press asked me, 'How do you feel about being in Cynthia Payne's book?'

'*Me*?' I exclaimed.

I was totally mystified but it turned out that she had a photograph of me on the set of *Sunday, Sunday*, surrounded by 50 pairs of shoes. Apparently she used to keep that photo on top of her television set because some of her punters liked to look at my legs!

Pictures of me seemed to be turning up in funny places. My son Michael once said to me, 'Why on earth is there a picture of you in *Stringfellows*?' The reason is that I had been there for the after-show party of a rock and roll theatre show and had been having a marvellous jive with my pal Cliff Richard. The next day a newspaper ran the picture with the headline 'Rock Around The Crock'! It stayed at Stringfellows for years...but it was always good for street cred!

What I will say about the thousands of interviews I've done is that I'm so grateful to all of them for the ongoing interest and passion I have for the business I'm in. There are dozens of other happy memories and very talented guests that I could write about but if I did I'm afraid this book would be too heavy to carry around. So I'll leave it there.

CHAPTER 9

LOVE AND LOSS

No life is untouched by sadness and the greatest tragedy in mine came in 2004, when I lost my precious daughter Caron to cancer. But I was to experience loss before that: Dad had already died from a severe stroke and in January 1987, freshly back from a holiday in the Seychelles, I got a call from Caron.

'It's Nanny, Mum,' she said. 'She's had some bad news. She found a lump in her breast. The doctor's run a biopsy. She's going to have to have the breast removed.'

I couldn't take it in that my beautiful mum was to have a mastectomy.

I took the next flight to Belfast. It was the longest two hours I had ever spent, and I arrived at the hospital just as Mum was coming out of surgery, where my sister Lena and I sat waiting for the news. It had come utterly out of the blue and was a terrible, terrible shock. When she did come round from surgery, Mum was distraught. She was a fastidious woman about her appearance and although the doctors assured us they had got it all out, Mum's obvious distress made me dread for the future. I returned to London, horribly worried about what would happen next. We didn't really know that much about cancer in those days. It was always referred to in hushed tones as the 'Big C'. Well, the Big C certainly hit home.

After a terrible week at work worrying, I returned to Belfast, dreading what I would find. I walked into the ward and there was Mum, her IV drips tucked into an M&S bag.

'I told them I'm going shopping!' she trilled.

Thankfully, all her old spirit returned: she started referring to her specialist bra as her 'falsies' – 'feel this, Gloria! Just like the real thing! Better than before!' – and she returned to her home in Portadown almost as good as new. The only real difference was that she said she wouldn't visit me in London any more in case she fell ill away from home, which I completely understood.

That April though, I was heading out for a quiet dinner on my birthday, when friends who lived in Sevenoaks, Debbie and David Noble, rang and suggested we pop round to their hotel for a drink first. We were just having a pleasant chat at the bar when I looked across the room and noticed a large gathering of people. Suddenly the crowd parted in the middle. I did a double take. I knew every one of them... And then, to my surprise, I saw Mum sitting in the middle of all of them! It was all down to Caron, who'd gone across to Belfast and brought Mum back with her. It was one of the best and most thoughtful birthday presents I have ever had and you can imagine how I wept buckets of joy. It was so thoughtful of Caron to organise such a surprise. But that was Caron.

My mum and I continued to have many good times after that as her confidence to travel grew and grew. During one of her subsequent visits, I was due to present at the *Royal Variety Performance* and I managed to get a couple of tickets for her and my sister Lena. It turned out to be one of her greatest highlights and for me it was fabulous to have her there to witness something that ordinarily she wouldn't have experienced. I remember we got dressed in all our finery at the London Weekend Television studios, Mum in her best black dress accompanied by a short mink jacket that I had bought her the previous Christmas. Adding some diamanté jewellery she looked wonderful and as we were leaving the building, one of the doormen who I knew well shouted across the lobby, 'Your mum's outshining you tonight, Glo!'

Mum collapsed into a fit of self-deprecating giggles. It was one of her defining moments.

Soon after she got back to Portadown, though, I began to sense that we might be approaching another difficult period because she snapped a bone in her arm just by grabbing on to the handle of a bus. Once in hospital, it emerged that the cancer had spread to her bones and the lymph glands. It was a real blow. Lena was brilliant and saw Mum every day; I went over as much as I could but it was frustrating living on the other side of the Irish Channel with a 'live' broadcast to do every day. It did help in one way, though, as at least Mum was always looking forward to the next visit.

One Sunday night I was driving back from the airport, with my mind completely on my mum back in her hospital bed, when I suddenly saw blue lights flashing. To my horror I discovered that I had put my foot down to the floor and the police had caught me doing 118 miles per hour. Obviously I was not proud of what had happened, horrified in fact, and I sat there shedding many tears. I tried to explain that my mum was extremely ill with cancer and the policeman was quite sympathetic, but he had a job to do and I was booked. I got out my driving licence and handed it over.

'Is this right?' he asked.

'Yes, it's completely right.'

The copper was confused because the name on my licence was Mary Winifred Gloria Keating, with no Hunniford in sight. As it turned out I didn't have to go to court as my lawyer handled it, but I got a two-week ban and a £500 fine. I was very relieved that it didn't get into the papers and though my kids thought that blue streak gave me some street cred, it was a serious lesson well learned.

Once again, Mum amazed us all with her resilience. One day when I was over she announced, 'I want to go home. I want out of hospital.'

I was cautious.

'I'm not sure, Mum,' I said. 'Why don't you give it a weekend as a trial and see how you manage?'

'Oh nonsense! I'm fine, I want to go home.'

So we did what she asked and moved her bed downstairs into the sitting room. Lena, who lived nearby, looked in on her every day. But Mum's broken arm hadn't healed properly and one day she fell out of bed and onto her bad arm. She didn't have the strength to push herself up and ended up trapped between the bed and the wall. She was only saved when a neighbour, Jack, who checked on her regularly found her and lifted her back into bed. That marked a turning point in Mum's illness. She was a very dignified person and was mortified that Jack had seen her in her nightie, but worse perhaps was the realisation that she really couldn't cope on her own. She went back to hospital after that. It really was the beginning of the end.

The women in our family have always been so close: I had an exceptionally strong bond with Caron, as I did before her with Mum too. She was the first person I turned to when I was a child; she was a stay-at-home-mum and had always been there for me. And now I had to accept that I was losing her. It was a dreadful time: I'd find myself weeping just before I went on air, and then I'd have to pull myself together and turn into bright and breezy Glo. At least my work took my mind off everything, if only briefly. And anyway, listeners don't want to hear a dismal voice, they just want to be entertained with music and chat. But I have to admit it was a real Jekyll and Hyde existence at the time, and it was tough with the heaviness of my mother being so ill and having to put on a happy mask. But that mask became a regular feature when Caron got her cancer.

Towards the end of June, as the cancer got worse, Mum started hallucinating, although she was lucid at least some of the time. No matter how bad she got, I couldn't bear the thought of losing her. But it was inevitable now. She wasn't eating very much but, one particular weekend I spent with her, she did manage some ice cream and jelly for me and I felt so glad she had eaten. What I didn't know was that would be her last meal because when I returned to Sevenoaks on the Sunday night, almost as I walked through the door, the telephone rang with the news that she had gone into a coma. I headed straight back to Belfast, but when I got to her little ward at the hospital it was empty. On 6 July 1987, Mum passed away.

In Ireland, tradition is that the body is brought home and kept there until the funeral. Over the next few days I sat for hours and hours beside my mum's open coffin, somehow taking comfort from the fact that Mum was still beside me, clearly at peace. But despite the fact that I was a forty-seven-year old mother-of-three, I couldn't shake off the feeling that I was an orphan. I'd lost both parents now and parents are the people you grow up considering to be immortal. They are the ones who are always there for you, who will always protect you and give you that unconditional love and when you lose your parents it is the first time that you really have to confront your own mortality.

After the funeral, Lena and I cleared out the house, which involved a good many more tears. Mum had kept a selection of scrapbooks: first collecting clippings about Dad's magic act, then another about my acts as a child, another about me as an adult and another about Caron, who had by this time got a job as a presenter on *Blue Peter*. Mum even had one about herself, because by that time she'd become a bit of a local celebrity on the back of her television appearances like *The Des O'Connor Show* and *This Is Your Life*, and also interviews that the two of us had done together for magazine articles.

Then there were more tears when we came across an unopened box of chocolates tied with a big frou-frou bow. This was the wonderful occasion that I wrote about in Chapter One, when Mum came to London and appeared on a special Mother's Day chat show with Des O'Connor. The mothers of Michael Parkinson and Russell Harty were also there. It was such a lovely occasion; they were all put up in a smart hotel and given a limousine to use with none of the offspring allowed to be around.

The next day I had taken Mum to tea at The Ritz, which she loved. She kept on saying, 'Oh I never thought I would be in such a posh hotel like The Ritz'. As we sat down the maître d' at the Palm Court, an Irishman called Michael, came over and said to Mum, 'Madam, I thought you were simply wonderful on *The Des O'Connor Show* last night.' Of course she was absolutely thrilled, all the more so when as we were finishing tea, Michael returned with a huge box of Ritz chocolates, decorated with a lace bow and placed on a silver salver. 'Madam,' he said, 'just because you were so wonderful on television last night, I wonder if you would accept this on behalf of the management.' That was the box of chocolates we found, that Mum had kept as a treasured souvenir, never opened. I often think of the gestures people make, like reading out personal requests on the radio or as in this case a small gift, and just how much it means to the individual.

★ ★ ★

A couple of years later, I experienced another rather difficult period for a number of reasons. Everyone in the public eye receives unwanted attention, but I had been fairly lucky. Apart from the abuse I received as an Irish woman in the early days in London on the radio at the time of IRA bomb attacks, I had had remarkably little in the way of hate mail or crank calls. Perhaps they had come in and I was shielded from it by the station but it was certainly nothing I ever knew about.

But there were little incidents. There was one man who waited for me outside Broadcasting House every day for five years: while it had always been the case that people wanted to pose for pictures or to get an autograph, this one took it further. On one occasion he ran over to greet me and then bent over to try to kiss me. I shoved him backwards and said, 'Don't ever do that again!' And he didn't. And so, until the end of 1989, that was about as much trouble as I had ever had.

But by now, this same man had begun writing to me at the BBC when I was doing the afternoon radio show for Radio 2 and he fantasised that when I played a romantic piece of music or read out a romantic greeting, it was a secret message from me to him. He'd write: 'I know you want to see me. I'll be at the such-and-such hotel at 4pm.'

I ignored it, of course. The next day, he'd send an irate letter telling me he'd waited three hours and asking why I didn't turn up. Flowers and cards started to arrive at the BBC and when he told me he'd booked us on a Christmas cruise on the QE2, I began to realise that this was getting completely out of hand.

It was when he started lurking in the foyer at Broadcasting House that I began to get irritated, but it soon got a lot worse. He had worked out that I lived in Sevenoaks, so he began taking the train there and asking about where I lived. He was a rather frail, vague-looking man but obviously bright enough, because he went to the taxi stand and spun a sob story that he was invited for lunch but had lost the address. The taxi man was totally taken in and actually drove him to the house. Far from the menacing character I'd made him out to be in my own mind, he was a pathetic creature, balding and meek, altogether sad. I was perfectly polite and told him to go away, which he did, shuffling off down the road.

But he came back. One afternoon I was in London in the middle of the 'live' radio show, but Michael was at home studying for his A levels. He rang the doorbell and told Michael I wanted to see him. Michael tried to talk some sense into him: 'Look, why are you doing this? Don't you have any family? Do they know you're doing this? You know Mum doesn't want you here. She doesn't want to see you so please go away.' The man refused to budge so Michael knew he'd have to change tack. On a different occasion, Michael said, 'This is useless what you're doing, it's just a figment of your imagination. It can't lead anywhere, don't you see that? I want you to leave right now!' When that still didn't work Michael threw a bucket of cold water over him. He stood there, soaking wet and utterly dejected. But even that was not the end.

I felt very anxious when Michael told me. It's one thing someone writing to you, quite another when they arrive on your doorstep. But he just kept turning up. He was a sad old man in his late seventies, and when he was told to go away he always did. He was obviously mentally disturbed. Part of me pitied him, but it was also a great invasion of our privacy so I decided it was time to report it to the police. After about a year of his visits, I got an injunction out against him, saying he had to stay at least 150 yards from my workplace and 500 from my home. Nor was he to write letters or make phone calls.

It made no difference. The letters kept arriving. He started putting eerie things in them talking about my dogs and that he knew what a bunny boiler was. But finally, after I had a bad accident with my shoulder, of which more below, matters came to a head. The stalker arrived at my door one day during this period and it really freaked me out. My arm was immobilised in a sling and I knew I'd be quite unable to defend myself if anything happened. I spoke to my solicitor and we decided to take him to court. I waited in the ante room and the QC told me that as he'd persistently broken the injunctions, it was likely he'd go to prison. I didn't want to be responsible for that, I just wanted him to stop. It was obvious he needed medical help, not locking away. The judge said if he ever came near me again it would automatically be prison. To cope with it I had security gates and a camera fitted at home instead. Despite all this, he still kept coming, but now at least I could see him through the camera and tell him to go away which, luckily, he still did.

Around this time it emerged that my stalker had been charged a few years earlier with sending a hoax letter bomb threat to Margaret Thatcher, as well as harassing Princess Margaret and the Director-General of the BBC. He was undergoing treatment for mental illness and finally he must have got tired of it or developed an obsession elsewhere because he stopped coming so often. It was only when Stephen and I got married that he took a big hint and stopped altogether. However it had all made me so paranoid that by this time I became over cautious.

When I was on air one day my housekeeper Elsie rang the BBC about a very suspicious package that had been delivered to the house. Panicking a bit, I told her to ring the police. The package had been placed in the garage well away from the house, but we were busy asking Elsie, 'Is it ticking? Is it making a sound?' But when the police came and blew it apart, it turned out to be only a pile of books sent from a publisher. Many a laugh Elsie and I had later over a cup of tea.

★ ★ ★

All in all, there was a lot going on in 1989. Back from a skiing holiday and feeling as fit and healthy as I ever had been, one night I headed off for a game of tennis with my friends Pam and Div Harris, after which we were going to go on to dinner. We used the indoor courts at Michael's school, and I was raring to go, which proved my undoing. Div lightly popped the ball just over the net and I had to make a split-second decision whether to run for it but my adrenalin was really pumping now and I was playing with someone much better than me. Looking back, it seems as if time slowed down into a series of freeze frames: I could see the ball coming towards me. Just as I leaped towards it, I caught my toe on the indoor surface and did one of those runs where you don't fall down and yet don't stand up either. I staggered on and eventually ended up crashing into the metal post that supports the net.

It was almost as if it was happening to someone else. I heard the crack of bones right across the court and gradually I became aware that I was twisted head over heels into the net. The others were standing over me, ashen with shock, terrified I'd broken my neck. I hadn't but I knew it was bad and managed to roll onto my back, not yet realising that my arm was grotesquely twisted out of position, almost as if someone had pulled it off and stuck it back on again, but the wrong way round.

By the time the ambulance arrived, I was experiencing pain of a type I'd never had before. I was in such searing pain I could hardly bear to have the attendants touch me, but somehow they managed to raise my arm into a blown-up support and I was helped into the ambulance. By this time it was obvious that I'd broken my arm, but we didn't realise how serious it was until I'd been X-rayed at the local hospital in Tunbridge Wells. The orthopaedic surgeon finally came to me with a serious look on his face: 'I don't know how you've done it but you've broken the ball and socket in your shoulder into 15 pieces and the humerus is also broken in your arm. In other words, you've mutilated your arm and shoulder.' After that no wonder my arm was hanging backwards. It was a massive, massive break and I'm very lucky to have an arm that functions at all today.

The doctor was blunt about it: my only chance of having a working arm was if it was operated on by an expert in the field, otherwise I'd be left with only about 25 per cent movement. But there appeared to be few shoulder experts in the medical field; he couldn't recommend anyone and he didn't know anyone who could carry out the operation. So I decided to do some research of my own and because of my past work as a journalist in Belfast, I had a lot of home numbers for surgeons in Northern Ireland. Ironically, the various injuries people suffered in the Troubles meant that Ulster surgeons had developed an unparalleled knowledge and skill in dealing with knee-cappings, brain injuries, shootings, bomb blasts and so on, and so it was the best possible place to start.

Back at home from the hospital, I rang one of these surgeons, based in Hollywood, County Down.

'My arm is literally hanging off, what can I do?' I asked him.

'Look, I think I read in the *British Medical Journal* of two people who do shoulders,' he said. 'I'll ring you back with the numbers. But if you don't get any joy, try and get on the plane and come over to see me, and I will see what we can do for you here.'

In the event I didn't have to take him up on it. I was in far too much pain even to lie down so the next day I immediately

206

rang both of the surgeons he had suggested. The first one to call back was the wife of one of the surgeons in the *BMJ* and that's how I ended up in the hands of Mr Ian Bayley, one of the best orthopaedic surgeons in the UK. He was called 'Shoulder Bayley' by his colleagues and thank heavens I found him because I was in such a bad way by now that I couldn't even dress on my own.

I got to his office and after an examination and yet more X-rays, he indicated that the situation was serious. 'It's not a question of *will* I operate, it's the question of *can* I because you've smashed the ball and socket badly,' he said. 'But I'm willing to give it a go.'

The operation took place at the Clementine Churchill Hospital in Harrow on the Hill, and in a strange way I was actually looking forward to it because this was the only hope I had of getting my arm back to some kind of normality again. It took three and a half hours of painstaking surgery: the ball of my shoulder had exploded, with bone splaying off in all directions. The surgeon scooped up the fragments, pulled them together in a mesh of wire and stapled them with dozens of metal clicks. There were a further two giant steel pins from the shoulder to the elbow. 'There's no problem with the humerus mending,' the doctor told me when we were done. 'That's elementary. The big question now is the shoulder. How it heals will determine the amount of movement you'll have.'

I lay low for about nine days, zonked by the anaesthetic and the pain, but the old Northern Irish work ethic soon kicked in and I made my decision to go back to work. However, my right arm and hand were so badly swollen that I had no movement right to my fingertips and, despite all the metal pinning me together, I was worried I'd dislocate something and my arm would fall apart again. I couldn't dress myself properly, couldn't apply make-up and couldn't do my hair so I enlisted the services of anyone who happened to be nearby to help me. Michael and any other unsuspecting person became quite proficient at backcombing!

When I got back to work the BBC moved me to a special basement studio, with an angled pillow to prop me up, and a constant supply of painkillers and herbal tea. The BBC were so kind in sending a car for me each day but my shoulder was so sensitive to any movement that I had to ask them to send an automatic – even manual gear changes produced a jolt to my shoulder that I could barely suffer. But I was determined that this accident was not going to strip me of my job and change my life.

It is at this unlikely juncture that the maverick comic genius Kenny Everett enters the story. I had known him for years and he was very instrumental in my career for a number of reasons: we were about the same age and we were both represented by our agent Jo Gurnett through the Terry Wogan agency. He and I remained great colleagues until his death in 1995 and we did a lot of work together. Kenny was at the absolute height of his career at that point, so famous that he had to have Jo with him at all times, even when he went out to the supermarket. People just would not leave him alone, so he needed someone there for protection.

Before my accident we'd agreed to do a programme called *That's Showbusiness*, with Kenny as a captain of one team and me captain of the other. At first I thought I wasn't going to be able to do the show. We had a chat about it to Jo, who was sympathetic but pointed out that if I didn't do the first episode I'd have to miss out on the rest of the series. I rang the producer, John Kaye Cooper, and said, 'I'm so sorry, I'm still looking forward to doing the series but I'm in a terrible state here.' Remember, I was literally numb right down to my fingertips and my arm was in a sling.

But John was extremely understanding: 'Look, I would rather you come and do the series even in a sling than not do it at all,' he said. So, unsure as I was and despite being as helpless as a baby, I had some lovely sequin jackets bought for me that would cover it.

The show was filmed in Manchester and to begin with Jo had to travel with me: I flew there once a week for 13 weeks, with my angled cushion on the plane to absorb the vibration.

Jo also had the room next to me at the hotel: it had a connecting door so that she could come through and give me my copious tablets, pain killers and settle me into bed. However, one week, she wasn't able to go and so Kenny had to have the room on the other side of the adjoining door. He would come in to put me to bed, angle the cushion, give me my tablets and the rest of it, and the absurdity of it struck us both. 'Can you imagine if the *Sun* could see you and me, you putting me to bed,' I said as Nurse Everett fussed over me. We both thought it was hysterical – and of course 'all in the best possible taste'.

It took four years for my arm to heal fully as there were various setbacks involving further operations. The ball and socket were healing beautifully, but ironically the humerus – the bone between the elbow and shoulder – which initially had the better prognosis, was not. There was talk of a bone graft from my hip, which would have put me out of action for another two months, which I just couldn't bear the thought of and, being a complementary therapies fanatic, I said to the specialist, 'If I don't do this will my arm fall off?'

In the middle of his laughter he agreed to give it six months… As it transpired, I never had to have the bone graft and I've continued to be a devotee of complementary treatments ever since.

It was now 1990 and I had gone back to filming *Sunday, Sunday*, which is where Kenny Everett steps in again. He always did the first programme in any series I did so he was there when a new series began. I was out of my sling by this point but my arm and shoulder were still extremely tender. I introduced Ev and he bounded out on stage saying, 'Darling, darling, darling, darling, how wonderful to see you!' He grabbed me to do a tango thrust over his knee, but he moved too fast and knocked me backwards. I went crashing to the floor and knocked my shoulder against the blunt metal edge of the steps. The audience burst out laughing, thinking it was all part of the act, until they saw me lying there, skirt around my ears, contorted in pain, crying, 'Oh my shoulder, my shoulder!'

Kenny of course was absolutely devastated; he'd gone quite white and was clearly terrified I wouldn't survive the programme. I was immediately picked up and taken off the set, but something inside me pushed me on; I was determined I'd go through with it. Dr Theatre usually takes over and I have always had a 'show must go on' mentality, just as much now as ever. 'Look,' I said to the crew, 'if I don't go on again right now, I'm never going to get through it.' So I made myself go back on and acted on some kind of autopilot, until finally the show was over and I was taken to the nurse's surgery. At that point I burst into tears. There was some suggestion

I'd cracked my spine, although fortunately subsequent X-rays showed there was no further damage. Kenny, meanwhile, was deluging me with flowers and cards: 'In future maybe I should just write to you,' he said one day.

But something very odd had happened when I had that second accident. Caron, who had recently got engaged to her manager Russ Lindsay, was driving over Albert Bridge at the exact moment it happened. She felt a jolt within her and just knew something had happened. There was always a strong connection between us – call it ESP or whatever you will – but she turned the car around and drove straight to the studio. She knew exactly where I was. The nurse was just dealing with me as she walked in and I said, 'Who called you?'

'Nobody but I just knew that something had happened to you', she said.

It was very odd but she instinctively knew something had happened and that I needed her.

* * *

Despite Kenny's antics I regained 80 per cent movement in my shoulder and while I had to give up skiing, to my own great surprise I was able to go out on a tennis court again. 'Live' on air one day Cliff Richard said, 'Why don't you get back in to tennis? Come to my tournament in Birmingham', referring to a tennis trial he put on to find young players. As I was on the spot I heard myself say, 'Yes, of course I'll be there.' Sue Mappin, who ran it all, helped me enormously, getting me over my worries about using my arm again and even organised some tennis practice at Wimbledon itself. On the day of the tournament the vast crowd at the arena had been watching the young players, including a particularly talented four-year-old called Jack. He was superb. I'll always remember later when I was playing doubles with Cliff and not very well, a joker from the crowd said, 'Cliff, you should bring back Jack!'

Joking aside, that eventful year still had something more in store. It had been a trying one for me but lovely for the kids: Caron had got engaged, Paul had started a very successful sound company, which he still runs to this day, and Michael had passed his A levels and got into Bristol University. *Time to celebrate*, I thought. And so, on the evening of 10 December, we held a special dinner in the great room at Hever Castle, which has long been a family favourite for all of us, with not only family present but a selection of close friends too.

Before the dinner itself, we held drinks at the house, where we had a beautifully decorated Christmas tree sparkling away, casting lights on the ceiling, candles all lit and creating a warm glow. The atmosphere was warm and relaxed, and after that fraught year I was feeling happy: everyone I loved was there. We went on to the castle, but I noticed Caron was looking a bit restless. She'd brought her new puppy Bailey to Sevenoaks for the first time and had, somewhat reluctantly, left it with my own considerably burlier canines.

'What if something happened to him?' she fretted.

'Oh nonsense, he'll be perfectly fine,' said Michael.

'Come on, Caron,' said Russ. 'Don't you think you're getting a bit carried away?'

But Caron was certain that something was going to happen to her puppy and so, ignoring all pleas to reconsider, my determined daughter said she was leaving early to check up on the pup. She asked Michael for a house key, but he was distracted. So she asked me and I got up to go with her, but was promptly taken up in conversation with another guest.

'Mum,' said Caron insistently for the second time, 'the key.'

'It's in my bag in the cloakroom but I'm coming shortly anyway,' I said. But I got waylaid again and so Caron, Michael and Russ all left for the house without a key.

When I got back about twenty minutes later, I knew immediately that something was wrong. I could see a strange yellow glow in the hall. The front door was wide open and the hall was thick with smoke. Caron, Russ and Michael had been heaving buckets of water everywhere, with everyone increasingly confused and panicky. You do not know how frightening a fire can be until it happens to you. The fire brigade arrived and took over and they contained the damage to the hallway. It was quickly established that it was the Christmas tree's faulty lighting that had started the blaze.

Caron later told me that they'd pulled up to the house to the sound of frantic dogs barking and, still with no key, the only way they could get in was to break the glass of the back door with a broom handle. And thank heavens for that. The fire chief told me that the brass railing at the bottom of the stairs in the front hall had bent with the heat, the floor was on fire and the combustion was such that if anyone had opened the front door, it would have issued a blast of oxygen that would have caused an explosion and could have killed the lot of them. Had someone been watching over us, making sure Caron didn't get the front door key? Was that Caron's sixth sense again, knowing they had to get back to the house? I have often wondered.

We foolishly stayed in the house that night, breathing in smoke: I went to bed blonde and woke up with jet-black hair.

In fact the house was blackened from top to bottom and I went on finding deposits of soot for years afterwards. There was widespread damage and everything, carpets, curtains, clothes had to be replaced.

'How on earth am I going to be able to clean and replace everything?' I asked the fire chief.

'Lady,' he said, 'you are lucky to have a house to replace everything in at all.' More than that, the family was safe, the dogs were safe; we were all safe. But still, it had been really quite a year. Little did we know that worse years lay ahead.

CHAPTER 10

THAT'S GLO-BIZ

One of the great truisms of life is that nothing succeeds like success and, given that I was now appearing regularly on radio and television, I was offered more and more projects in return. These included the aforementioned *Pebble Mill*, *Songs of Praise*, *Highway* and *We Love TV* and in the early 1990s I filmed a six-week run of *Gloria Live* on BBC1, which replaced *Kilroy*. This was different from my other work as it took me back to my roots as a news reporter: a current affairs programme, which covered everything from the Strangeways Prison riot of 1990 to the Middle East.

It was extremely full-on though: I would read up on the issues the night before and watch the news avidly. And as we covered four topics in each programme, all topical, that was a lot. I would then be up at 4.30am every morning, in the Lime Grove Studios by 6.30am for a meeting with my editor Charles Miller, do an hour and a half of make-up and rehearsals and then go on air 'live'. After that, it was on to Broadcasting House for my Radio 2 show, followed by a return to Lime Grove to talk about the next day's show. I wouldn't get home until eight or nine at night, then I'd study my notes, fall asleep and start the routine all over again the next day.

It wouldn't have been sustainable to go on working at that pace all year round so I was to a degree relieved when the six weeks were successfully over. I had mixed feelings when they wanted to run a second series, though we softened it slightly to include much lighter subject matter as well (and to make my days slightly less exhausting!).

One of the strangest things that happened during that series was to do with a story about two British drivers who were arrested in Greece under suspicion of transporting huge pipe bombs on a truck. The story was all over every aspect of the news and the families in Britain were screaming how unfair this was, how their sons would never do such a thing and when would they be released. As it turned out, my driver for that programme was a man from Athens called Anthony. And when he told me stories about having been married to the previous prime minister of Greece's daughter, I was always a bit suspicious. However, as we chatted in the car and were talking about this particular story, he said, 'Do you want me to ring my former father-in-law, maybe he knows the lawyer involved?'. Much to the chagrin of my editor, he said, 'Well let him follow it through and see what happens.' Well, true to his word, within an hour, Anthony had managed to line up the lawyer and had news that these men would be released from prison at eleven o'clock that morning. Despite our programme's scepticism it all seemed to be authentic.

So we managed to get the relatives, including one of the

boys' mother and sister, in the studio with us 'live'. And here's what happened. We let the nine o'clock news go, not having told the newsroom anything about our scoop, went on air 'live' and, as it was the hottest story of the day, we went straight to Athens where we did an interview about the situation, and this lawyer confirmed that they would be let out of prison mid-morning. All the while the cameras were tight on the faces of the immediate family and when they heard the news, the reaction of tears and emotion was palpable. What a scoop. The newsroom wasn't particularly happy that we hadn't told them and when we came out of the studio at Lime Grove after the programme, the street was packed with international film crews and journalists.

It just goes to show you should always listen to what your driver tells you.

* * *

One day in the early nineties, I got an unexpected phone call from my agent Jo Gurnett asking if I would like to stand in for Terry Wogan, or my grandfather as I used to call him, on his nightly chat programme on BBC1. Terry was such a legend I couldn't contain my amazement at being asked to take his place for two weeks. We had all the top stars of the day: Angie Dickinson, Wet Wet Wet, Natalie Cole, but one day during our daily meeting, the producers said in rather hushed tones, 'How would you feel about interviewing Salman Rushdie?' Now, as a news buff this was music to my ears but, bearing in mind he was in hiding under a fatwa, I thought that might be difficult to organise. However, it was true: the Wogan team had somehow managed to get the first 'live' interview since the fatwa was issued. It was an unbelievable scoop.

Now, what I really knew about Rushdie was extremely limited, so I went back to a senior producer on *The Jimmy Young Show*, whom I really respected, and I hired him out of my own money on a freelance basis to do the research.

Three years earlier Rushdie had published *The Satanic Verses*, provoking Iran's Ayatollah Khomeini to issue a fatwa demanding his death. Rushdie promptly went into hiding and in the ensuing furore, numerous protests, killings and attempted killings took place. Only four of us in the BBC – the editor, the producer, security and I – knew he was going to appear on the show. Security went through the roof: Special Forces made an advance visit to establish the quickest and safest route into the studio, while sharpshooters took up position throughout Television Centre. When Rushdie arrived, just before the show was due to begin, he did so with a Special Branch guard, who were ready and waiting to take him immediately when the interview ended.

I did my homework extremely thoroughly, with the help of my learned radio producer, but I soon began to realise that although Rushdie had always been understandably presented as the victim in this case, there was more to the story than first met the eye. For a start, there was the fact that the taxpayer was stumping up for his 24/7 Scotland Yard protection and then there was his ex-wife, the American writer Marianne Wiggins. She had denounced him as a weak, self-obsessed man who failed to campaign for other writers who were prisoners of conscience. I decided I was not prepared to give him an easy ride.

When Rushdie arrived, no doubt expecting a cosy chat, I was ready for him. I walked on to the signature music and the first thing I said was, 'Tonight, live on *The Wogan Show*,

Salman Rushdie.' Well, you could audibly hear the sharp intake of breath from the audience. I sat down and began to ask him what it was like to move safe-houses so many times – in the course of a few weeks in Wales he moved 29 times. Then I went for it.

'You realise, of course, your protection is costing £1 million a year. I'm sure the average taxpayer would wonder why we should pay for Salmon Rushdie's protection?'

He didn't answer me directly, instead saying, 'If Terry had been here I was going to remind him of the time I used to write television commercials for him.' Then he went on to say that he was sick of hiding, the fatwa had been in place for too long and he hadn't meant to offend anyone.

'Given all that,' I said, 'are you still planning to release the paperback, considering you've already made £6 million on the hardcover version?'

'Of course I am!' Rushdie bristled.

'Well, you'll only reiterate the offence,' I said. 'You're going to drag it all up again.'

'But that is my right. The principle hasn't changed. For three years people have been lying about me and saying terrible things, that I did it all on purpose.'

'The argument is that it was all calculated to sell books.'

'Every author's work is calculated,' Rushdie replied. 'But when it comes to satire, should you sentence the creator of *Spitting Image* to death? For three years I've had to hear people blaming the victim. I do not take responsibility for my own murder.'

I felt it was time to raise things a notch and referred to reports that it might have delayed the release of the hostages who had been kidnapped in Beirut in the 1980s.

'That's a terrible thing to say,' snapped Rushdie. 'I've been a hostage to the hostages. I haven't been chained to a radiator, but I've been hunted by killers. The danger is not a joke. I am not to blame. I am not prepared to go into hiding any more. We will fight against it and we will win. I see my future as returning as a serious writer.'

And with that he was whisked off in a furious huff.

It made a huge sensation at the time. The switchboard was immediately flooded with calls, some pro, others anti. The literati, of course, were totally supportive of the freedom of speech of any writer and the other half of the public went, 'Good on you, Glo! Why does he think he can write whatever he wants and offend people?'

There was some degree of shock in the papers the next day that I had been so aggressive: 'Miss Hunniford subjected the author of *Satanic Verses* to an astonishingly tough inquisition,' said one. 'At one point, with an uncharacteristically fierce expression on her face, she attacked his motive for writing the book. To think Gloria was uncharitably described on this page not long ago as being like the ever-smiling senior stewardess of an island-hopping Celtic airline. An injustice to be sure!' It was a compliment, of sorts.

As for Rushdie himself, he continued to bristle with fury. Shortly afterwards, he went on Radio 4's *Woman's Hour*, where he complained to presenter Jenni Murray, 'For three years I have been vilified to a degree that few human beings ever are, by everybody from the Ayatollah Khomeini to Gloria Hunniford.' Well, I'd certainly never been linked to the Ayatollah before but that also ran in all the tabloids and in due course it went into a frame and up on the wall. As my kids would say, street cred.

* * *

As my own career moved on, of course I had the great pleasure of seeing Caron following in my footsteps and making a name for herself in television. She had started out in Northern Ireland, where she presented *The Video Picture Show*, *Channel One* and *Greenrock*, but her really big break had come when she became a *Blue Peter* presenter in 1986, a role she had pursued for four years. After Bristol University, Caron had been very confused about what to choose as a career. My advice was, 'Write to all the programmes you know and love and send them a concise biography and a photograph of yourself. State how you know they aren't necessarily looking for someone at the time but would they keep your details on file just in case.' And that's how she got her really big break when she joined *Blue Peter* in 1986. It turned out that Biddy Baxter, the famous Editor, had no idea that Caron was my daughter until the papers got hold of it and made quite a fuss. Bearing in mind I had served years as a mother buying sticky-back plastic and pipe cleaners to make Tracey Island, it was surreal when she was about to do her first programme. That day, I was in London Weekend Television and because I didn't want to miss a second, I made them switch their televisions to BBC.

Biddy Baxter was legendary in making all her presenters do quite dangerous stunts and activities, and when I think of the Health and Safety rules today and duty of care it seems almost unbelievable what they did. However, on occasions, I think I was an overcautious mother because when Caron said her first piece of filming was side-car racing, I thought it was like George and Mildred with the sit-in side-car attached to the bike. Instead of that, Caron came home black and blue and explained to me that she hadn't spent the afternoon as Mildred, but leaning out dangerously on a platform from the bike as they raced round corners. On another occasion, when she was off the coast of California diving with sharks, I was watching, virtually screaming at the thought of the danger when Caron said, 'Mum, I'm beside you, I'm here, I'm OK.'

She went on to join BBC Radio 5 and presented a number of other programmes including *This Morning* with Richard Madeley, when Judy was ill. One particularly enjoyable job was when Caron presented the Barcelona Olympics with my old friend Terry Wogan. They became great friends and after Caron died, Terry got in touch with me to say he understood about losing a daughter because his little Vanessa had died of a heart condition when she was just three weeks old. The fact that he totally understood really helped and I knew he would always be there for me any time I wanted a chat.

Caron and I worked together on a programme called *Family Affairs* on BBC 1 from 1992, dealing with various child/mother/parent/grandparent issues, and our two gen-erations blended very well. We were always surrounded by little children on the programme, which we found great fun and one day a little girl of six or seven was sitting on my knee when I was reading a link. She said in a big loud voice, 'You're not making that up, you're reading it from that over there', which of course meant I could barely read the autocue, I was laughing so hard.

On another day the children were decorating gingerbread men and when I asked one little one what exactly she was doing, she said, 'Don't be silly, I'm decorating her boobies!' Contrary to the old saying, I actually do enjoy working with children.

During that series the producer decided we would feature families who were separated by war. It was particularly exciting and challenging for me to do as I was sent out to Split, in what was Yugoslavia, to do my first satellite broadcast at the height of the Yugoslav War. I remember watching the endless trucks of technical machinery coming off the plane. We were met by a female major in the army, who said to me straight away, 'Your hotel is a transit one. So many people come and go. Make sure you lock yourself carefully in your room.' It didn't exactly make for a comfortable introduction to the scenario.

Over the next few days we linked up many of the British troops in Split with their wives and children back in the studio with Caron. Those links are always very interesting to watch so it was a real adventure for the programme and took me back to those times when I'd travel to Germany to interview the soldiers for their families back in Ireland.

Then, on the day we were leaving, the producer said, 'Knock on the door of my room and we'll travel to the airport together.' As she opened the door, my eye immediately went to the beautiful turquoise blue carpet on the floor, magnificent white furniture in the room, along with a huge four-poster bed topped off with a stunning view of the sea from her balcony.

I could only think of how I'd spent the last four days in the grottiest room I've ever had the misfortune to be in: dirty brown carpet, a grey, cement-like sink with shocking lino on the floor. The bed was especially suspect and I slept every night with my dressing gown on, wrapped around my neck so that the sheets didn't touch me at all, and a pair of socks so my feet never got near the sheets either. When I explained to her about the enormous contrast, she glibly replied, 'Oh yes,

I do feel a bit guilty. Technically this was your room but I got here first.' (I was back in Split in Croatia recently for a holiday and thankfully it was a rather more salubrious occasion!)

I truly enjoyed working alongside Caron; it just seemed to add another facet to our relationship. It was rather interesting when Alan Boyd, once head of entertainment at LWT, called us both in to discuss the possibility of presenting a new magazine programme on Channel 5. Caron listened carefully to the idea and, without even glancing in my direction, she immediately said, 'To be honest with you, I want to make my own way in my career because Mum will always be Mum, and she has more experience than me and I feel as if she might pull rank.' It was just another example of my strong-minded daughter.

So, *Open House* went ahead on Channel 5 with me as the only presenter and it ran from 1998 to 2003. When I decided to do it Channel 5 was a very new, relatively unknown quantity, and many people thought it mainly consisted of very questionable late-night viewing. A number of colleagues even asked, 'Are you sure you want to work for Channel 5?' But the answer was that yes, I was. Alan was a dear friend with whom I'd worked at LWT and I trusted him and his judgement. Besides, their money was as good as anyone else's.

It was to entail five programmes a week. My second husband Stephen, of whom much more shortly, and I were in Dublin when everything was confirmed, and we talked it over.

'It sounds like a good opportunity,' he said.

But I didn't really want to go back to working five days a week and so we came up with an alternative format, which actually became a blueprint for many programmes to follow. We did three 'live' shows a week, on Tuesday, Wednesday and Thursday, but Monday and Friday were recorded on Wednesday and Thursday nights. This meant that we made five programmes over the course of three days, leaving the weekends free. The emphasis was on news and current affairs and delving into the issues behind them, along with a mix of celebrity guests and performers. It was headed up by Paddy Haycocks, a well-known broadcaster and producer, who is fabulous at holding people together as a team. In fact, I hold Paddy's judgment in such high esteem that even today, if I'm unsure about anything, particularly politics, I ring him to chat it over.

I'm pleased to say the show took off in a fantastic fashion. Because it was new and Channel 5 was new, we could be as flexible as we wanted. We had a format to accommodate news but, on the other hand, if the guest was big enough we could make it a special and give the whole programme over to, say, Neil Diamond, Lionel Richie or Donny Osmond. And behind the scenes, the team really bonded.

The show was always fun to do under Paddy's tutelage as editor. Brian Conley was a regular guest and I can hardly believe that Donny Osmond used to deputise for me when I was on holiday. We had a guest chef on every day, and so we launched the careers of many new chefs... but it didn't seem to do anything for my cooking!

However, after a few years a new controller came in and decided that he wanted to give the budget to Terry Wogan for a morning programme and so our show came off air. Ironically, the new programme failed in popularity and was taken off. I felt so sorry for the crew, as we had never been out of the top ratings and had been very successful, but it was a blessing in disguise for me, I'll admit, as it allowed time to go to Australia to be with Caron who was living there at this time.

Looking back, it was a halcyon period, with a tight team with an inventive, flexible format. But times change. For five years the whole team stayed together, which is quite rare in television. We worked and played hard and to this day I regularly bump into some of them, now in high places or working on prime-time programmes. Then there are the *Open House* reunions every so often and a chance to catch up and reminisce. I feel so lucky looking back on the thousands of guests we had day-to-day for those five years and the times we had.

★ ★ ★

In a chequered career like mine there have been many other memorable programmes. *The Heaven and Earth Show* was one that ran for nine years on Sunday mornings but I only presented it for the last couple of years. The show was fascinating to do because it was not so much what people thought about religion but what they thought about morality. It made for a very good debate about all sorts of topical issues.

One of the most interesting series, which I did for the Biography Channel was called *Gloria's Greats*, which focused on the lives of well-known people, many of whom I had already met on Radio 2. I'd also done *Ladies of the House*, which featured politicians like Barbara Castle, Betty Boothroyd and Edwina Currie, and it was fascinating to hear about their motivation for going into politics. An innovative independent producer Paul Stead and I had worked on a number of television projects like *Time Off With*, where we built a programme around how celebrities spent their days off so I knew we'd come up with top names. We interviewed the late Sir Roger Moore at La Colombe d'Or, which was his favourite restaurant in St Paul de Vence in the South of France; we went to visit Cliff Richard in his magnificent home in Barbados and also featured the great Cilla Black in her family home in Spain. It was very poignant when she died so suddenly in 2015, because Cilla, during that programme, had talked in detail about how much the whole family enjoyed their time in Spain and that some of her husband Bobby's ashes were under a tree in the garden. I was so shocked and saddened when I heard that she died at that house, which in her time had brought her so much happiness.

It was during all this time, though, that Caron first became ill. She didn't want anyone to know about her cancer and I always said if anyone found out, it wouldn't be from me. So only family and a very few close confidantes knew what we were going through, but it did make it very difficult at times. Not only did I have to put a brave face on at work, but some of the interviews I had to do were so painful. I remember interviewing the former Scottish goalkeeper Bob Wilson and his wife Megs, whose beautiful daughter Anna had died from cancer at the age of thirty-one, but as I was talking to them, a voice in my head was saying, *If only they knew what is going on in our family life. My daughter is also suffering from that hideous disease.* And everything they had to say resonated so much with me. I couldn't let on though and had to carry on as normal. Looking back, it is incredible how you manage to get through these things. But something or somebody seems to give you the strength.

CHAPTER 11

THE SECOND TIME AROUND

I wasn't looking for a second husband when I met Stephen Way. Like all young brides, when I'd married Don I'd expected it to be forever and although by the early 1990s we were long divorced, I was perfectly happy as a single woman, forging an independent life for myself. I had a good job, a roof over my head, my children were well settled in their various jobs and I was even looking forward to being a grandmother as Caron was pregnant. But when the moment came, everything fell into place perfectly and I learned that there's a lot to be said for second marriages; the second time around you're looking for different things from a partner from when you were a teenager. Although you always worry about your children's welfare, the 24/7 responsibilities of bringing up a family have gone and when you're older, you're looking for kindness, conversation and humour as much as good old sexual attraction.

Stephen was a salon owner and I used to drive past his salon in New Bond Street when I was going home from the BBC studios to Sevenoaks. In his teens he was Vidal Sassoon's assistant. It was an amazing breakthrough period for hair design. Throughout the Swinging Sixties, people like the dress designer Mary Quant were making the headlines with her miniskirt and her haircut in asymmetrical designs. Being the much talked about artist, people in the salon could only talk to Sassoon through Stephen. There was a strict regime within – everyone had to be well dressed in suits and shirts and Vidal was the guru. At that time, because of his innovative methods, the public, known as 'Varderers', used to pay £25 to stand high up on the balcony, looking down to watch and learn from Vidal and his team. One day, in this revered and somewhat silent atmosphere, a postman burst through the door, swinging a sack of mail over his shoulder and carrying a letter in his right hand. He shouted across the salon, 'Which one of you is Victor Baboon?' You can imagine how everybody dissolved into laughter. Even Sassoon had to crack a smile.

Eventually Stephen set up on his own in 109 New Bond Street, where he gained the accolade of being the longest sole trader after operating his business there for forty-three years.

It turned out a mutual friend of ours was to act as Cupid when he invited us to the same gala evening. Harold Leighton was a very well-known hair technician who travelled the world and, strangely enough, when Northern Ireland was on his schedule he would always drop in to Ulster Television to tell us about new, innovative products or hair fashions. So when he heard I was going to work in London in the eighties he said, 'You must make me your regular stylist.' He was based in Harrods, so of course I loved going to the hairdressers even more.

Now spin forward to my first glimpse of Stephen Way. One night in 1993 we were individually invited to a big drinks party to mark a new production of the musical *Hair*, held at The Lanesborough Hotel on Hyde Park Corner in London, with a preview afterwards. As I was arriving with my friend Libby, I saw Stephen getting out of a taxi with that strong stride of his and I remember thinking, *I hope he's going to the same party as us*. He was.

We had a brief chat at the pre-show party and it turned out that Stephen also knew of me as he was a Radio 2 listener. In fact, I was very amused when he told me much later that before we met he'd always thought of me as a Frank Sinatra/Tony Bennett sort of a person, whereas he was a Rolling Stones and Neil Young character. But we hit it off immediately and chatted for a long, long time. Apparently he thought that I was really smiley, happy and pretty. And, above all, interesting. Well that was a relief.

We went on to watch the show, both of us secretly pretty pleased that the other was going. Then the after-show party was held at Browns in Covent Garden. Stephen was there too and we started to talk again for a rather long, concentrated time, before my son Michael interrupted us and said, 'Mum, Johnny Gold wants to see you.' He led me away.

'Actually,' he said, 'Johnny Gold doesn't want to see you but I thought you needed rescuing. You've been talking to that man for a long time so I decided to interrupt.'

'Thanks, Michael,' I said cynically. 'That was actually going rather well.'

Fortunately Stephen wasn't in the slightest bit put off and soon came back. And in many ways we haven't stopped talking since.

It was a bit of a *coup de foudre* for both of us and at the end of the evening he said, 'Can I give you a call?' To my delight, he rang the next day.

Stephen remembers that, as a keen photographer, he was working at a place called Downtown Darkroom at the time and recalls it like this:

> I said to the man who ran the place, 'Can you tell me when it's twenty past two?'
>
> 'OK.'
>
> 'What time is it now?'
>
> A short time later I asked, 'What time is it now?'
>
> 'What's the matter with you? It's a quarter past two. What are you doing, we're developing pictures.'
>
> 'I told you, I have to make a phone call.' So I went upstairs and rang and later found out she was fitting me in around her live radio show – I suppose a bit like a diary entry.

We saw each other that very night, going to see Michael Feinstein do a solo performance at the Café Royal and I remember liking the fact that Stephen took my hand to lead me through the traffic. Even at that point I felt that he was very protective.

So despite the intervention of my younger son, Stephen and I started seeing a bit of one another. But I wasn't ready for a serious relationship at that time – remember, I'd only legally divorced Don a few years earlier – and Stephen was

Above left: With my second husband Stephen. This sun-kissed shot was taken on holiday in the early flushes of romance.

Above right: Emerging hand-in-hand from Hever Church on my wedding day.

Below left: Caron and I on my wedding day at Hever Castle. Of course, the memories of Caron's wedding at Hever came flooding back.

Below right: A very proud Michael hugging me by Hever's Italian Lake.

Above: The group photograph with both sides of the family. If Michael looks a bit weird, it's because he missed the photo call and I had him added in later. Those little boys at the front are over 6 feet tall now.

Below: In our business we naturally make a lot of showbiz friends, and we were lucky that so many came to the wedding, including (from the top): Lesley Joseph, Phillip Schofield, Su Pollard, Peter Powell, Anthea Turner, Mr Motivator, Julia McKenzie, the late Desmond Wilcox and Esther Rantzen, Barbara Windsor, Jim Davidson, the late Victor Spinetti, Faith Brown, Sean Rafferty, Hannah Gordon, Chris Jarvis, Canon. Roger Royal, Brian Conley, Brian Kennedy, Sir Cliff Richard and Barry McGuigan.

Top left: Caron, Charlie and newly-born Gabriel on the hammock in my back garden in Sevenoaks. I miss those days when all the little ones would come down at weekends.

Top right: Despite Caron's illness, there were so many carefree days in Cornwall and subsequently Byron Bay. Here's Caron, pretty in pink, ready for the Fowey Regatta.

Middle left: Right up to the end Caron insisted on living life to the full. In the week before she died, here's Caron making a Gingerbread house with the boys, whilst at a hotel in St Gallen, Switzerland where she was undergoing treatment.

Middle right: Byron Bay was very good for Caron, Russ and the boys. Despite everything else that was going on, they had many happy times together. For a while, Byron acted as a little bubble away from it all.

Bottom left: Whilst trying to heal, Caron turned her Australian summer house into a place of meditation and reflection.

Bottom right: Sir Cliff with his guitar strumming, when he visited Caron in Byron Bay. She let very few people into the inner sanctum, but Cliff is like family.

Top left: Caron, Michael and myself in Byron Bay, Australia. Caron took great solace from the visiting Tibetan monks. They brought incredible light, laughter and innocence to the house. This is the Rinpoche who gave Caron such comfort when he said, 'You have not been singled out'. For he too had suffered from many illnesses, despite devoting his life to prayer.

Top right: I love this photograph of Caron and I looking so intently at each other. It was heart-breaking every time we left Bryon Bay, never quite knowing what the future held or when we would see each other again.

Middle left: Sibling love. Caron and Paul having a lingering hug as he prepared to leave Australia on his way back home. Those farewells were so tough. This photo sits by my bedside.

Bottom left: Caron atop Säntis, the highest mountain in Switzerland's Alpstein massif. When she was undergoing treatment in nearby St Gallen, we'd often take the cable car up the mountain. Despite being ill, up there was a welcome escape, with heavenly views.

Bottom right: Caron always believed in Angels and thought of white feathers as their calling card. So this picture holds particular significance. She'll always be my precious angel.

Above left: On the set of *Strictly Come Dancing*, with Michael, Charlie and Gabriel. I loved the glamour of it all and couldn't get enough feathers, glitter and sequins. Taking part helped me clamour out of my deep, dark hole following the loss of Caron.

Above right: Me and my boys, in St Paul de Vence – my happy place in the South of France.

Below left: *Rip Off Britain* has been a huge success and commissioned for another two years. With co-hosts Angela Rippon and Julia Somerville.

(© BBC Rip Off Britain)

Below right: The lovely 'Loose Women'. Thankfully everyone got the white memo.

(© ITV)

Left: On Paul and Lisa's wedding day at Hever Castle, with the whole family. Lisa looked gorgeous, as did her girls Summer, Angelica and Chloe. Sally and Russ's girls Flora and Tilly made the perfect flower girls.

Right: Paul, Lisa and the girls. As he walked out of the church, Paul punched the air and shouted, 'I did it!'

Left: I adore this shot of the four boys – Gabriel, Beau, Charlie and Jake. I always thought they looked like the next boy band!

Right: Stephen's very good-looking and truly lovely grandchildren, most of whom live in Cornwall.

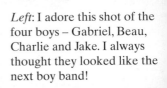

Left: This photo shows every combination of what represents a modern family. Sixteen of us celebrated my birthday in Barbados. Every meal time was an immediate party.

Above left: Stephen and I with Charlie and Gabriel's half-sisters, Flora and Tilley. Here are my King Charles Cavaliers, Gemma and the lovely Roxie whom we lost earlier this year aged just five.

(©Sally Meen)

Above right: With Paul and Michael at our shared holiday home in the South of France. It's where we run away to as often as we can and spend proper family time together.

Below left: A dramatic shot of Charlie, Gabriel, Michael and Stephen.

Below right: A recent shot of Charlie and Gabriel at home in Sevenoaks. They're so naughty and always have me in fits of giggles.

Top left: With the whole family at The Langham hotel for a private dinner the night before the investiture. It's a shame that they couldn't all come to Buckingham Palace, but it was a lovely pre-celebration.

Top right: Paul, Michael, Stephen and I in front of the famous Grand Entrance of Buckingham Palace.

Middle left: I'm sure that I broke protocol by clasping the Queen's hand, but having such admiration Her Majesty, I got carried away in the moment.

Middle right: I love this shot with the Yeomen of the Guard. The Head Yeomen said that he loved my hat – who knew he was so fashion-forward?

Bottom left: Proudly holding my OBE in the palace courtyard. It was such an honour to be recognised for my work with Caron's Foundation and I couldn't have done it without the support of so many people.

Bottom middle: My special surprise cake, made by the Executive Chef at the Ritz where we had an incredible celebratory lunch.

Bottom right: One of my favourite photos from the day, which my son Michael took. The shot really sums up the day and Michael thought that I looked like Hollywood royalty.

not yet divorced from his first wife and I didn't want to get caught up in a complicated situation. Rather than anything long term, I was just happy to enjoy Stephen's company and go to the theatre or have dinner with him occasionally on the basis of friendship rather than anything else. I fancied him, loved his company, but that was as far as it went – for a while at least.

But that basis of friendship that we built up over the next year was to provide a very strong platform for our relationship and I've always loved the fact that from the very beginning we had a strong liking for each other and not all based on lust.

* * *

It was around this time that I embarked on my first ever pantomime which, to be honest, I did to pay the taxman. It was running in Southampton and Brian Conley was the star name, playing Buttons in *Cinderella*, while I was the Fairy Godmother. On the first night, I was extremely nervous, but apart from the fact that, right in the opening scene, my magic wand flew out of my hand right across the stage and had to be retrieved by lots of tiny dancers, it went quite well.

A lot of pantomimes run three times a day, but in my case during the first three weeks of the run I was still doing my daily show on Radio 2. This made me very popular with the rest of the cast as, to begin with, we only had to do one performance a day. What a luxury during the panto season, although it was a bit of a punishing schedule for me: broadcasting at Radio 2, leaving at 4pm, making a mad dash to Southampton, doing the panto and then dashing home to do it all over again the next day. I then took three weeks off from Radio 2 over Christmas and New Year and rented a house from my good friend, Libby Lees, outside Beaulieu, in the New Forest. It wasn't that far from the Mayflower Theatre in Southampton and it also meant the family could stay over the holiday season.

Brian is a master of comedy and panto and it turned out to be a really fun experience. One night during the run Stephen came down to see it, bringing a little gift of a ceramic box to wish me luck. We went out to dinner afterwards and he clearly thought he was going to be invited back to the house for coffee! However, I explained to him that I had brought my trusty housekeeper Elsie with me and she had nothing to do but prepare a meal for me when I returned from the panto so I was going to head straight back to the New Forest. Stephen clearly didn't believe me and thought I had another boyfriend harboured away. Nothing could have been further from the truth and we laugh about it now, but to this day I'm not sure he believes that Elsie was the only other person in the house that night.

Elsie in fact regarded it as a bit of a holiday. We were staying in a beautiful old rectory and during the day we would go into Beaulieu to do some shopping and have a cup of tea and a scone. She was free during the day and the family still chuckles at the memory of seeing her languish on the settee, smoking a fag, drinking a cup of tea and reading the *Sun*. On one occasion Libby's housekeeper, Mrs Purdey, was cleaning the black-and-white tiles in the hall behind which Elsie was sitting. Elsie looked over her shoulder. 'Oh, Mrs Purdey, you've missed a bit,' she said pointedly, clearly enjoying pulling rank on her fellow housekeeper.

The pantomime season was soon over and I went back to my normal routine. By now, Stephen was clearly keen to move to the next level. He kept asking me, 'Gloria, when are we ever going to get it together?'

'When the time is right,' I'd say.

Eventually the time *was* right when I went to Dublin for work and Stephen came with me. Things moved on to a different level, but it just happened: I wasn't exactly waiting for him in Janet Reger underwear. After that we knew it was serious.

Gradually I began to introduce him to the family. Everyone clicked at once. Caron said that, given I had spent half my life at the hairdresser, all my dreams must have come true now that I had one of my own. Michael remembers the first time we all met: 'We were having a drink at a country pub. Mum and Stephen drove up in his pink dune buggy. Neil Young was blaring from his eight-track and they climbed out, Mum wearing sunglasses and a leopard-print scarf and Stephen wearing black leather trousers and I thought, *Yep, this is going to work*.' My older son Paul and Stevie get on exceptionally well and, coincidentally, his wife Lisa's dad was also a salon owner, so they have a lot in common.

Stephen comes from a family of nine and has two children himself, and remembers Caron's husband Russ also making a point of welcoming him to the family, which he appreciated. I was introduced to Stephen's boys, Dominic and Matthew, as well, initially just as a friend but gradually it became obvious that we were closer than that. But again the blending was easy. His two boys loved snooker, so Russ invited them to the audience of a television show he was producing to do with snooker, *Red or Black*.

When all the children met each other, I was thrilled that they all hit it off from the start. Matthew is a great big giant of a rugby player and I remember him almost picking Michael up in a bear hug when they said hello to each other. Caron even went on to ask Stephen to be the godfather of her younger son, Gabriel, which means a great deal to him; she and her family were living in Barnes at that point and she was always very generous in inviting us round to join in with the 'craic' as we would say in Northern Ireland

On another occasion Matthew was rather overawed when he was invited with us to a James Bond premiere, which is always a star-studded occasion.

'What should I do?' he asked.

'Just look after Gloria,' Stephen replied. And as Matt was as imposing as any of the security guards, we were well looked after that night.

That was very much the way Stephen was brought up. When he was growing up, his own father used to say to him and his brother, 'You're boys and they are girls and you have to respect the fact they are girls. You must never abuse them, or use your weight and strength against them. Boys, they have the right to use the mirrors, the bathroom and everything else first before you.' His sisters were treated like princesses in that family and that is the way he has treated women ever since, which makes for a great husband. And considering his chosen profession in the beauty industry, his father's advice stood him in good stead.

We simply got on terribly, terribly well. We moved in together the following year, and a year or so after that we went on holiday to Barbados where we stayed in a lovely villa with a private pool, just the two of us. Now, I am not a swimmer, as you know. I do not swim. But we had this private pool at the villa, so Stephen said, 'Come in. I'll teach you to swim.'

'No.'

'Come on, Glo, it's a lovely day, the pool is warm and I'm here.'

So I got in the water and I did maybe seven strokes before I started to go under. I grabbed Stephen round the neck really tightly with such passion and quickly asked him to take me to the steps. As I was in the process of getting out he looked at me.

'Will you marry me?' he asked.

'Yes,' I spluttered. Actually, it was totally unexpected, but there was no hesitation in my mind.

Later, he told me that that was the only time he'd ever seen me looking so vulnerable. 'So I thought I'd better propose,' he said. 'I thought, I've got to marry and look after this one and, anyway, no one had ever held me so tight.'

[By the way, I haven't been swimming again – not even once – and Stephen has been looking after me ever since.]

As it turned out, I had to adjust to the idea of marriage. Don had just died, but we'd been separated for so long at that time and we'd both moved on in life. But it was more than that. Prior to my divorce from Don, I had never lived alone in my life, I'd never even been left with babysitters when I was a child and I had to teach myself to live on my own as my children had flown the nest. But I had done it and I was happy with my life, and enjoying the freedom. So now I had to teach myself to be married again.

I never expected or particularly wanted to get married once more. I felt as if I'd done that, had my children and was about to have grandchildren, and felt quite fulfilled so I wasn't on the lookout for another husband...but I feel as though I've known Stevie for ever.

★ ★ ★

Stephen and I married at St Peter's Church at Hever Castle on 6 September 1998 and, if I could, I would relive that day any time. Hever is such an historic landmark in itself; it automatically creates a very special atmosphere. The church was packed with all our family and friends and they all knew each other so well it almost had a party feeling. I arrived in a horse-drawn carriage, with well-wishers lining the narrow pathway to the church door.

We had really wanted to get married in church, it was very important to us. As I was already classified as a widow it wasn't a problem for me but it was different with Stephen as he was a divorcee. When we were doing all the planning, we had spoken to a vicar who had himself been divorced who had said: 'Why is it so important to you to get married in church?'

We said, 'It's important for us as individuals but also to say to our family: This isn't a passing fancy, it's a very serious thing we're doing.' We wanted to be married in front of God and our children.

When I got to the door of the church I couldn't wait to get up the aisle towards Stephen. Somebody had said the night before, 'Have you any last-minute qualms?' and I remember replying with conviction, 'Absolutely none.' I just felt so very fortunate that we'd found each other at that time in our lives.

My two sons, Paul and Michael, gave me away. They walked me up the aisle with broad smiles, which were probably even broader when the vicar said, 'Who giveth this woman?'

'We do,' they said enthusiastically.

All our children were there and most of their children –

at that point we had eight grandchildren in total between us (now it's ten), including Beau, the second son of Paul and his then partner Sandy. He had actually been born the night before the wedding and was the best present of all. Stephen and I had done the traditional thing of sleeping in separate rooms but we laughed when we met each other in the corridor at 6am, each with a cup of tea in our hand to go and see our new grandchild.

Stephen's two sons, Dom and Matt, were his best men and Caron was my maid of honour. All the children bar the new baby were involved in the ceremony. As page boys they looked divine in their little gold and cream suits and Dominic's daughter Elicia, being the only girl, in her angel-like white dress.

We were married by Canon Roger Royle, whom I had known well through Radio 2. We could not have had a more sincere, vibrant, interesting and amusing wedding service. Many people afterwards said if only more churches had a vicar like Roger the pews would be full every Sunday.

In a way the wedding service was a bit like a programme because Roger Royle was used to broadcasting: Cliff Richard read the lesson about the importance of love, the well-known Irish singer Brian Kennedy, who had toured with Van Morrison for years, sang Van's 'Have I Told You Lately That I Love You', which is one of our favourite songs ever. Then my lovely friend and flautist James Galway who thought he was going to be in Japan suddenly said he and his wife Jeanne would be able to come after all and they asked, could they play in church? As Roger said at the time, 'You know you're at a cool wedding when Jimmy Galway is the extra.'

We had the reception at Hever Castle in a great marquee. In the planning I remember we had quite a debate about what we were going to do, which Stephen recalls with amusement:

'Gloria,' he asked, 'What sort of music should we play?'

'Well, there are different types at the church service,' I said. 'There's the welcoming of guests and there's the party afterwards, so we need something different.'

'But what do you think in the church? I really like violas and violins, oboes. Bellini...that sort of thing,' said Stephen.

'And afterwards?' I said.

'Well, we could have a trio, maybe piano, guitar, drums.'

Stephen recalls that I sat up straight in my chair and, looking him straight in the eye said, 'We should have the BBC Big Band.' And, amazingly, that's what we had, all 21 pieces. I had worked with these fantastic musicians on *Friday Night is Music Night* and other programmes but on the day they had to mute the trumpets just a bit. It was glorious. And then, with Stephen's sons being twice the size of mine, the four of them doing a Blues Brothers routine certainly made the reception memorable, alongside Jim Davidson and all his risqué jokes plus Frankie Vaughan singing 'Gimme the Moonlight'. As you may have gathered, it was a fantastic day.

We spent our honeymoon in Italy. Friends of ours had a villa just outside Lucca and we enjoyed a blissful week there. And since then it has been a very happy relationship.

If I'm under stress Stevie will do everything to make my life smoother, whether it's cooking a meal or whatever and I do the same for him. He has a theory that the person in most need at a particular time has to have priority and support, and I love him for it.

And isn't it bliss that I married a man who had 25 hairdressers working for him? I landed in heaven, really. Apart from loving him I feel very comfortable with him. He doesn't irritate me – except when he leaves all the kitchen cupboard doors open and his shoes everywhere. If there's anything wrong I can't harbour it anyway because it sits like a lump in my throat. If I have disagreements with anybody I don't want to sulk about it or forget it or let it fester. I want to talk about it and sort things out. And we have the same principles in life. Stephen and I both consider family to be the central core of our lives.

We do have some laughs together too. One night Stephen and I were strolling along the Embankment in London, which sadly is where you'll find lots of homeless people and those begging for money. As we went past one, he vigorously shook a polystyrene cup at us. Stephen said, 'I'm so sorry, I just don't have any change'. Then the man said, 'Oh, it's alright for you, Jerry Springer,' at which point I nearly collapsed on the pavement with laughter. And then I heard him say, 'And you too, Judith Chalmers.' It's one of our favourite stories to date.

It's a very strange feeling when the public think you are a certain person and on one occasion, Caron, her husband Russ, Stevie and I went to a very famous restaurant in London called Efes. Caron and I knew the owner of the restaurant really well and he usually made a fuss when we went in. But on this occasion, all the attention was on Russ and slowly but surely, every waiter started coming up to him saying, 'Oh Mr Ghost, I know you're trying to have a private meal but would you sign my video?'. Russ insisted he wasn't Patrick Swayze but they would not have it; the more he resisted the more insistent they became. So in the end, you can only fight it so long and ultimately Russ had to line up with all the waiters and kitchen staff to have his photo taken. For years, it was up on the wall. Years later, a business associate of his went there and enquired as to why his photo was on the wall, to which Russ replied, 'oh, it's a long story'!

* * *

Like me, Stephen believes that getting married at an older age has many advantages. 'When you're very young, you're tied up in your career,' he says. 'And I was married the first time at the beginning of my career. When I met Gloria, it was nearing the end of my working life and we promised each other that we would slow down a bit to spend as much time as possible together and not travel to far-flung places without each other. However I don't see Gloria keeping her promise about that slowing down!'

But I agree with him, you just know the hurdles you have to get over when you are in a long-term relationship with someone. Which is just as well because only nine months after we were married in September 1998, Stephen had a small heart attack. He was the last person in the world I would have expected to have one. He's a very physically strong man, very conscious of exercise and healthy foods, but his brother George, who had seemed in the peak of health died very suddenly two weeks before from a heart-related illness.

Stephen loved and admired George a great deal and I believe the shock and emotion may have triggered his attack. A lot of doctors feel that heartache and emotional shock can have a great knock-on effect, and only a year before their sister Paula had also died from a heart condition. But it was to be a very good wake-up call and I now keep a very close eye on him. I can see when he's tired and I'll say: 'Just sit down for a while. Rest and read a book.'

If that wasn't bad enough, in 2012 Stephen had a stroke. I was just about to leave the house to do *The One Show* and I was on the phone to the producer when Stephen hobbled in from the garden with one shoe on and one shoe off.

'I am not myself,' he said. 'I feel like cotton wool.'

My dad had died of a stroke so I suspected straight away what was wrong. I rang the doctor, who told me to take him to the hospital immediately. Thankfully, my driver from the show was outside and Stephen was able to get down the stairs to the car so instead of heading to the studio, we went straight to Pembury Hospital, near our home. It turned out that he'd had a haemorrhagic stroke, which occurs when blood from a damaged blood vessel leaks into the brain. But the weird thing was that Stephen was completely lucid and could still talk to me.

'How long ago did he have the stroke?' the emergency doctor asked.

'About an hour and a half ago.'

'How long ago? How long ago?' the doctor persisted.

I just wanted to scream, 'Do something'.

But then the doctor explained, 'If we get to the patient within three to four hours of it happening, he can be given a clot-busting injection. It improves the chances of a full recovery, but there is a risk of it killing him.' This was a thrombolysis and while it increased his chances of survival, there was also a 7 per cent chance of it causing bleeding in the brain.

By this time Stephen had lost the power in an arm and a leg and we had to make a fast decision. But while it was very frightening, we also knew the injection could give him the best outcome. The nurse at the other side of the bed looked at me and said, 'He has to have it.'

So in the middle of the trauma Stephen gave his permission for them to do it. What a tense life-in-the-balance moment.

Within 36 hours he had fully regained the power in both limbs and a week later he was able to leave the hospital. He really was so lucky. If it had happened 10 minutes later the situation could have been far worse because I would have left for the television studio and who knows what state he would have been in when I found him that evening. As it was, the only lasting consequence was a tingling in the fingertips and a slight loss of sensitivity.

But it is when you're older that the 'for better or worse' kicks in. Young love is based almost entirely on lust and attraction but it's when you're older you realise that what you also want and need is a deep understanding, kindness and friendship; Stephen and I had had a strong friendship for a year before it moved to the next level and so we had a good basis for our relationship.

Apart from Stephen's heart attack early on, this was a happy time in my life. Having lost both my mother and my father by this point, I once again had the sense of being in a strong and happy family unit, this time based in England. My children were near to hand and over the years we've all got closer to each other. As Stephen's sons live in Cornwall, one year Michael and Paul said to him, 'We would like to make you a Father's Day lunch. We want to say thank you so much for looking after Mum.' I'm so relieved they all get along so well.

Over the years, Caron would insist we all got together on a Sunday in Sevenoaks and those were some of the happiest, most carefree days we had. The kids would be so happy playing together in the garden, building tents and cubbyholes, while we adults would be inside making lunch and chatting about the week's news. It brought me really close to my grandchildren and allowed me to get to know their little personalities and likes and dislikes. We have a strong bond that exists to this day, of which more anon.

★ ★ ★

I have written a lot about my professional life and the impact that it's had but my favourite job has always been being 'Mum'. Family is at the core of my wellbeing and happiness. While of course I am greatly fulfilled by work, if I was ever forced to choose, family would win out every time. It was at the very heart of my own mother's DNA and integral to my own upbringing. It's rooted deep down within me and, in the main, Irish mothers never want their children to live too far away. My mum May always said that 'the family that eats together stays together.' So nothing gives me more pleasure than seeing all the family round the table for Sunday lunch in Sevenoaks. I love those long meals, where absolutely everything gets discussed and then, as the evening progresses, there are stories, tall tales and even a spot of singing. While painful for some I insist that everyone does a turn or else we call the party police.

Over the years the inner circle has obviously expanded and now we have what's become the new phenomenon of the modern family. In that respect the Hunniford/Way/Keating/Lindsay clan doesn't disappoint. What has been fantastic is that we have all been on holiday together quite a few times, on occasions sixteen of us. But it works and it's glorious for me seeing all the generations together.

Between Stephen and myself we have ten grandchildren. Six are in Cornwall from Stephen's two sons; Elicia is the eldest at twenty-four and is now a cancer nurse, Elliot is twenty-three, the twins Billy and Jake are twenty-one and then the little ones, Lily is seven and Jack is five. Sorry for all the names but I'd be a terrible grandmother if I leave one out! I have my four grandsons from Caron and Paul, Charlie is twenty-three and Gabriel is twenty, and then there are Flora and Tilly, who Russ had with his second wife Sally Meen. While they aren't blood grandchildren, they do call me Nana nonetheless. Charlie said that when the girls were born it made them feel more like a family unit and the girls have always adored and looked up to their big brothers. Paul's sons are Jake, who is twenty-one and Beau who is eighteen. As you can see, there are a lot of boys in our family. However, since Paul married Lisa we've added her girls, with three gorgeous step-grandchildren, Chloe who is twenty-seven and twenty-two-year-old twins Angelica and Summer.

I've always maintained that having children was the best thing I ever did and, on reflection, if I had my time again, I would have had more. Not only do I love my children dearly, I really like them as people. I seek out their company, look forward to spending time together and am deeply proud of who they've become.

THE SECOND TIME AROUND

Caron of course left the biggest void in all our lives, but we talk about her all the time and she blessed us with two gorgeous boys. How proud she would have been seeing them grow into such genuinely thoughtful, kind and funny young men. Apart from being brilliant company, I feel closer to Caron when I'm with them as I see her in their mischievous ways. They have a *really* naughty sense of humour and consistently make me laugh out loud; they often tell me the kind of hilarious stories that I am sure most grandmothers aren't privy to, stories that are wonderfully inappropriate but in a good way. She would have adored their sparkling personalities, quirkiness and sense of individuality. Though on certain occasions like landmark graduations and birthdays, I can't help but give way to anger when I think how much she'd have loved to be there. How much *we'd* all love her to be there.

The boys were only ten and seven when she died and are now tall, handsome and smart men. Sometimes it seems like only yesterday when Caron left us and yet on other days it feels like a lifetime ago. It's so very difficult to fathom but regardless, Charlie and Gabriel bring us all so much joy.

Now that I reflect upon it, in their adult years Caron, Paul and Michael all managed to carve out their own extraordinary path. Not that there is anything wrong with a conventional nine-to-five job, but they all became very independent, rarely asked for hand-outs and worked hard to create their own niches. Maybe it goes back to that Hunniford DNA and a good Ulster work ethic.

Michael followed in Caron's footsteps by going to Bristol University to study English and Drama. That particular course was hailed as one of the best in the country and he had great fun messing around with *Little Britain* star David Walliams, who was in the same year. David would spend his time prancing around and doing Frankie Howard impressions of, 'Nay, nay and thrice nay. Ooh no, please, it's wicked to mock the afflicted,' and years later would go on to play the leading role in the BBC biopic of Frankie's life. Michael pursued the written word and 25 years ago formed a company called Ink, which now publishes inflight magazines for more than 30 airlines. A bi-product from his life in the sky is that we all profit from the obscene amount of air miles that he accrues.

While studying sound and set design at college in Guildford, Paul continued with his passion for drumming. In one early production at college he got to design the stage and we all fell about laughing when we went to see the show. Suspended from the ceiling in the middle of the stage was a drumming platform, with Paul front and centre, and no prizes for guessing where all the lights were pointing. Poor old Michael Ball, who was a classmate of his, singing his heart out on the stage down below, was practically in darkness. I'm sure there was a lesson to be learned because Paul went on to found Delta Sound, now one of the largest audio companies in Britain. He has provided sound for prestigious events such as the opening and closing ceremonies for the London Olympics, momentous Royal events like the Queen Mother's 100th birthday, Jubilee celebrations and, more recently the Queen's 90th. When working at the G8 summit he once made me laugh by sending a photo of the mixing desk which just had gaffer tape with handwritten markers that read, 'Merkel', 'Obama', 'Cameron', 'Hollande' and 'Putin'. I texted back, 'Do they take the radio mics off when they go to the loo?'

Paul's sons haven't followed him into the sound business: Jake is currently at university in Cornwall majoring in

Sportswear Design and Beau has just completed his A levels. We all think that Beau is the left-field entrepreneurial one. He'll probably make millions and lose it a few times, but he's definitely one to watch.

And in 2015 our modern family was extended further when Paul married the lovely Lisa at Hever Church. Although we have a massive connection with Hever, weirdly Lisa and her family do too. Her late mum Angela, who sadly died seven years ago of cancer, absolutely adored Hever and would often go there with her husband Louis and the children. So it was especially poignant that they married in the church that held such significance to us all. Lisa was previously married and, as I mentioned, has three grown-up girls. As such we'd only hoped that the vicar would agree to a blessing. One Sunday morning I asked the Reverend Jane, 'Given that Stephen and I were married here and that Caron was married and is buried here... Is there any chance you'd conduct a service to bless my son Paul and Lisa?'

She refreshingly replied, 'Bless them? Why don't I marry them? There are far too many stuffy old rules and regulations in the Church today. We need as many people as possible to be part of the community – so it would be my pleasure.'

You couldn't have wished for a more fitting person to conduct the service than Jane, this very forward-thinking vicar who has now sadly moved on to a new parish. The character and spirit couldn't have been more perfect if Richard Curtis had called central casting. Even Dawn French's *Vicar of Dibley* wouldn't do her justice. Jane was a vision with her curly red hair, brightly coloured nails and shiny Doc Marten boots, which she wore under her tunic.

Given Paul's day job, he had quite the eclectic playlist

in this very small medieval church. I recall that when Josh Phillips from Procol Harum was playing 'When A Man Loves A Woman' at the beginning of the service, Reverend Jane had her eyes closed, but was it with tears of happiness or just that it was a refreshing song in this old church.

As already stated, I adore big family gatherings and part of me has always envied Shabbat, the traditional Jewish Friday-night dinner. Not attending Shabbat just isn't an option, unless you want to face the wrath of a scorned Jewish mother. Michael has often teased me that I'm like a Jewish mother, in that I can major in guilt and always have a full fridge. It's true. I still buy for a family of five.

A few years ago a friend invited us for Shabbat at his home in London. I was introduced to his lovely daughter who had just had a baby and then, rather confusingly, I was introduced to her girlfriend, who had also just had a baby. So this man who headed a very traditional Jewish family explained that his daughter and her girlfriend had had the babies with their gay male best friend. And the guy said that if he was going to father the children, he wanted to be really involved and so he looked after the babies every other weekend.

The boy's mother was thrilled. Ever since he came out, she'd always taken it that she wouldn't have grandchildren. So, true to his word, every other weekend he takes the children, the mothers have time off, everyone is happy and as long as it works for them, why not? Long live the modern blended family.

CHAPTER 12

LOSING CARON

It is 13 years now since Caron died in 2004 and, in hindsight, the strength of my sons and my husband Stephen has seen me through the extreme heartache and the deep black hole of losing my gorgeous daughter to the hideous disease of cancer aged just forty-one.

By the late 1990s, life was pretty idyllic: my career was going well, I had found real happiness with my second husband Stephen and I was watching my children grow and thrive as they carved out successful lives of their own. Caron was so happily married and had started building her family with my first grandson Charlie and she had just given birth to another glorious son Gabriel. She was a much-loved television presenter by this time, having launched her career on BBC1's *Blue Peter* and going on to co-present *This Morning* with Richard Madeley. Bias aside, she was a beautiful girl and so it seemed that she pretty much had it all. Then the bombshell hit and the steamroller rolled in.

I've written about this time before in my previous books, *Next to You* and *Always with You*, and it remains the most heart-breaking moment of my life. A dagger came to slice through all our joy, a dagger that was to change everything irrevocably and plunge all of us into a terrible darkness.

Caron was first diagnosed with breast cancer in 1997, shortly after her dad's death. I found out when Caron and I were having one of our many gossipy chats, and she casually mentioned that she had found a lump in her breast. Bearing in mind that she'd recently given birth to her second son Gabriel, I, along with her doctors, thought it was just a milk lump, so we told her not to worry about it too much. However, her doctor rightly said, 'If it doesn't go away within six weeks, I think we should have that lump out and have it analysed.'

And when it didn't go away, she reluctantly agreed to go into hospital to have the lump removed. I went with her and her husband Russ and I'll always remember her saying to us, as we stood at the end of the bed, 'This is not the way I want to spend my day. I'm only doing this because you and Russ have insisted.' So Caron went through surgery and then came down to Sevenoaks to recuperate for a few days.

It was actually Russ who first found out that Caron had cancer: he described the feeling as being 'like a baseball bat to the stomach'. I remember it clearly. It was a beautiful day, Caron was upstairs in bed reading and Stephen and I were out in the garden impatiently waiting for Russ to ring with the results. When he gave us the horrific news that the lump was cancerous, I was dumbfounded: my beautiful young daughter had breast cancer. I couldn't recall ever feeling worse, and that's even with everything we'd been through with my mum. I remember standing in the sun in the garden, looking up at the window, Caron completely unaware, and thinking, *life will never be quite the same.*

We waited for Russ to arrive from London and he had the undeniably heart-breaking task of breaking the news to Caron. She later said, after hearing the news, that she couldn't help but think of the famous John Lennon quote, 'Life is what happens when you're busy making other plans'. It was such a deeply stressful time, not just for Caron, but for the whole family. Russ and Caron went straight to the oncologist who said that the lump was small so everyone was hoping for a cure. Caron had such a positive attitude to life, so she quickly told herself that the cancer could be removed and life would get back to normal again. But I've always believed that no matter how good the prognosis is, with any cancer patient there will always be that niggling doubt that with any pain or ache, it might come back…and sadly, that's what happened to Caron.

Despite having surgery to remove the lump, the doctors said they didn't think they'd got it all so they had to perform another procedure. As the cancer was still classed as 'low grade' at this time, Caron decided against a mastectomy and she remained ever optimistic, as indeed we all did. She even went back to work, but decided not to tell anyone outside of the inner family circle. This turned out to be categorically the most difficult secret of my entire life.

Within a relatively short time though, the cancer had spread even further and was becoming more aggressive so Caron agreed to a mastectomy, as well as chemotherapy and radiotherapy. I remember her saying to the medical team, 'Don't give me any prognosis of time, just tell me what I have to do.' And, to her credit, she did.

One day though, not long after Caron's surgery, I got a call from her specialist and we met at Michael's house in London; I could never have imagined what he was going to tell us, that Caron only had, at the most, 18 months to live. She wasn't there at the time of the conversation and we all agreed not to tell her. It may sound an odd decision but we knew it would have broken her spirit completely. As it happened, she ended up battling her cancer for seven years and I've said before that I genuinely believe all the complementary medical roads she went down gave her something else to hold on to and undoubtedly a feel-good positive attitude until the end.

In fact, we never talked about death, only about life, but I knew that Caron's greatest fear was leaving her boys behind. It was the only time I ever really saw that darker side of her mind and I remember her telling me one day, 'Promise me you will always look after the boys.' She fought for them as much as for herself. And I've always said that her intense battle with all of her treatment gave the boys at least another two years with their mum.

She'd escape to her favourite spot in Cornwall – Fowey – with the boys whenever she could during the school holidays and even for long weekends. It's a very spiritual place and even during the low moments of her treatment, she felt better there and more peaceful. So on one trip back to London from a weekend break, when she and Russ were talking about what a great time they'd all had, Russ had a bit of an epiphany moment: 'Why don't we reverse everything, live in Cornwall and go up to London to work?'

Russ has always been known as a 'fixer': there was a house high up on the cliffs overlooking Readymoney Cove, a beautiful spot, and although the owners hadn't put their house up for sale, Russ obviously made them an offer they couldn't refuse. Within a matter of weeks they'd packed up their home in Barnes and moved into that beautiful house, called Menlo. It was the perfect move for them and they all settled in quickly and became a part of the community.

Life for them really was idyllic in Fowey, and clearly eliminated some of those stresses and strains of living in the city. Fundamentally, it allowed Caron to concentrate on getting better. There were also many times of joy in these years, when there were so-called periods of remission, and the whole family has some wonderful memories from our fun-filled time down in Cornwall with Caron. Stephen and I regularly went down there for weekends. It was 1998 by now and I would finish recording one of my *Open House* programmes at 10pm on a Thursday night then Stephen would come and pick me up at the studio and we'd drive the six hours to Fowey. Sometimes we stayed at the local hotel but we often stayed with Caron and her family at Menlo.

One day Caron said to me, 'Mum, there's a lovely little house for sale down the road.'

'Caron, I'm not buying any more houses,' I replied.

But in the end we did. Despite my hesitation, I wanted to be close to her and not on top of everybody else at Menlo when we came to visit. And I knew it was important for Caron to have her space as well and time to heal. I still have such fond memories of Caron and the children coming past the house on their way home from school, sticking their heads through the kitchen window and saying, 'Any chance of a cuppa?' Our house was painted bright yellow and Gabriel called it the 'Yellow Yellow house'; in fact, when we painted it the local fishermen said they'd lost one of their land markers.

* * *

During that halcyon period, Caron explored many complementary therapies and discovered a meditation treatment called 'The Journey'. The author and motivational speaker Brandon Bays founded it and ran the courses, and the idea was to remove the emotional blocks that we've all built up within us during the course of our lives. Caron really relished those sessions and told me that it allowed her to get rid of 'stuff'. So when Brandon suggested Caron go to Australia to attend one of their sessions, there really was no holding her back. The whole family went and rented a house on the beach at Watergose Bay, near Byron Bay, on the eastern coast of Australia.

There was nothing not to like about being on the beach every day, bodyboarding and splashing about with the boys in the surf, and in Byron Bay, Caron had found her spiritual – and practical – home. They only intended to go for a holiday and were out there for three weeks. But they all loved it so much that they ended up staying for nearly three months. It was during this time that Caron decided to make a commercial and personally poignant video about her journey, from her head to her heart, and it's something I'll always cherish.

When they eventually came home I knew in my soul that she'd be going back there and return she did, because, during one of her routine tests back in England she received the devastating news that the cancer had spread to her other breast.

When the doctors told Caron she had to have a second mastectomy, she couldn't face it and virtually ran away to Australia. It's impossible to say what would have happened if she had agreed to it but I know that Russ believes dealing with the outcome would have likely damaged her whole sense of self-esteem that she'd have lost so much of the optimism that was making her strong. And by now she was so firmly set on her extra path of spiritual healing that, on the day of this new prognosis, she immediately said, 'I have to go back to Australia to pick up on that strength I feel in Byron Bay.' So she booked a solo ticket there and then, and we all stood by on the London street outside Michael's house, a few weeks before Christmas, in disbelief as Russ drove her to the airport. It was such a knee-jerk decision that she didn't even have anywhere booked to stay but it only took her a few days to find a place to rent so Russ put his job on hold, packed a few things up in Cornwall, and he and the boys quickly followed. It's incredible to look back and think of that now, the lengths that Russ went to, but it will always stay with me how loved Caron was, and how supported too.

This is what Caron wrote in her journal when she reached Byron Bay:

> *Finally arrived in Byron, in the rain. It feels very good to be back here – there is something in the fabric of this place which I recognise and connect with right away. Of course I miss my mum and the family, but this is where I want and HAVE to be – at least for now.*

It was agony having my daughter 12,000 miles away, never mind battling cancer. At first I hated Australia. I couldn't help but think, *if it's sunshine she wants, why can't she be in Italy, Florida or somewhere nearer home.* And they were to remain in Australia for over two-and-a half years. Stephen and I managed to visit eight times – and this was despite Stephen's busy business in London – and of course Paul and Michael visited as well. I think Paul was in denial about what was going on. A few close friends of his had survived breast cancer and he always thought his big sister would get better. I know that he was worried how Caron would be when he flew out to see her but, actually, they had a great time and made some special memories together.

Michael made the trip quite a few times too. On one of those occasions when Stephen and I went out, we decided we'd keep it a surprise from Caron that Michael was also coming. I remember arriving at Brisbane airport quite late in the evening, driving the hour and a half to Byron and then hiding Michael in the house in the garden – the house Caron had rented used to be a B&B called Taylors and helpfully it also had this little garden house outside of the main home, which helped with our plans brilliantly. Michael was up with the kookaburras, bursting with excitement, and sneaked into the house and into Caron's room just as she woke up. You can imagine how confused she was but thrilled at the same time; it was a lovely moment. Later that day, I remember she said, 'If you can be woken up at seven and see your brother standing by your bedside from the other side of the world, then anything's possible.'

Russ was now solely keeping the household together, supporting Caron in every way and looking after the kids so, when we flew over, we tried to help out as much as possible, running the kids backwards and forwards to school and helping out with the shopping and cooking. It made me feel as if I was doing something helpful too, while Caron got on with her daily yoga session, acupuncture, oxygen treatment, reiki, sound healing, reflexology and colonic irrigation.

I have a special memory from that trip, when we heard that the Tibetan monks were coming to chant in Byron Bay. Sadly,

LOSING CARON

Caron was not feeling well enough to go and see them that night but, luckily, we met a girl called Maureen from Belfast, who was travelling Australia and organising the monks' itinerary. Turns out she used to watch me way back when on Ulster Television, so with the good ol' Northern Irish connection, she said, 'Well, if Caron can't come to us, we will go to her.' Caron absolutely loved the monks being there. She always said, 'They don't have much and they're not looking for much,' but I know they gave her incredible strength any time they visited.

In fact, they became regulars at Taylors and on one occasion, in the garden house, they made one of their intricate mandalas. They spent nearly a week blowing different-coloured sand into this incredible design, which we then watched being destroyed. I couldn't get my head around this ritual, all the time they'd spent to make it, but it's not in their faith to hold on to anything. Once it had broken we were all given little boxes of the holy sand to take with us. I knew it meant so much to Caron.

The story of the monks doesn't end there: Russ had built an office under the house but apparently hadn't treated it correctly against termites. To cut a long story short, after Caron died, the termites eventually ate the house except for the hardwood window frames, the kitchen units and bathroom fittings. So the whole house had to be razed to the ground and the new owner (who had actually bought the house for the monks) wanted to build a modern house to avoid any problems in the future. He said to Maureen and the monks, 'You can have whatever you want that's useable,' so all these things have been incorporated in their new building, in the rainforest not very far away from the original house.

Michael recently went to visit while on a business trip and he said it was so emotional to see them using all of Caron's things, like her Cath Kidston table cloths, her cushions and rosebud china, and even a small table which she had made out of driftwood, on which she had painted a red heart, that now sits in front of their worshipping altar. The monks' incense and candles adorn it every single day, and they call it the eternal flame. So in the end Caron's story is still carrying on and we will always remember the monks chanting for her for two days, to aid her healing, the last time she saw them.

13 years down the line I can appreciate what Australia as a country and Byron Bay, in particular, gave to Caron. It allowed her a freedom that she wouldn't have had in England; this was before social media so the paparazzi weren't able to snap her walking with her cane for support, for example, which would have affected her greatly. I can look back now and think of the happy times we all had together in the rainforest, on the beach, and those moments of joy splashing around with the children in the pool.

At the same time as lapping up life in Australia, Caron was always searching for other options and therapies and discovered a clinic in St Gallen, Switzerland. It incorporated complementary treatments and vitamin C infusions alongside bits of chemotherapy and orthodox treatment, so fitted in with her philosophy. As one might expect with the reputation of the Swiss, the clinic was pristine, well-ordered and had a wide selection of treatments to choose from. She went to the clinic a couple of times and she'd fly to Switzerland directly from Australia. I remember on one occasion picking her up at the airport, watching her walk with difficulty, but after a few days at the clinic, the change was extraordinary.

And typical of us, we'd then go shopping. I recall one time she bought a lovely pair of red shoes and fishnet tights. She

got all dressed up for dinner that evening and the maître d'
of the hotel, who had taken a protective shine to Caron, said,
'Madam, you look utterly amazing.' It was such a boost to
her confidence; I'll never forget it. She also bought a heart-
shaped ring on that trip; I wear it every day and each time
I look at it, it brings back such happy and sad memories of
that time.

* * *

The beginning of the end came in Switzerland. It was at
Easter 2004, and because it was Easter Sunday, Caron had
wanted to go to a café in a beautiful spot in the mountains.
She'd been staying at a hotel near the clinic for a month and
this had become her favourite place. Most of the family was
there: Russ and their children, Charlie and Gabriel, Michael,
Stephen and I, and we all remember watching Caron with her
boys, building gingerbread houses and then watching them
playing in the snow, as if nobody had a care in the world.
However, after lunch her strength just seemed to wash away.
We all headed back to the hotel and settled Caron into a chair
so she could paint Easter eggs with her family, but halfway
through something changed. She seemed to run out of steam
so Russ took her back to her room. One of the nurses from
the clinic came to the hotel to give her a treatment and tried
to massage some warmth and comfort back into her legs but
they were cold and unresponsive. She looked at us and said
Caron needed to go home. And so, after two and a half years
of being away, it was time for Caron to come home.

Michael took Charlie and Gabriel back to England to
stay with Russ's parents, while Stephen and I went back to
Sevenoaks to get the house ready for Caron. She was now

in such ill health that it was decided Russ would drive her home so she could avoid the stress and discomfort of flying. That night though, Caron was wracked with pain, tossing and turning and mumbling in her sleep, as Russ looked on, helpless to do anything. Occasionally she even seemed to be delirious. Caron now had tumours up and down her spine so we'd all seen her in pain many times before, and they'd had some harrowing times in the last few months, but Russ has said that there was something different this time.

The next morning Caron seemed to have recovered a little, although she still couldn't get out of bed. She persuaded a reflexologist called Andrea from the clinic to come and give her a massage in her hotel room as, by now, there was no way she could have made it to her. Once there, Andrea confirmed that Caron's body had started to 'shut down'; as if all her vital organs were beginning to stop working. The nurse came soon after and told Russ to get her home as soon as possible.

This was 11am on Easter Monday but it took until four o'clock that afternoon to get Caron dressed and packed and all the bags in the car – they'd packed for a four-month trip so there was a lot of stuff. It was an incredibly hard time; Caron was in such pain that she was virtually immobile and kept getting back into bed for some relief. She couldn't sleep though, and she definitely couldn't eat. Our decision had been right: it was time to bring her home.

Caron could barely walk; she didn't even have the strength to get on a porter's trolley so that Russ could push her to the lift. But there was no choice so, with the aid of her cane and Russ, Caron made the walk to the lobby, step by agonising step. It took almost an hour.

Russ had made the car as comfortable as possible for

her, with the seats laid back and blankets to create a bed. Apparently Caron was so relieved to get in, she told Russ, 'I'm not getting out of this car until I get to Mum's house.'

For the first four hours of the journey Caron did nothing but sleep. Russ said that she mumbled a bit and fidgeted but, apart from that, she was mainly peaceful. He certainly didn't think she was dying, but he didn't take for granted the incredible journey they had before them to make it back home. To cope he broke down the journey into sections: get out of Switzerland, cross France, get through the Channel Tunnel. In fact, he admits now that his goal was to get Caron back to England alive. He was praying to make it back. He's even told me that he thought about what he'd have done if the worst had happened. Would he have just motored through, pretending she was asleep? Indeed, he said that's exactly what he told himself he'd do, there was no way he was leaving his wife's body in a French morgue.

The journey sounded absolutely horrendous and I admire the strength he had. But an amazing sunset guided him westward and home, and he said he followed that burning sun all the way through Switzerland and France.

Mainly Caron lay still but, halfway across France, something miraculous happened and she suddenly came to, looked at Russ and smiled. On that car journey, just as with other times over those last six months when Russ had thought, *this is it*, something, somewhere had given her a boost and she seemed fine. Outside, there was no one on the road but them. Russ has described it as 'an extraordinary cocoon, a Tardis, taking them home. A quiet moment to share after all the panic that had gone before'. I think he knew that, given that when they reached my home Caron would be surrounded by family and doctors, they were unlikely to be alone again. So they started to talk about everything, their entire life together. As Russ says, there was never a time when they didn't chat and this was no different, except for the fact that Caron was dipping in and out of consciousness, in what was an honest and emotional conversation. I remember talking about this with my friend, the late journalist Lynda Lee-Potter a few months later:

Although he can't remember the specifics of what was said, he knows it still never reached a dramatic 'I am dying' moment. It was softer than that. Kinder. What they did was reminisce. They laughed about some of the strange and funny things they had done together. Their time in Cornwall. Their adventures in Australia. In this magic capsule, suspended in time, they discussed all they had achieved. They had enough time to say things to each other that they wouldn't have said at any other time in their relationship. Caron was incredibly loving and, more than that, appreciative of everything Russ had done for her. She said some wonderful things to him that will stay with him for ever. Was she finishing things off, tidying up life's loose ends? Russ feels that somewhere in her system Caron knew she didn't have a lot of time left. There was pride in what they had done together, the love and support they had given each other and everything they had achieved. In fact, what took place between them was communication on such a deep level it didn't have to be spelled out. They didn't have time for that: Caron would drift off to sleep again.

Once they had crossed the channel Russ says that he felt Caron knew she was home somehow. He saw her visibly relax:

It was a surreal experience...it wasn't as if their lives flashed before them, but somehow they had said goodbye, without ever voicing the word. Mainly, of course, they talked about their two wonderful sons, about the joy, light and pride Charlie and Gabriel had, individually and together, brought into their lives. They talked about what special souls their two sons seemed to have, what they might contribute to the world and their wonderful personalities. Throughout Caron's illness she had been searching for a miracle to extend her life. During that car journey they finally realised the miracle had been there all along. Charlie and Gabriel, their phenomenal children, would take Caron's spirit into the future and beyond. They were the miracle. They were Caron. Against the background of seven years' soul-searching, trauma, questioning and pain, Russ and Caron had striven to remain a happy family unit. They had succeeded in doing that. Caron had only ever asked for one miracle: to live. But she was granted a second: a happy life.

★ ★ ★

When Russ and Caron finally reached our house in Sevenoaks, it had just gone 1 am. They had been driving for nine hours non-stop and, being in the same position for much of that time, Caron had seized up so it was a struggle to get her out of the car. In the end, we had to get a chair so she could be carried, with Stephen and Russ lifting her out and carrying her through to the kitchen. Even the slightest movement caused her incredible pain so it was a real feat. Even then, despite all the pain, her mind was still alert: as she looked around the house she noticed I'd put up a painting she'd bought for me Christmas and said, 'That looks lovely there.' She sat at the kitchen table on the chair she'd been carried in on, and managed to drink a cup of green tea in her favourite pink spotted cup and even eat a little of Stephen's home-made vegetable soup. There were such mixed emotions. I was so, so happy to have her home but it was devastating to see her in the condition she was in. Even then, that sense of humour broke through as Russ and Stephen manoeuvred Caron up the stairs, wobbling from side to side, all giggling at the same time.

It was after 3am by the time we managed to get Caron into bed. Once she was settled, Russ called me in to say goodnight. I could hardly believe that my beautiful girl was back in Sevenoaks. Once she'd gone to sleep, Russ, Stephen and I just stared at each other back in the kitchen; there were no words left to say. No one slept that night. Russ lay down alongside Caron and I spent the night pacing outside in the corridor.

I'd slept for what felt like ten minutes but I was up and ready as soon as the sun rose. Having my daughter home with me kept me going. I was so happy to have Caron back in her room and was even thinking about her being back in Cornwall that summer, all together as a family.

Caron awoke at about 10.30am and I heard her soft voice through the door, then Russ came out and told me I could go in. It was wonderful to see her sitting up in bed but I knew that looks can often be deceiving. After speaking to her for a while I went downstairs to make her breakfast: sliced melon and tiny squares of rice bread, served with tea in the 'magic' teapot, with a tiny plate and cup from her childhood, which always used to make her feel better. It was wonderful to just be able to do something. I sat beside her and held her hand, safe in the knowledge that she was really here beside me and not far away in Australia. Her hand was warm in mine but her breathing was laboured.

I'd rung our lovely family GP, Richard Husband, as soon as I was up and he'd promised to come round once his morning surgery finished. But when he arrived, he gave us little to hold on to. 'I'm so sorry,' he said. 'I had no idea how ill she was.' He arranged for his surgery nurse, Cathy, to come to the house and administer a drip to help Caron's breathing, and as Cathy was also an experienced nurse he said she'd be able to give us an idea of just how serious Caron's condition was. I remember thinking, *What did he mean? How bad did he think Caron was? She'd been here before, she'd rally again. Wouldn't she? Wouldn't she?* But the doctor couldn't answer our increasingly frantic questions. When Cathy arrived, our worst fears were confirmed.

'She doesn't look good,' she said.

We'd heard those words before though and each time Caron had pulled through so we clung to that tiny bit of hope.

Paul hadn't been able to join us for Easter in Switzerland as he was skiing in France, but we'd rung and told him everything and that we were bringing Caron home. For some reason that Tuesday morning Paul had decided not to go out on the slopes – it was like he knew he was needed elsewhere. And as soon as Russ rang him to tell him they were home and to update him on Caron's condition, he set off for the airport immediately. There was the same eeriness with Michael too – he'd gone to work as usual that morning but, when Russ called him, some sixth sense had already led him to leave his office and he was en route to Charing Cross for a train to Sevenoaks. It's something he will always be profoundly grateful he did.

For the rest of the day, we'd all sit at the end of Caron's bed, talking to her and one another. Other times, we left her to sleep and get some rest. I remember being alone with her and just standing and watching her as she slept. Michael was able to spend a little time on his own with her, and she was strong enough to talk with him as well. When she'd fallen asleep he went downstairs to get a cup of tea but by the time he'd come back, just a few minutes later, Caron was absolutely still. For a split second he said that he thought the worst had happened and remembers just staring at her, willing it not to be so, but then he heard a gasp and her chest rose again. He didn't tell us this at the time but, soon after, he came to get us all so we were with her for the rest of the day. That afternoon the nurse came back and Caron's breath got more erratic.

'She hasn't got long at all,' said the nurse.

By now we knew what was happening but we couldn't help still hoping for a few more months. After all, the plan was to spend the summer in Fowey.

The boys were at a fairground with Russ's parents but he knew he had to get them over to Sevenoaks. It was so fraught; Russ's parents didn't have a mobile so he had to track down the owner of the fairground, ask him to seek out his parents and tell them to bring the boys to Kent straight away.

It's hard for me to revisit this traumatic moment in my life that I first wrote about in 2005:

At about six on 13 April 2004, two extraordinary things happened. Caron's breathing changed again and Charlie and Gabriel arrived at the door. The nurse told us that

LOSING CARON

Caron was starting to slip away. We all looked at each other in terror. I saw my own boundless fear reflected in Russ's eyes. Inside my head I was shrieking, 'This can't be happening! Stop it! Stop it!' Caron had just got home. It wasn't fair. It wasn't the way it was supposed to be. Russ raced downstairs to the boys. He told them on the way up that Mummy was going to find it really hard to pull through this, then brought them to her room. As incredible as this seems to me now, although she was dying, an extraordinary smile had spread across Caron's lips. The little boys hugged and kissed her, talked to her for a little while, then went downstairs. It was unbearable to behold. Russ, Michael and I stayed with Caron, clinging to her until her last breath had left her body and still this amazing, enigmatic smile held fast.

It was peaceful. It was diabolical. There is not a word in the world to describe how it feels to watch your child die. It wasn't that my heart was breaking, rather that my soul was shattering. I was dying with her but, unlike Caron, my body wouldn't let me go. Despite the terrible carnage in my heart, Caron radiated a still, quiet peace. She was only 41. Finally the nurse said, 'She's gone…' But she hadn't. Not quite. Her body was warm. She lay there, smiling reassuringly as if to say, 'It's OK, everything is going to be OK.' No she hadn't gone. Not then. Not ever.

The doctor was there – I hadn't been aware of his arrival. After that we kept saying, 'How on earth are we going to tell the boys?' He took us aside and said, 'You watch. The children will lead you.' They were incredibly strong and prophetic words. Because they did. Together we went downstairs and I saw Russ say the hardest, most awful words any father might ever have to say to his child. Mummy was not coming back. Hearing him speak so gently to his beautiful boys, hearing him try to explain the inexplicable, was almost equal to watching my daughter die. It was too shattering to watch.

It was a beautiful day, filled with shafts of amber sunlight. I remember Michael taking Charlie and Gabriel to a window. He said, 'Every time you feel the warmth of the sun on your face, Mummy is with you.'

I didn't think any of us would survive that day. But the doctor was right: the children do lead us. They are the future. They carry Caron deep within them. Every time I look at the boys I know her spirit is still alive. I can see and feel her. I can sense her presence. They were the reason for us to get up the next morning.

And these words remain true to this day and will do so forever.

Paul arrived in Sevenoaks about an hour after Caron died. He immediately knew something was wrong and he found it so hard to realise he had missed her – in fact, I remember that he almost screamed when he saw us and the devastation on our faces. 'Please tell me she hasn't gone,' he cried. Nothing had prepared us: not the seven years that had passed since her diagnosis, not the devastating prognoses; not the mastectomy, or the chemotherapy, or even when we were told that the cancer had spread to her bones so she had to walk with a cane, or the crippling pain she suffered. She'd always come through before.

I still can't remember all the details of the moments after Caron died, though – we were all in such shock. I do know that I wouldn't let Caron be taken out of the house to a funeral parlour so she stayed at home, in her room, where all of us could go and sit with her and Paul could say his own goodbyes. Other friends came too; she was never alone. We filled the room with flowers and photographs, and we lit candles everywhere. I remember that night, going to sit beside her on the bed and saying goodnight to her as I had always done. She looked so beautiful, finally so free of the pain that had wracked her body for seven years.

If I could have kept her at home forever I would have done.

* * *

Caron's funeral was held at St Peter's Church, in the grounds of Hever Castle, where she and Russ had got married 15 years previously, where Stephen and I were married and where Paul was to marry over a decade later. Crippling pain seared me on that day when I knew I would never see my beautiful daughter again – at least not in this world.

The cortège left the grounds of the castle and we walked the short distance to the church. Russ and I were holding on to Charlie and Gabriel so tightly as we led the family mourners, and I vaguely remember a battery of photographers and journalists standing at the side. I couldn't have cared less who was there because I was weeping uncontrollably that we were having to say goodbye to our beautiful girl.

The small church of St Peter's and the grounds outside were filled to capacity with Caron's family and extended circle of friends, and in many respects the actual service went past in a blur. But, as always, with any serious situation there were a few unscheduled moments. Russ, who gave an incredible eulogy to Caron, was ticked off at one point by the vicar, who was looking at his watch indicating that he had already spoken for 45 minutes. But because Caron's cancer had been such a secret from her friends, there was so much that Russ wanted to say and explain. At the end of his eulogy he invited everybody back to Hever Castle for refreshments and I'll always remember Gabriel breaking the silence when he shouted out, 'Will there be any Fanta there? I'm thirsty.'

I was incapable of actually speaking at the service but Russ kindly read a letter I'd written to Caron:

My dearest and most beautiful Caron,

What a joy and privilege for over 41 years to have you as my most precious and loving daughter.

I feel so proud to be your mum and I could not have wished for a more glorious daughter; spirited, caring, loving and full of fun.

You showered endless love and joy on our lives and brought light and rainbows to us daily. Although our relationship has always been exceptionally deep, during the last seven years there have been constant new depths and discovery, but through all your pain and suffering, you have brought such warmth, love, laughter and friendship.

Watching you bravely battle with cancer has taught me so much about positivity, tenacity, dignity, spiritual growth and integrity. You are a total inspiration, not only to your family, but to all those lives you have touched.

You and Russ have given us the precious and ultimate gift in two beautiful boys, Charlie and Gabriel, and you will live on through them. They will be a daily reminder of your spirit and individuality and all the values that you have taught them. Alongside Russ, Paul, Michael and Stephen I will forever love and look after your cherished boys, as you would wish.

I miss talking to you every day, you were the girl I loved talking to most in the world. The heartache of losing you will never be healed, but you have left us with millions of exquisite thoughts and memories.

In Australia you used to say that you could not wait to have a cup of tea out of your favourite cup, at the kitchen table in Sevenoaks and with your incredible instinct and typical Irish timing, you made it back. Perhaps out of the endless memories, a few of the more recent ones will always shine out. Four weeks in Switzerland when, in the middle of concentrating on your healing and treatment, you also managed to organise my birthday celebrations, the Easter egg painting competition and a blissful Mother's Day, just you and me. It was the first time in three years that we had spent Mother's Day together and what a glorious day we had in the Swiss Alps, scoffing apple strudel and chatting non-stop.

How I treasure your gift, which you managed to paint in Australia despite your pain and frustration; beautiful tulips in a country frame which you carefully inscribed with love and kisses and lovingly placed in your suitcase for our special day together, which was yet another example of your generosity of spirit, which you radiated in abundance. You always did believe in angels and now you are one of God's brightest and most beautiful, so fly freely, my darling Caron, in your release from pain and know that every second I will carry you in my heart.

With all my love forever,

Mum

★ ★ ★

After the bleakness of the funeral, it's hard to know how anything carried on as what you would deem 'normal'. Russ and the children stayed with us for a few months before they had to go back to their home in Cornwall, which actually helped a great deal. The children were a healing focus because they had to be cared for and looked after and they were utterly amazing; one minute they would be talking about losing their mum and the next they'd be jumping up and down on the trampoline having a great time. It did wreck my heart when I overheard Gabriel saying to a girl who was helping us clean the house, 'Did you know my mummy has just died?'

When they went back to Cornwall, as they had to for the children to return to school and for Russ to pick up on his working life, our house in Sevenoaks was eerily empty. I went in to what I now call the black endless hole and every time I tried to claw my way to the top, I seemed to slip back down again.

In those first weeks and months of grief, I do not know what

LOSING CARON

I would have done without Paul, Michael and Stephen. Their support was constant and unwavering. Stephen understood something of what I was going through because when he was a boy in Ireland, his eldest brother was shot by a sniper after the war had ended and peace had been declared. He saw the raw pain on his mother's face and witnessed at first-hand the toll it takes on a mother to lose a child. The reality is you cannot carry a child for nine months, give birth to a child and then ever get over losing that child. Because while all bereavement is painful, and I would never underestimate loss of any kind, I believe that losing a child is the worst kind of searing pain. While there is an enormous sadness in losing your parents, it is the natural order of life, whereas seeing your own child die is not. When I gave birth to Caron for the first time I understood the deep love and responsibility you feel for your child and your determination that nothing should happen to this child – and then it does and you can't stop it. In our case Caron and I were also particularly close. I was with her at the birth of her own children and saw how strongly she fought against the encroachment of this hideous disease for their sakes as well as her own.

Looking back, in the depths of my own grief – I call it 'the selfish grief' – I didn't seem capable of taking on anybody else's loss. Then a friend told me a story. After her daughter had died, her son stopped her one day when she was rushing out the door and said, 'Mum, I'm your child as well.' That shocked me into reminding myself that my two sons needed me too. After all, they had lost a beautiful sister, one who had mothered them as well as being a sister to them and they were in great pain. At that point I made a positive effort to get back to some semblance of normality for the sake of my family.

These words from Caron's diary also provide me with comfort, she said, 'The thing I love about the human spirit is that no matter how dire the circumstances, there always comes a point when you can have a laugh and forget about what is happening, even for a minute, realise you're still alive and all things are still possible.'

I also keep on display permanently in my hall a poem that brings me great comfort every time I pass it. It was sent to me by Roy Castle's wife, Fiona, right after Caron died, and in turn I have passed it on to many friends in times of emotional need:

> *Sometimes, when the sun goes down, it seems it will never rise again...but it will!*
>
> *Sometimes, when you feel alone, it seems your heart will break in two...but it won't.*
>
> *And sometimes, it seems it's hardly worth carrying on...but it is.*
>
> *For sometimes, when the sun goes down, it seems it will never rise again...but it does.*
>
> 'Sometimes' *by Frank Brown*

★ ★ ★

Caron is threaded through many conversations: people I meet in the street who have also lost a child, others who fondly remember her from *Blue Peter* days. I have to admit that I don't understand people who say, 'Do you often think about Caron?' I honestly want to scream, 'Are you mad? I think of her every day, sometimes dozens of times a day.' She would have loved that dress. Wanted to buy that painting. Or laughed at that joke. In so many instances, I say to myself, 'What would Caron think?' Because she was the girl who I enjoyed talking to most in the world. We could discuss anything and everything as she always had such an unusual way of looking at things. She was naturally funny, always made me laugh and was so intelligent that I learned from *her*. And all through her battle with cancer, her tenacity and positivity were such that *she* became the teacher.

There are so many landmark points of life Caron never lived long enough to see, but we like to think her spirit is around us all the time. My grannie used to say that the spirit lives on and I never understood that until now. Caron always had a very strong belief in angels and indeed had done a number of documentaries about the subject. At the beginning I wasn't quite sure about my own belief because, when we couldn't find a parking meter, she'd say, 'We'll ask the parking angel'. To which I just laughed. But you know, we always seemed to find a parking meter. Even to this day, Stephen and I often say, 'Where is that parking angel?' and, d'you know, it works every time.

What she did believe though was that if you found an isolated white feather, that it was an angel's calling card. Now, we're not talking about a bunch of white feathers that land on the lawn, we're talking about a single white feather in a somewhat obscure place. I find them all the time. But I now believe that it's Caron's calling card and I have collected jars of them over the years.

Some people are very sceptical of the very subject but I don't care because I believe if it brings you a degree of comfort at the time, so what? And it's interesting to see that so many books are now written about angels and many shops stock nothing but angel-related gifts and literature.

Since Caron died, I have consciously tried not to go down

the anger route because it would be so easy to get angry at God for not saving my child, but my faith is very important to me and I have wanted to hang on to it. However, in recent times I do find myself getting very frustrated and angry on certain occasions. When Charlie graduated from university, I felt really upset that Caron didn't get to see it.

She would have been so thrilled that he was at university, studying literature as she did, with the two of them chatting about books together. And when Gabriel worked as a model in his gap year, she would have been fascinated to see the wacky fashion photographs that emerged, but on the other hand some beautiful ones as well. And now that he's started a new job in Marketing, she would have been bemused by the stories he has to tell. Charlie has also just started creating advertising campaigns and he was rather touched when on holiday recently, I told him that his great-great grandfather had been an Advertising Manager for a group of newspapers. He was very amused to hear that my dad Charlie had to dream up the ads, decide the slogans, hand draw everything and then present perhaps three adverts to the clients, hoping they would like and buy one. It's such a contrast to the way Charlie works now, with all the specialised technology available to him. However, I think he was pleased that he's following in his great-grandfather's footsteps.

Charlie has Caron's sense of humour and is always teasing us, but he's a fantastic boy to talk to. Gabriel was only seven when she died, like a little waif caught in the headlights, but now he's a strong, 6'4 handsome young man, bearing many of Caron's features.

In hindsight, was it fate that I was at both of their births and is it any wonder that I enjoy seeing them so much?

CHAPTER 13

A RECOVERY
OF SORTS

Caron's death had been headline news and people were totally shocked at what they were hearing because although she was a public figure, she had managed to keep it secret. And so a stream of letters began to arrive. First they came in sacks, then they came in crates. Some came from people who had known Caron but others came from people who had only heard the news but had suffered a similar bereavement themselves and wanted to say a few words to tell me that they understood what it is like to lose a child.

The letters became a lifeline and an enormous source of comfort. One woman wrote:

Dear Gloria

I am so sorry to hear about the death of your beautiful daughter, Caron. She was always a ray of sunshine on TV and will be sadly missed.

I lost my own son Philip, aged 33 to leukaemia in January and know a little of what you are going through. It is very hard to lose your child.

We have found that we have gained our strength from Philip's. I am sure you feel so proud of Caron's courage and the love she bestowed on those close to her and we find we can draw on that. Philip told us he didn't want us to be unhappy as he had had a full and exciting life so we should be happy for him.

I am sure all these brave young people feel the same and I hope you will find this a help in the coming months, as we do.

Yours sincerely,
Brenda

Some people wrote apologising for the intrusion: in fact, it was the exact opposite. Those letters became a lifeline. I stopped counting after their number reached 8,000, but I read every one: they came from friends of Caron's, from people who had had her picture up on the wall, from fans of *Blue Peter*. Some wrote about her very individual sense of style. People gave me advice and it did help enormously, not least as I began to realise that I was not alone. Other people had experienced this blackout I was feeling and sometimes the message could be bleak. One correspondent wrote:

My advice to you is to take each day as it comes and to give in to your bad days. Let it all out and then you'll appreciate your slightly better days, but in my experience it does get worse before it gets better. Let your family and friends help when you want it, but also have days to yourself. You will be emotionally exhausted after trying to put on a brave face for the world. You will get stronger and the confidence will come back eventually and one day you will smile again.

Another early letter was very blunt, but although they made me reel at the time, I later realised that they contained some very powerful advice:

I'd like to tell you it gets better but it doesn't – you have to learn to live round it and through it, because there is no way you can ever replace the loss of a child, nor would you want to. The easy part of grief is to sit in a quiet room, looking at photographs and weep, but remember if you weep from now till the day you die, it won't change anything and it won't bring Caron back.

At first I wanted to throw that letter away from me. The thought that I would always feel like this was unbearable. But she went on, 'I truly know how you feel. I too lost a child – my son. It is now 22 years since he passed on. I still think of him every day.' Twenty-two years, I thought. Am I going to wake up and feel this pain every day for the rest of my life? But, ultimately, those words were to help me because I realised that the beginning of healing only starts when you know you will never be healed. The pain of losing Caron was never going to leave me. But it would mutate into something else.

And then, in August 2004, I received a letter that was to be one of the most constructive and life-changing notes I ever received. It was written on jotter paper and, having received many letters written on jotter paper in my radio days, I knew they didn't always contain pearls of wisdom. But this turned out not only to be profound, but to mark the start of my healing.

Dear Gloria

It is 1.48am on Wednesday 25th August and again I find God is using my quiet time to interrupt my sleep. I am being driven, quite strongly, to write to you again.

I now better understand that I will not get peace and rest until I capture, on paper, the words being given to me to convey.

Caron is so much in my head, particularly at this time of the early morning. Why and how is not important or frightening any more; it is simply how it is. The connection is made.

The next chapter is still important. You must stop and listen to what needs to be done. Think about how Caron's life is to be carried forward and used to make sense of her early passing in some way. Place your faith, love, energy and skills to move Caron into another dimension for all to reach and touch the essence of her spirit.

A RECOVERY OF SORTS

The world continues to search for a purpose but you have a key to unlock the treasure, the treasure that Caron brought with her into this world. It is not lost; she is not lost – you must believe this. It is not a coincidence that you are in the limelight. Caron is also known and loved – these events have been lined up purposely. The wider world can see and connect to what they know; it will just give the next chapter validity and credibility.

The difference that can be made is huge. Caron's courage, kindness and days of pain will not be forgotten or lost for one second, as there is too much to lose.

As difficult as this is, the next chapter awaits. You need to start work. This is a great opportunity to honour Caron, to move forward in a more positive way, in the right direction, to make sense of something that on the surface makes no sense at all.

Look deeper, feel deeper, search deeper. You will be given the answers and the direction. Our loved ones are gifts from God. They come to us, even if only for a short while, to share essential messages with us. Think and remember.

There is nothing to waste here. Caron can teach us and she was sent for a purpose – to share messages of truth. Her faith was in place and is important now. Take quiet time to reflect and interpret her message. Others need to hear the things that she is trying to convey.

Caron is not lost to you. Remember her soul is bigger than death – and death is never the end. To stay healthy and focused, you must work with this loss and not against it in order to carry her spirit forward. Caron needs to know this is how it will progress, otherwise her passing is for no reason and that can't be. It is not the truth. In your heart I believe you understand this. I hope whatever I have taken down makes sense to you.

With much love

God bless
Ann

This extraordinary and profound letter was to make a huge impact and difference. It really knocked me back on my heels, but I woke up in the middle of that night and I immediately knew what I had to do: I would start a Foundation in Caron's name that would provide assistance and support to all different types of cancer charities. And so 'The Caron Keating Foundation' was born.

Now, 13 years down the line, it represents the positivity in my life, and it really is my healing. We are a totally family-run charity, with only the expense of a part-time secretary. I am the administrator and Paul, Michael and Stephen and indeed the whole family are very much involved in the organisation of our events to raise money. They all have their part to play. In recent years after my brother Charles retired, he too got involved in the IT side and running the website.

We don't set out to make millions because we are a kitchen table-top organisation but somehow we have. For example, the most recent pay-out was over £400,000 to over 74 different cancer charities. We are focused on smaller issues: we don't do big buildings or enormous grants, but we will, for example, donate £2,000 for a helpline or £30,000 for early detection equipment, which is the biggest single sum we have paid out to date. We will also fund complementary treatment rooms in hospices, some of them named after Caron. We give small donations that really make a difference and we have donated to all kinds of different cancer charities – breast cancer, bowel cancer, skin cancer and so on.

I read every bit of paper relating to the Foundation and it is a long drawn-out process deciding who gets the grants. I make notes on every application we get and discuss them with my GP Dr Richard Husband, who helps us make our choices. The positivity it engenders is phenomenal and it is gratifying to read on the website accounts by people whom we have helped.

In November 2014 we held a dinner at The Dorchester to celebrate Caron's 10th anniversary and the Foundation. So many friends and colleagues shared their tributes with us including Phillip Schofield, Janet Ellis and Mark Curry, with whom she'd presented *Blue Peter*. Cliff Richard, Rod Stewart, Michael Ball, Neil Diamond and Rob Brydon were among others there.

Of course we couldn't function without the help of many generous individuals who support us and we appreciate any donation, from £5 to £5,000. There is one loyal fan of Caron who runs marathons and is a football fanatic: he regularly sends donations of £5, £7, £25. There are a couple of girls who have suffered breast cancer themselves and hold dinners to raise funds. We are also funded by larger organisations, like

Hard Rock who has supported us for 10 years now and holds an annual dinner and auction. It is owned by the Seminole Tribe of Native Americans in Florida and I once asked one of their senior members,

'We're absolutely thrilled about the support you give us, but why us, since we're such a small organisation?'

'Because we can see exactly where the money goes,' he said. 'You are family-run and we are very family oriented.'

We are so proud as a family to be able to do this in Caron's memory and I think Caron herself would be amazed and proud of what is being done in her name. It not only helps various cancer organisations, but enables us to find a purpose from the deep loss. When a project from Northern Ireland comes up, it is deeply gratifying to be able to put something back into the region where Caron grew up. In particular we support the Big Bus campaign run by Action Cancer in Belfast: this is a bus built in Northern Ireland that can go anywhere from an estate to a factory to the backyard of a supermarket. When it's stationary, it is hydraulically controlled so that the centre of the vehicle expands into a clinic and it is here that women who are outside the NHS age group for screening can have a mammogram. This can really help women in, say, an estate where they are living with young children: instead of going to hospital, they can just go down to the end of their road to be screened.

Given that both Caron and my mum had breast cancer, this really appealed to me. And in a lovely touch, they were the charity who generously put me forward for an OBE, of which more later. That was a very humbling moment for me and brought the point home of how many people have helped and supported *me* to get this far.

★ ★ ★

Life would never return to normal after Caron's death but somehow you have to survive. As I mentioned earlier, Russ, Charlie and Gabriel stayed on in Sevenoaks but when they had to go back to their home in Fowey to pick up on school and their life there, I had to find a way forward. My way of coping has always been to work. When everything else was like quicksand, work has been a constant. Inside my head, whether it was my mum's words or the letters that poured in, all I could hear was 'keep busy'. It wouldn't be for everyone, but it has always worked for me and so about two months after Caron died, I was asked to do a week as a guest presenter on *This Morning*. Of course the show was like going back to family as I had worked on it previously, Caron had been a host, and I had always regarded it as a safe space.

They were very tactful in how they handled it. They brought me on to the show on the Friday beforehand and we talked about the loss of Caron. I broke down and so did Phillip Schofield and Fern Britton because they knew Caron very well themselves. But there it was – out in the open and the next week I could get on and front the show. It was good in that anything that takes your mind off grief, if only for half an hour, is constructive. In my case reading, research or talking about other people's lives helped.

And then about 18 months after Caron died, I was asked to be a contestant on *Strictly Come Dancing*, when the show was entering its third season. Initially I thought that this was an absolutely terrible idea, but slightly to my surprise I couldn't find anyone to tell me not to do it. At that time, I was in such a dark hole, I thought I would never laugh or smile again, which my boys thought was very sad. Everyone started urging me to take part. In fact the crux came when Paul and Michael said: 'You'll be doing something for yourself, Mum. It's a chance to put a bit of joy back in your life, give you something to concentrate on and bring back that smile.'

They were right. This was very early on in the series and if you could put one foot past the other, you were on. I was paired up with Darren Bennett, who was then about twenty-eight years old, and that age gap slightly worried me on the more sexy dances. I was imagining that my husband and grandchildren would tell me I was being a silly old bat. The redoubtable Arlene Phillips soon put me right, though.

'Stop worrying,' she purred. 'Enjoy a young man's body. Forget that he's twenty-eight.'

And, much to my surprise, it did just that. It lifted me out of a state of mind that I thought I'd never get out. In a way there was no time for weeping. There was the constant training as and when I could fit it in, between promoting *Next To You*, a book started by Caron about her life growing up in Northern Ireland and dealing with her cancer and finished by me.

Along with work and family, there just weren't enough hours in the day. And how I hated that film crew being around during every second of rehearsals. In many ways I never gave myself a proper chance on the show by not setting aside enough time for rehearsals. I found out, for example, that the athlete Colin Jackson was doing a minimum of eight to nine hours a day and, naively, I was doing half an hour here and there when I could fit it in. In the event I lasted for three weeks – I was just so grateful I wasn't the first to go.

Despite the nerves it was an incredibly exciting and happy experience and people often ask me, 'What do you talk about when you're waiting for the music to start and that fabulous walk down at the beginning of the show?' We would stand in order and the chef James Martin would always be right behind me as we stood behind the steps for our glamorous entrance. People might be surprised to learn that we were generally chatting about his organic carrots and how he'd planted five acres of them. In the middle of those nerve-racking minutes all those simple anecdotes began to cheer me up.

There was a wonderful atmosphere around the show. I used to tease the other contestants: the girls were all about size six to eight and were constantly asking the wardrobe people to cut another few inches off their skirts.

'That material you've cut off?' I asked. 'Could I add it on to my costume?'

Our first dance was the waltz, and of course I knew how to do that. It was my era and, anyway, our Latin teacher in Portadown College taught us ballroom dancing at lunchtime. I wore a white organza type dress with a faux-fur cowl collar and the white was quite flattering around the neck. You think you know a bit about ballroom dancing until you get to the *Strictly* rehearsals. It's a totally different discipline and alien to what I'd learned before.

To be honest, I was just glad to get through that first dance, but I was horrified when I discovered that our second dance was to be the super-sexy rumba. 'Please, do not make me run my hands down your body,' I begged Darren, and so he devised a rumba that mainly consisted of outward hand gestures instead of the slow, sexy movements.

'Oh, Gloria, Gloria, I would say that was a very unusual rumba,' remarked the acid-tongued Bruno Tonioli. 'More like a queen waving to her subjects.'

Once again somehow we survived through to the next round, in which we were to do a jive. That was my era too so I'd had high hopes for that and, let's face it, we had jived our way through the sixties. But, despite our efforts, we were voted off. *Strictly Come Dancing* had done a huge amount to lift my spirits, though, and to this day all the *Strictly* contestants get asked back to watch the show from the audience, so I get to relive the whole thing without the nerves. The camaraderie is fabulous but I always thought it was a strange phenomenon that one minute the judges were slating your mistakes and the next you're in the bar afterwards and everyone's as nice as pie! All in all, one of the best experiences of my career.

Despite all this, though, there were still many instances when I was overcome as we all struggled to come to terms with what had happened. I was asked to appear on *Desert Island Discs*, for the episode that aired on Christmas Eve 2006. I was very flattered to be asked to appear on that legendary show and found it very hard to choose the eight discs – in the end they included the overture to *Gigi*, which I had watched on that early trip to Canada when I was only seventeen, 'Move Over Darling' by my childhood heroine Doris Day and 'Miss You Nights' by Cliff Richard, which he'd sung at Caron's funeral, and the one I would choose should the other pieces fall beneath the waves. Kirsty Young was in her first year as the presenter and was very well researched, but when she asked me about that drive home from Switzerland and Caron arriving back at the house, I started weeping and couldn't find the words. I had to leave the studio to compose myself before I could carry on.

The first of anything is so difficult. Birthdays, anniversaries and Christmas, in particular, becomes a bit of a nightmare when you've lost somebody the previous year. It is almost impossible to recreate the type of Christmas you've had before. Not for the first time, it was Cliff who came to the rescue. One day, right out of the blue, he said to me, 'How are you going to manage Christmas?'

'I just don't know. Will I send cards, will I not send cards? Will I buy gifts, will I not buy gifts?'

'Did Caron like Christmas?' he asked.

'She absolutely loved it,' I said.

'Then go for it. Make it bigger and better than anything you've had before. Do it as a huge celebration for Caron and her boys.'

I looked at him and thought, *Of course, why don't I?*

And so we did: we had not one Christmas tree but six, along with two six-foot tall all-singing all-dancing Father Christmases, wildly over-the-top decorations and candles everywhere. Charlie and Gabriel and the rest of the family loved it and it was a huge success – but more importantly, it gave me the key to coping with all those significant events.

★ ★ ★

It was typical of Cliff that he should come to the rescue with his advice. By this time, he and I had been close friends for about 45 years, stemming from those early days in Northern Ireland, when he agreed to do an interview with me, something that made an enormous difference to my early career.

I was very impressed by him right from the start. I admired his stance on religion and his life values, and even when other people were aggressive to him and didn't like the fact that he was so successful, he always remained sympathetic and open. Back then in the early days I did a few more interviews with him and it began to feel as if Cliff and I had a good relationship. This stepped up a gear when one day I got a call from his manager, inviting us round to tea and tennis at his then home on the St George's Hill estate in Weybridge. It was the first private invitation into his inner circle, which he guards very closely, and from that moment he was primarily a friend, not a professional interviewee.

Our friendship developed. He came round occasionally to our house for dinner, and a group of us, which also included the late Jill Dando, continued to socialise. One night when he was performing at the Royal Albert Hall, he had asked me to find a chef for a party he was holding afterwards. He also asked if I wouldn't mind holding the fort and lighting a few candles before everyone got back after the show. Now, I am a candle nut – I love them. I found every single candle in that house, candles that had been there for years and never been lit, candles absolutely everywhere and lit the whole lot of them. By the time Cliff and his guests got back it looked like the Blackpool illuminations. He still teases me about the time I nearly set his house on fire.

We went to a lot of events and parties at his home, which he eventually sold, before moving to another mansion in Sunningdale in Berkshire. I was so happy when he received his knighthood in 1995, as it gave him credence in many circles, including showbiz that perhaps he had never had before. He is a good man and has always given 10 per cent of his earnings to charity. He is a truly generous person.

When he bought his house in Barbados, Stephen and I went there for the first New Year's Eve and we had a terrific time, but there was a huge downside: I am now extremely allergic to mosquitoes because of that visit. I was a little alarmed to see the kitchen window was open and swarms of mosquitoes were coming through.

'Could you maybe close the window?' I suggested to the cook.

'This is Barbados,' the cook said, and shrugged.

Cliff's sister Joan was there with her then husband and he and I both got really badly bitten – all over my face and body and even on my eyelids. At the local supermarket I asked what I should put on it and was told to use citronella. I didn't realise how strong that stuff was so I caked myself in it to stop those mozzies biting. At about 2am that morning, my husband literally had to drag me out on to the balcony as I couldn't breathe and it turned out, as we heard the next day, Joan's husband was just the same as I had also given him some of my stash. It may prevent bites but, boy, that citronella is strong!

Cliff couldn't understand why all of this had happened but when he investigated he found out that builders, who had been finishing off his new house had gone off for Christmas and New Year and left the lids off all the water tanks. They were heaving with an infestation of mosquitoes, which had to be dealt with professionally, and has left me with an allergy to them to this day. It's a story that we often laugh about, but it was no laughing matter at the time. LA was our next stop after Barbados and I remember getting into the bath in the hotel and almost crying out, 'Thank God, no more mosquitoes!'

★ ★ ★

Cliff has an ability to make people feel better even in the most difficult circumstances. After the shock of Jill Dando being shot in 1999, it was a sad, sad time as we had all been friends, and it was scary, too, because at the beginning it was mooted that television presenters were being made into targets. For a while I was very, very fussy about who was at my gate and who rang the bell. But Cliff was a great friend of Jill's as well; we'd all had such fun together. Jill's death just shattered us, but when we were coming back from her funeral, there was a terrible queue on the M5 so we turned off in to a little village and went into a local pub. I said, 'Why don't we tell all the stories that made us laugh around Jill, silly things we did and all that?' And it changed the horrendous sadness to great memories. We didn't think that we'd laugh so quickly around the table, but we did and Cliff helped with that.

As we became closer we shared all sorts of things and when Caron became ill, it was a secret kept from almost everyone. Cliff was one of only three people in whom I confided, the others being two girlfriends, because I totally trusted him. I found some solace from him because of his ability to chat things over and his faith is so strong, in turn it gave me some strength to cope.

Caron and Cliff had always got on well, too. When Caron and her family were living in Cornwall, we bought a house nearby. Cliff came and stayed for the weekend and again was able to offer some comfort to Caron. When she and her family were living in Australia, Cliff had come to Brisbane to perform. We were also out there at the time and so he came to stay with us for four days. It was a halcyon time for both of us. I was able to unburden myself to Cliff and Caron could talk to him as well. One night the two of them stayed up talking all night and to this day Cliff has never told me what they talked about.

A RECOVERY OF SORTS

When Caron died in April 2004, Cliff attended the funeral and sang 'Miss You Nights' in tribute to her, which was so special because we have strong memories of him singing that around the dinner table in Australia. On that day, he was really speaking from the heart. He quoted from the Bible about the greatest gift of all – love. A truly deep friendship exists between us and he has been a great man repeatedly for our family.

So therefore it was against that background many years later that I heard with utter disbelief that Cliff's apartment in Berkshire had been raided by the police with the BBC hovering in a helicopter to cover the shock event. Operation Yewtree had been set up to deal with historic sex abuse allegations in the wake of the Jimmy Savile scandal and it had emerged that Cliff had been accused of assaulting a fifteen-year old boy at a Christian rally three decades previously, allegations that I never believed for a second. But Cliff's many friends rallied round fast. First, mutual friends, Jackie and her husband Richard Caring, rang me and recommended a particular lawyer. Then I rang Cliff. 'Now sit down and listen to what I have to tell you,' I began. 'Don't say anything, this is what you have to do. I've been told on good faith this is the best lawyer for you.' So I was with him from the very beginning.

Cliff told me later that the shock of seeing the police going into his apartment was absolutely devastating. The first he knew of it was when a friend called him and said, 'Turn on the TV.' Imagine sitting in Portugal on holiday watching your home being raided. Cliff told me later that he fell to his knees and wept but fortunately he had a friend with him who said, 'Get up. You know you've done nothing wrong.' And so he did.

295

But that was only the start of a nightmare for Cliff. He was quite horrified with the allegations and he was in a state of total shock. To have this crazy, unfounded situation hanging over his head was enough to drive him to total frustration and devastation. He had no idea who his accuser was and there was little or no information coming back from the police. He was appalled at what he regarded as a completely false accusation and couldn't believe anybody would put him through such agony. The reality is I would trust Cliff with my life and I have never seen him put a foot wrong, ever. And so began nearly three years of torture for him being accused wrongly of something he just hadn't done. I believe that so many members of the public were horrified at the treatment he was given, with the total invasion of his home and privacy, but as sometimes happens Cliff said he never had so much support in his life from fans, friends, family – and the press.

Cliff has lots of really good friends and they kept travelling down to Portugal to see him but in many ways, if you think about it, he was imprisoned. Over the next two years until the time when the charges were finally dropped and Cliff was totally exonerated, we talked frequently about what was happening and how the situation was evolving.

Finally, in June 2016, the Crown Prosecution Service said there was not enough evidence for a case and that no further action would be taken, while the police and the BBC were both heavily criticised for their conduct. But Cliff was understandably tormented even about that because he felt that the CPS had left him open to 'no smoke without fire' insinuations: 'My reputation will not be fully vindicated because the CPS's policy is to only say something general about there being "insufficient' evidence",' he said in a statement afterwards. Although he was relieved he was very frustrated about the 'insufficient' evidence part because as he pointed out, 'How can there be evidence for something that never took place?'

During that time, although I knew he would be vindicated I obviously wouldn't have asked him as a friend to give me his first interview, but one day he said, 'Look, Glo, when all of this is finished I have a lot of things I want to say, so would you do the first interview?'

Would I? What a scoop. If the football and other sport hadn't been on at the time I believe it would have been transmitted in prime-time. As it was there was a lot of hype around ITV that we had the exclusive. So much was made of it in trailers in the days leading up to the transmission – *Good Morning Britain* took a piece with him and so did the *Lorraine* programme – all of it as a lead-up to a special one-hour in the *Loose Women* slot. Cliff didn't disappoint as he had so much pent-up emotion. He hadn't slept or eaten well for years and now he could be totally open about what he had been through.

The whole case has had a serious and lasting impact on him: 'Although I've been cleared, one of the first things that comes up when you go into the computer is not about my singing, but that case,' he told me. The frustration and pain he feels are as a direct result of that shock. 'I didn't want to go out of the front door when it was all going on,' he said. 'I thought I would never sing again. I've only just been able to start sleeping after all this time.' Even now he cannot believe what has happened to him and it eats away at him – quite literally. At the time he lost so much weight that when he hugged you it felt a bit like skin and bone.

Cliff had an enormous cloud hanging over him for years and he had palpably lost his joy for life. We were constantly on the phone when it was going on and he would go over the details over and over and over again because it was tormenting him. His friends had the ultimate faith in him but it still ate away at him inside. Cliff is understandably upset about how he's perceived in the rest of the world. 'I perform in Asia, New Zealand, the Middle East, and the clearance factor doesn't stretch that far.' However, when Cliff appeared at the Royal Albert Hall while he was still under a cloud, he really didn't know how people would react when he came out on stage: what actually happened was that the audience stood up and applauded. So much so that he could hardly get the show started.

'You know what?' I teased him. 'That case probably means you've got a whole new fan base, who just came along to show their support.' But the impact on him has been so severe and I don't think he'll ever fully get over it.

Cliff has only ever been back to that apartment in Berkshire once and then only for about five minutes to pick up some clothes, and he then sold it at a loss. He's currently suing the BBC. I believe that it all only happened because there was such a backlash over the Jimmy Savile scandal and the Operation Yewtree investigation was on a roll. Then when Rolf Harris was found guilty, suspicion was cast on all entertainers from that era, but in Cliff's case nothing ever added up. The rally in which he was supposed to have assaulted someone actually took place two years after the accuser said the incident took place.

In the years during which he was under suspicion, others came forward to make false claims, including a serial rapist and a blackmailer – whose identities are protected by law – and in one especially ludicrous suggestion, someone alleged that Cliff had roller-skated into a clothes shop in Milton Keynes, assaulted someone, roller-skated out and then roller-skated back in two hours later to do the same again. 'Have you ever heard anything so ridiculous?' Cliff said in an interview afterwards. 'Surely, if it were true, he would only have had to push me in the chest and I would have fallen over?' In actual fact Cliff filmed his video for 'Wired For Sound' wearing roller-skates in a shopping centre in Milton Keynes and the accuser was clearly a fantasist who couldn't separate fiction from reality.

While this was going on, no less than six retired policemen got in touch to say they were there that day with him and that there was no way he could ever have been involved in something like that. A lot of people in the public eye were coming under scrutiny at that time and someone clearly thought he'd be a good name to pick out of a hat. And the results have taken a devastating toll on a truly good man.

Those of us who are close to him became very worried as we saw the physical toll it took on him, too. When we transmitted the exclusive with Cliff the scars were clearly there. 'I didn't sleep – I probably only got around three hours a night,' he told us. 'Still to this day I just can't understand why someone would want to do that to another person.'

I just think Cliff was totally relieved to get everything off his chest. He was so honest about his feelings, his pain and frustration about being under suspicion for such a long period of time. From my point of view, I had never doubted him for a second. I always knew he was an extremely good person at heart and for many, many people there was a huge amount of relief when he was cleared. The public support was stupendous.

During the interview, typically for Cliff, we did have a few light moments and he suggested he could get a facelift for himself – and a job lot for the rest of us...! He is in a better place now but I don't believe he will ever fully get over his ordeal. He has recently started to sleep peacefully again but it was a disgraceful hounding of an innocent man. You know, what I admire about him is that he's already looking for a venue to stage a celebratory 80th birthday concert? If that's not tenacity and positivity, I don't know what is.

CHAPTER 14

I'M STILL HERE, HUNNI

Many a brown envelope has dropped through my letter box, mostly in the form of unpaid bills, but when a rather distinctive official-looking one arrived in May 2017 marked 10 Downing Street, I opened it more enthusiastically than usual. I read it, reread it and then screamed for Stephen to come in from the garden. Then we both read it and reread it to make sure that what we were reading was real. And yes, the unbelievable accolade had been given...an OBE in the Queen's birthday list.

The official wording released to the press was as follows: 'An OBE for Miss Mary Winifred Gloria Hunniford for services to cancer charities through breast screening services and cancer support'.

I was so honoured and thrilled when I read the news, not only for me but for the whole family. I found it almost impossible to keep it a secret – after all, I do open my mouth regularly to broadcast to the nation. But you have to keep it completely under wraps until the news is made public, or the accolade can be taken away. You're informed quite a way in advance, but all those weeks meant only Stephen and I knew anything about it. Then a week or so before the formal announcement, I was with Paul and Michael having a business meeting and, when our colleague left, one of my sons said, 'So what's new?'

Well my big news came blurting out so fast there wasn't a dry eye between us. We drank in the news together, after which we drank something else – a little stronger than tea. However, I then had to put them on their absolute honour not to tell anybody until the news was made public. The questions came fast and furious. Well, I didn't have immediate answers but within a relatively short time the honours list was published and then a few weeks later, Buckingham Palace was confirmed.

Apart from being utterly delighted by the honour I feel extremely humbled by it and immediately thought of all the people in my life who have helped me get there. I'd never previously known how the honours system operated, I always thought that there was a mysterious team of Downing Street officials who voted for various public figures and that's how the decisions were made. Not so apparently. I mentioned earlier in the book that Caron's Foundation had regularly supported the Belfast-based charity, Action Cancer. It transpired that they had nominated me for an honour and then later I heard Douglas King, who is the main fundraiser, had been in touch with Stephen, who in turn had to ask various friends and business colleagues to write citations. People like Paddy Haycocks, my editor at *Open House*, Canon Roger Royle, who married us, Sally and Ben Kelly, two Queen's

Counsels who are great family friends, and Johnny and Cathy Comerford, who were Caron's best friends. When I eventually got copies of their citations it was of course very flattering to read effusive comments about myself but at the same time I felt that I didn't really deserve it. After it was announced in the press, this is what Gareth Kirk, the chief executive of Action Cancer, had to say:

'Her commitment to breast screening services has undoubtedly saved lives of women, who without Gloria's encouragement would not have come forward for screening. She's a force of nature and no job is too big or small. She uses all her own time and is an endless ball of energy in her quest to save lives. We think the kindness she has is in her genes. She's turned the most terrible tragedy a mother can face, into her life's mission to stop anyone else losing a daughter.'

It was all so humbling.

My only sadness was that Caron wasn't around to join in with the spirit of the whole thing. Knowing Caron's penchant for fashion, even stemming back to her *Blue Peter* days, I can only imagine how many shopping trips we would have had together in preparation for the big day. Family, friends and even strangers were so kind when the news finally broke, with cards and flowers flooding the house in Sevenoaks, which once again reminded me how generous of thought people can be on meaningful occasions like this. And, not that our family needs an excuse for a party, it is the perfect reason for a big celebration to mark the investiture.

* * *

From the moment, I revealed to my sons that I had been honoured with the OBE, the questions came thick and fast, 'Will it be at Buckingham Palace?', 'What do we wear?', 'How many family members can attend?', 'Will it be the Queen who bestows the honour?' The excitement leading up to the 13th October investiture day was palpable. I have to say, it was quite a dilemma deciding what to wear – which colour, length and what design? In the end, I went to designer friends of mine based in North London, Revie and John Jourrou, who in the past have created various outfits for me for momentous occasions. Revie was the first to say, 'Don't go for strong colours' (which I tend to do, because I like a bright look). She said, 'Keep it simple but impactful'. So, in the end, we decided on an off-white three-quarter length coat and matching skirt and top, with a beautiful piece of black trimming that Revie had been keeping for a special occasion. The hat, I knew, would be easy to have designed because for Paul's wedding two years prior, I discovered a wonderfully talented milliner, Vivien Sheriff. At that point, I was taken to her atelier in the New Forest and it was stunning to watch Vivien and her team put together the most exquisite hats. As she has a lot of styles on pedestals to show, I was able to try on various hats before deciding on *the* one. It was already made up in marvellous pink hued feathers but Vivien adapted it to my black and white colourway. And even the Head of the Yeomen of the Guard at Buckingham Palace courtyard on investiture day said, 'Madam, I love your hat'. However, I'm jumping ahead of myself. Back to the planning and lead-up to the big day...

In my heart, I would have loved to have taken more family members but of course, each recipient is only allowed to bring three guests, who were my two sons and husband Stephen. So, I decided to have a pre-investiture party the night before. There is a beautiful private dining room in the The Langham hotel, which I love and often admire when I'm passing through the hotel. I decided that would be perfect as the building itself brought back so many memories. The dining room faces the front entrance of BBC Broadcasting House, where I started my Radio 2 journey back in the 80's. Over the years, I'd conducted hundreds of meetings in the hotel, done live broadcasts and even held special family and Caron Keating Foundation events there. So, it seemed fitting to invite my twenty nearest and dearest to a celebratory dinner. We decided to stay in the hotel for a few days in order to really enjoy the build-up. It was hugely exciting seeing my specially designed outfit hanging on the outside of the wardrobe and getting ready for our pre-investiture family celebration. It turned out to be such a fun night and we were able to make as much noise as we wanted! However, for once, we were somewhat sensible and went to bed early in readiness for a 6am start the next day. I decided to have the full works, so one of our regular make-up girls from *Rip Off Britain* arrived at 6.30am, followed by a *Hello!* magazine photographer who was covering the 'getting ready process' and departure for the palace. I can't begin to describe the butterflies in my stomach as the hour drew near. We had already been told by previous recipients whom I knew that if you get there earlier than required, your family have the chance of getting a better seat and view of the proceedings. So, although the invitation said 10am, we were second in line outside the Buckingham Palace gates at 9.05am. Very shortly, there was a long queue of people behind us and amusingly, lots of foreign tourists started taking photographs as I sat in the waiting car. They probably thought that I was some foreign dignitary. Anyhow, for everyone's amusement I waved and let them snap away.

When the huge palace gates swung open, everything was so well planned in terms of where to park and which door to enter via. We were thrilled to discover that everybody enters through the famous covered portico Grand Entrance, often seen when foreign leaders attend a state visit and where we've all seen the royal family ascend many, many times.

As we made our way up through the palatial surroundings, we were informed at every turn where to go. Recipients and their guests were all held in an overwhelmingly beautiful long gallery, with oversized original oil paintings as far as the eye could see. Michael had just finished watching *Victoria* and *The Crown* and commented on the enormity of actually being inside the palace. We eventually came to the point where recipients were directed one way, whilst their guests were invited to take their seat in the Throne Room. Of course, there was a lot of wonderment at the totally magnificent surroundings as neither of my sons had ever been inside Buckingham Palace. It was just so exciting for them to be in the inner sanctum, to look at the splendour and glory of a building which we'd all looked at on television and in films all of our lives.

My son Paul is always extremely chatty with everybody and before long he discovered from a rather official-looking gentleman that it was Her Majesty The Queen who would be bestowing the honours that day. That was the first confirmation we'd had as to which member of the royal family would conduct proceedings as nobody is told in advance. Apparently, the Queen doesn't do that many investitures these days, so we felt exceptionally privileged that she was in residence. To give you an idea of scale, on my day there were only 50 recipients whereas there can be up to 200 recipients, when a more junior member of the royal family is bestowing the honours.

What is really charming about the whole occasion is that those receiving the awards are put into one room all together and very quickly we struck up a common bond of anticipation and asked lot of questions about why we'd received our awards. When the time came, we were ushered further towards the Throne Room where there were various members of staff who are seasoned pros in explaining the process. It really is an exceptionally well-oiled machine, as everything works like clockwork. For example, we were shown towards the double doors of the Throne Room and told to proceed to an official guard halfway between the door and the podium. We should wait till our surname is called out during the citation, then walk forward to the podium where Her Majesty will be standing, then curtsey, take three steps forward so our toes touch the podium, and then (which was my worrying bit) we should reverse, taking three steps backwards, curtsey again, and then walk off. Of course, I was worried that my slightly dodgy left knee wouldn't be very good when curtseying and my reversing would be awful!

As it turned out, the Queen was exceptionally generous to every recipient and I felt as if we talked for a long time. As I was receiving the OBE for services to breast cancer screening and other cancer charities, she said to me, 'Remind me how you got involved in this kind of work?' When I said that I'd sadly lost my daughter Caron to breast cancer she immediately recalled, and I felt as if she meant it, 'Of course, of course, I remember now'. We talked for what seemed a long time about the work we do throughout the country in the Caron Keating Foundation name. But when the Queen puts her hand out to shake your hand, of course that's the signal that your time is up. However, I may just have broken a bit of protocol because I instinctively, when someone shakes my hand, put my left hand over the clasped hands. So, in the photographs it looks a bit like I'm never going to let the Queen go! And the other rather bizarre thought I had in the middle of this extremely special conversation was, I was dying to ask the Queen what her beauty regime was because her skin was so sensational close-up. Thankfully, I managed to resist but she did look superb and I have the utmost admiration for what Her Majesty does, bearing in mind her long 65-year reign. I know for sure that she made everybody feel exceptionally special that day, and that is certainly what contributed to one of the most memorable and proud moments of my life.

Afterwards, we were all led individually into the Throne Room to sit with our families and watch the remainder of the ceremony. One very special honour that was awarded that day was the St. George's Cross which was instigated by Her Majesty's father, King George VI, and I think that's one reason why the Queen was particularly keen to be presenting that day (which was very lucky for us). From the moment we arrived at the Buckingham Palace gates to the time we left, it was utterly thrilling and majestic (in the true sense of the word). I discovered later, that when Stephen and Michael were watching me receive the OBE, they both welled up and became quite emotional. Stephen had leant over to Michael and said, 'Gloria's mum and dad back in Portadown would have been so proud'. And when I reflect upon my very humble beginnings, Stephen is so right and I only hope that they were looking down and smiling.

When we came out into the courtyard, of course one is faced with television reporters and photographers and, naturally, I was keen to have a perfect record of the day. In advance,

I had ordered a video to be taken and a certain number of photographs, and then in the courtyard the families are also allowed to take whatever shots they want. One which really amused me was lining up with the Yeomen of the Guard. They are all so charming and happy to pose, but the Head Yeomen was incredibly tall and looked a bit like Bruce Forsyth. Next to him, I was a little Irish dwarf (but a dwarf with an OBE).

We were almost reluctant to leave the joy of being in the palace courtyard, given everything that had gone on in the previous few hours, but Michael had organised a special lunch at the nearby Ritz Hotel and there we were joined by other close members of the family. I'm sure the Executive Chef John Williams is used to many celebrations (in fact the Michelin star dining room is a favourite of the royal family) but that day he made us all feel very special by producing a marvellous six-course tasting menu, ending with a small OBE cake. By the time we left, we were very high on the excitement of the day, aided and abetted by copious glasses of champagne and an exceptionally good lunch. However, we had to remind ourselves that that night we were hosting a Caron Keating Foundation event at the Dorchester Hotel, kindly organised by Hard Rock. To top it all, as we were leaving The Ritz and walking past the Palm Court tea room, the pianist stopped what he was playing and burst into a rendition of 'When Irish Eyes Are Smiling'. The whole room stopped eating their scones and cucumber sandwiches and for one brief moment looked over. It was a very special moment, as I recalled taking my late mum there for afternoon tea thirty years before.

I've previously said in the book that running the Foundation is part of my healing after losing Caron, and to have a huge organisation like Hard Rock support a table-top run family

Foundation is utterly marvellous. They are on board again this year which will be the 11th annual ball they've organised to raise funds, which means an enormous amount to the work that we do all over the country. And really, this is why I feel so humble about receiving an OBE because so many other people, like the general public and Hard Rock, have done such magnificent work to support the Foundation itself. On that evening, Richard Madeley of Richard and Judy fame was the MC and part of the cabaret was a band called The Best of British, members of whom have been big bands like 10cc, The Faces and Rod Stewart's band. To add to that, Rod Stewart himself and his wife Penny came along to the event because a lot of their mates were in their band and, as always, they were very generous when it came to the auction. However, in the middle of all of the merriment, Richard introduced a crucial moment when the most enormous cake was wheeled in, depicting an edible version of the OBE award itself. So eventually, at around 1am, it was an extremely exhausted but extremely contented Gloria who fell into bed, having had the most incredible 24-hours that will stay with me vividly forever.

* * *

I was particularly pleased to see that Ringo Starr in this New Year's Honours List received his knighthood. I felt it was about time that he was honoured in this way and it sparked a few memories for me about my various encounters with the Beatles. Of course I remember going to see them in the 60s when they visited Belfast but, as you can imagine, I hardly heard one word because of the screaming. So now spin forward to when I had arrived in London to broadcast with Radio 2. Very often, I would read stories out of the paper if they had a bit of a twist or a funny pay-off line and on this occasion I had read from the paper that Paul McCartney, for a film or video he was making, had been busking in the street, unrecognisable of course, and he had only received a paltry amount of money. But the pay-off line was that he kept it. So you can imagine my surprise when my producer, later on in the programme, said, 'You've got to take this call because Paul McCartney is on the phone'. 'Yeah, yeah', I replied. 'No honestly, Gloria, he's on the phone'. So, thrilled to bits that Paul might just listen to the programme during the day, I took the call. After the initial pleasantries he said, 'By the way Gloria, you know that story you read out from the papers? It's absolutely not true that I kept the money so I want you to correct that'. So in the end I got a nice telling off for believing what I read in the papers!

A more straightforward occasion turned out to be during a Children in Need day for Radio 2 in the late 80s. Many celebrities would drop in to read requests from the public and it was absolutely their choice of music that was played all day. We were never quite sure who would drop in during our stint on the radio but I was delighted when Paul McCartney joined me during my time. He was as charming as ever, talking to the public and playing their music, and seemed to stay for quite a long time during which a photograph was taken of the pair of us which ended up in a book by Geoffrey Giuliano, one of the foremost writers on the Beatles and the Stones. I also got to know Paul's wife Linda very well, particularly when she started to write her veggie books, as she was a regular visitor to the Radio 2 studio. At that time, they had a home in Kent and she very kindly invited me to go over, which I sadly never took her up on. But Linda, with her fight against breast cancer, was an absolute guru to Caron and I remember distinctly when Linda lost her battle with cancer that Caron was very badly hit by that news. Caron had hung on to the positivity that Linda exuded with her healthy diet and determination to beat cancer; if Linda couldn't beat this hideous disease then who could?

Ringo and his wife Barbara Bach, I tend to meet at Chelsea every year, and we usually have a passing conversation about gardens and new species of flowers and plants. But I love their enthusiasm for gardening. Over the years there was much written about George Harrison's interest in his garden and he was equally passionate about his large garden in Henley-on-Thames. So you can imagine, it didn't take me long to accept an invitation to Ravi Shankar's 80th birthday which was held at the house and in the garden. By that stage, George had sadly died but his wife Olivia very kindly sent us an invitation because we'd also featured Ravi and his daughter Anoushka on Radio 2 many times. The garden was heavily swathed and festooned by the most exotic Indian-styled marquees. It was a superb evening weather-wise and to listen to Ravi Shankar's music in this exquisite garden, which had meant so much to George, was a totally memorable occasion. That night was the first time that I had seen a particular spectacle, an enormous helium balloon that created this glorious moon effect that was dropped from the sky and from it hung a trapeze artist. The moon would be lowered down and she would lightly touch the guests, then the balloon would be brought up again. It's hard to put down on paper just how beautiful it was, but it was such a magnificent affect.

For the final Beatle memory, we go to New York and the aftermath of the terrible shooting of John Lennon. I think we all remember where we were and the impact of hearing that news. It was just so hard to absorb. Sometime after that horrific incident, Yoko Ono released an album and through Radio 2 we were invited to meet with her at their apartment in the Dakota Apartment Building in New York. And if you remember, he was shot outside that building. It was with huge anticipation that we arrived there and first of all were shown to their offices on the lower floors. There was my producer Colin Martin and an engineer to record the interview with Yoko Ono, and we were eventually taken to their private apartments. I recall having to go through about three doors until we were taken to this huge sitting room which overlooked Central Park. Yoko Ono's maid eventually brought us a tray of tea and I remember thinking it was wonderful that we were left in that room for 45 minutes before Yoko Ono appeared to do the interview because it gave us time to have, what we'd call in Northern Ireland, 'a good nosy around'. The huge room was all white with the exception of some large green plants and a few very tasteful small pieces of mahogany furniture. The famous white piano was in prime position in the corner of the room and near to it was a very comfortable armchair which was turned against the room, facing out on Central Park, which meant the view was exquisite. Apart from marvellous artwork on the walls, there was a rather unusual piece and, as Yoko Ono explained later, it was a white dish that had chocolate ice cream in it where John had written with his finger, 'John Loves Yoko'. The ice cream had set like that so she'd had it preserved and cast, and put up on the wall as an art piece. Not knowing what to expect in terms of the interview, Yoko was very open and talked very freely about her feelings following John's death and her present attitude towards making music. It turned out to be a very private and exclusive interview at the time.

It was all a bit surreal but, again, one of the poignant ingrained memories of my life. This is yet another example of the privileges I've had through my work and although sometimes we moan about standing out in the rain filming, and damp British days, these memories are the upside of being involved in broadcasting and ones which I never take for granted, and treasure.

* * *

In addition to running the charity, I'm still working three to four days a week at the grand age of seventy-seven. My husband says I seem to be busier than ever, but then I've always been that way since I was seven. Michael worries that it's too much at times and insists that I do one day on, one day off, but of course it never really works out like that. He's even threatened to call my agent a few times!

Interestingly, when Miriam O'Reilly was dropped from *Countryfile* in 2009 at the age of fifty-two, allegedly for being too old for the programme, the press said it was all to do with ageism in the industry. To this day, every press interview that I do raises the issue. I've never knowingly experienced ageism, though maybe it went on behind my back, but it has never been discussed to my face. Mind you, I have always been realistic about my career, in that I never expected to be on prime-time every night and I've always been willing to branch out in different directions. An older person's perspective is as valuable – if not more so – than a hot young twenty-something. It's about balance and I feel that this open attitude has led to career longevity. Usually I find that when one door closes another opens. Ironically though, it was *Rip Off Britain* that led me back to prime-time TV. It was made and scheduled for morning TV and I don't think anybody thought in advance that the programme would be such a success.

When recession hit a decade ago, one of our BBC bosses made the decision to develop a consumer programme to deal with how the public felt about being 'ripped off.' He was pondering about who should front it as he was having a cup of tea in his office. He looked up and saw a *Cash in the Attic* poster and there we were, Jennie Bond, Angela Rippon and me. A few years later Jennie left and was replaced by Julia Somerville. And here we are today – all ladies of a certain age and I believe that's the strength of its success. There are 216 years of wisdom between us and we have certainly been around the block, suffered a bit and that's where age is a benefit. I always say you couldn't have three twenty-somethings' fronting the show because they wouldn't have the life experience, believability or credibility and therefore this is when having a few years behind you comes into its own. So, when pressed about ageism, I can only speak as I find and I'm fortunate in that I've never been out of work, never have to look for work and never had to hustle for it. So, there's that big dollop of luck again.

Since recession set in, whether it's energy prices, insurance claims or scams, people feel they are being ripped off and that's when they get in touch with us. We are three pretty formidable women, who can certainly kick down the doors to try and get an answer for the consumer. Let's face it, any dodgy businessman running a suspect company would certainly break a sweat if three old birds like us turned up. Of course off-screen, we have a meticulous and super-talented team working on the programme. With consumerism, and naming and shaming, the team have to be more than 100 per cent correct in order to deal with it on air. I believe part of *Rip Off Britain*'s success is that all the case studies are based on the viewers' own problems and scenarios. So if one person writes to us and is featured on the programme about, say, an insurance scam or claims for damages, then hundreds of viewers will identify with the same issue.

The brand has grown over the last ten years, which is a great credit to our senior editor, Rob Unsworth, who is often to be found at 2am pouring over scripts. It's not only the main *Rip Off Britain* show, but spin-offs like *Rip Off Britain 'Live'*, *Rip Off Britain Food*, *Rip Off Britain Holidays,* and everyone seems to have a story of something that's gone wrong. I even had one of my own – the first trip abroad we did for the programme meant leaving on one of those ungodly flights when you have to be at the airport at 4.30am, so that meant I was up at 3am. When I got to Tenerife, at about 11am their time, I got this manic call from Stephen to say that in my sleepy haze I had locked him in the bedroom! Well, apart from thinking, *what can I do from Tenerife?*, it transpired that though he had a landline phone he didn't have any numbers to hand and in order to get hold of Mary, my secretary and a key holder, he rang the vet thinking they'd have her number. The receptionist of course replied, 'I'm so sorry, we can't give out private numbers, is there anything we can help you with?' He heard himself saying, 'my wife has gone off on holiday and has locked me in the bedroom!' So realising the predicament she agreed to contact Mary, who let herself into the house, proceeded to the bedroom and I think it had been quite some time since she'd seen a man standing in his undies. But at least she came to the rescue!

On the serious side, there are shocking tales of people booking a villa, paying upfront in cash and when they get to the destination there is no villa. Or in another case, another family was already there. One couple, celebrating a 50th anniversary, fulfilled their dream of booking a holiday to Las Vegas and then lived the nightmare when they arrived to discover that the hotel had been knocked down. No matter how experienced a presenter you are, these stories affect you. I almost wept over the account of one young couple who had saved hard for tens of thousands of pounds for a deposit on their first home. They were scammed by a rip-off merchant who'd called to say that the solicitor handling their case had changed banks and that they should transfer the deposit to a different account. Sadly, they pressed the button on their computer and willingly transferred the funds to this new account and lost the lot. Totally heart-breaking and there was absolutely nothing they could do about it.

Being the host of such a consumer show made me pretty confident that I could sniff out a scam. So you can imagine my shock when I received a call from Santander explaining that £120,000 had been erroneously taken from my account. How could that have happened? Was this some kind of Ant & Dec joke, with hidden cameras in my kitchen? The money had been safely tucked away – or so I thought – in a savings account that I hadn't touched for a couple of years. The bank refunded the money almost immediately and my son Michael, in his pragmatic way said, 'Well what are you worried about? You got the money back!'

'Excuse me, Michael, I make part of my living dealing with scams on *Rip Off Britain* – I want to know more about how it happened,' I said. Apparently it is easier for four complete strangers to get their hands on my money than me. When I ring up any of my banks, I have to jump through hoops with umpteen security questions and passcodes, but in this case the main fraudster who was an unconvincing lookalike, managed to get the money transferred with a dodgy, fake driving licence. The only part of this whole sorry affair that tickled me somewhat were some of the *Mail Online* headlines and comments. The *Mail* wrote, 'They should've gone to Specsavers!: Gloria Hunniford's outrage after a "plump elderly" fraudster posed as the TV star and duped a bank cashier into handing over £120,000 from her account'. One comment went onto say, 'I don't know if Gloria Hunniford should be more upset about having £120k taken from her bank account, or being likened to the haggard, overweight imposter'. The imposter told the bank teller that she 'had a few bob' and wanted her grandson to enjoy the benefits of the very substantial funds she held in her account.

The woman looked nothing like me but she had a girl with her whom she said was her daughter and two young boys, one of whom she said was my grandson. They actually were what's called 'mules' to carry the money. They were strangers who had been recruited for the day. They didn't go to my local branch of Santander but to Croydon, armed only with a driving licence with my details on it and her photograph. Afterwards the police told me that the licence had probably been made in someone's sitting room. However, between them they managed to convince the bank teller to make them co-signatories of my account. I was left extremely upset, felt violated and confused. If Stephen, who also banks there had gone in and said, 'I would like to be a co-signatory on Gloria's account,' they wouldn't do it without stringent checks and my approval.

The case went to the High Court – the bank teller was let off, supposedly because she was pregnant. I've since discovered that UV light on the driving licence in the bank is not a fool-proof test either. The two boys were given suspended sentences and the two women are still on the run despite *Crimewatch* featuring it, as indeed we did in *Rip Off Britain*. The conclusion is that you can never be too careful and I'm afraid that I've lost all my trust in high street banks.

* * *

By sheer contrast to the consumer issues we tackle on *Rip Off Britain* being a panellist on *Loose Women* is the polar opposite. It's rather fun being a Loose Woman at seventy-seven and to hurl in the occasional shocking comment. The opportunity to be on the panel came when I had a chance encounter with the boss of ITV's Daytime Programming, Helen Warner. I met her at a fundraising party for Caron's Foundation and in the process she mentioned that she had spent a lot of time with Caron years ago working at LWT's *London Tonight*. 'Come in for a coffee some time and have a catch up,' she said. And so I did and as we nattered on about Caron and the things they got up to we started to talk about *Loose Women*.

'Did you ever think you would like to be a panellist?' she asked.

I'd often been a guest on the programme and I dearly love its format, so trying to be quite cool about it and not too overly enthusiastic, I heard myself say, 'Well yes, of course. If someone's ill I would love to stand in.' At the same time, I also suggested that some more newsy and serious topics would sit well. At my age, I certainly didn't want to be talking about shagging on the beach and getting sand up your bum! And so it transpired that my casual chat with Helen led to a meeting at the London Studios with the then programme editor, Martin Frizell...and from September 2015 I became a regular panellist.

As a format, *Loose Women* works very successfully because it incorporates the opinions of a wide range of women of all ages. There is the hardcore who are on air sometimes three times a week, presenters like Ruth Langsford, Andrea McLean, Janet Street-Porter who recently celebrated doing 500 programmes as a panellist, Coleen Nolan of The Nolans fame, Linda Robson from *Birds of a Feather*, and actress and cook Nadia Sawalha. Then there is a wider team made up of journalists like Jane Moore, Kaye Adams, Anne Diamond, Saira Khan and myself.

There is also the notorious Katie Price (The Pricey, as she likes to call herself) and then the wives of Sir Rod Stewart – Penny Lancaster – and Robbie Williams – Ayda Field – who regularly drop in juicy nuggets about their famous husbands, which of course always make a newspaper headline. So there really is quite the band of talent, all of whom have plenty to say. At times, it's just like a group of women having a natter and, due to the fabulous camaraderie, we almost forget that we're on 'live' TV. We have a very strong production team, who are very aware of the topical subjects under the guidance of our editor Sally Shelford. Sally is now expecting her first baby, so she'll soon have an even bigger insight into family day-to-day issues. The girls are so excited about our first 'Loose' baby.

There is no topic that won't get discussed, from the right and wrong ways of bringing up children, to depression in this modern age and even the menopause. I have to say that our husbands provide a great source of material. I'm amazed at just how often sex crops up on the show. You'd be shocked by how many quite elderly women stop me in the supermarket and say in hushed tones, 'Oh, I do love those *Loose Women*. It's my guilty pleasure.' I have to admit that if my mum knew I was talking about sex 'live' on TV she would turn over in her grave!

What I like most is the range of topics and opinions across the different generations. Sometimes it's pure fun and silliness, like the latest photo of Kim Kardashian's bum and at others it's the pertinent issues of the day which, on occasions, can strike close to home. I remember on one occasion we were talking about female hair loss and I broke down as I was suddenly reminded, quite viscerally, of the fact that Caron lost her hair in the course of her battle with cancer. She had such beautiful long hair and it was heart-breaking when it had to be cut off and then when she lost more through chemotherapy. There have been other soul-destroying revelations from some of the girls on the panel about being sexually abused when they were young. That goes to the heart of the programme – where the conversation is so real and personal that we can bare our souls and share the pain.

The team has an acute awareness of what's happening in the lives of the panellists. For example, we talked about Linda Robson's new grandchild, Andrea McLean's marriage to Nick, Penny Lancaster's second wedding ceremony to

Rod, Janet Street-Porter's CBE and Lisa Riley's amazing 10st weight loss.

I've had a few stand-out occasions of my own, perhaps none more so than in June 2017 when, for the second time, I was the subject of *This Is Your Life*, held to mark my seventieth year in show business. I hadn't a clue what was about to happen, as I assumed that it just a normal show with Coleen, Nadia and Ruth, but then quite suddenly the show turned into the set of *This Is Your Life* and my old Northern Irish mate Eamonn Holmes appeared. 'You thought you were here today to be a part of the *Loose Women* panel but, Gloria Hunniford, This Is Your Life!' he announced. Brian Conley came on to sing 'Congratulations', Cliff had pre-recorded a message and then the show put together a compilation of moments throughout the years, from my earliest days in broadcasting up to the present day. What I was not prepared for, though, was the way I would be knocked sideways by the footage of Caron looking so happy and healthy. Amid all the jollity of the occasion, I couldn't help but shed a tear.

In addition to work and family, another great constant in my life has been my dogs. I've always had dogs and at times they have been like children to me, especially after my own children left home. When I had problems with my stalker, one of my greatest concerns was not that he would hurt me but that he threatened my dogs: he pushed a letter through my letterbox saying, 'You don't have any rabbits but you do have two lovely dogs', of course referencing that famous scene in *Fatal Attraction*. Thankfully nothing happened but it was a shock. These days I have two Cavalier King Charles Spaniels, Gemma and Polly. Gemma's the older at ten and she had a sister, Roxie, who sadly died at only five. It happened at the beginning of 2017, despite the fact that she was the fittest little dog you've ever seen, so it came as an enormous shock that she just died in her sleep.

People who are not dog lovers sometimes can't understand how deep the loss goes but it really is like losing one of your family. Obviously one can't replace a dog, nor would you want to, but as I'd grown to love that breed so much I really wanted another but also as company for Gemma. Polly came to us when she was just eight weeks old and rather than embracing her into the house, Gemma was positively sniffy about her, though seven months down the line the two of them are inseparable. I even took Polly on *Loose Women* right after we got her to introduce her to the viewers; some said she was the cutest guest ever and perhaps they were right!

One of the biggest problems when you're working is having the right doggie care, a bit like childcare, and Stephen and I couldn't do what we do in life without our friend Lisa Ongley who even keeps our dogs overnight if needed. As she has dogs of her own, Gemma and Polly feel like they are off to playschool!

★ ★ ★

I often feel like I've had at least nine lives, from those early days singing aged seven, standing on trestle tables for a stage, to today. There was that year in Canada aged just eighteen, which having come from an entrenched Protestant/Catholic community in Northern Ireland, changed my whole attitude to life. Seeing all those nationalities living together in harmony completely broadened my horizons forever. There were those exciting years when television was in its infancy and I got to work both behind and in front of the camera. Then getting my own daily radio show on BBC Belfast and a nightly television programme for Ulster Television. Moving to London in 1982 was transformational, with thirteen wonderful years on Radio 2, one of best radio stations around. I met my idols like Doris Day, Charlton Heston and Audrey Hepburn. Somehow, I survived the pain of losing my precious and only daughter, which at one point I thought would take me out as well. My fulfilling second marriage to Stephen, which has brought me such deep love, contentment and friendship. The joy of seeing my children have children and actually witnessing some of the births was a privilege, let alone observing what fine people they have become. And finally, seventy-seven years later, I'm amazingly still in the business and, what's more, still wanting to do it. I have the passion, zest and drive to continue in a profession that has brought me so many glorious opportunities over the years.

Whilst I don't ever need to ski again or do a bungee jump, there are so many things I want to achieve. One more trip with Charlie and Gabriel to Byron Bay, to revisit the house that Caron and Russ left behind, may offer some sense of closure. When I reflect upon Caron's illness and knowing how it turned out, I wish that I'd given up work for a few years to spend every moment I could with her.

Being in my seventies, I am conscious of my mortality though I try not to dwell on it. If I search deeply, I know that it's one of the reasons why I continue to work so hard and pack so much into life. Having lived through the Troubles in Northern Ireland and realising how fragile life can be, plus of course, losing Caron, I am very conscious of making the most of every minute. I've often said that I wished there was a pill I could take so I didn't need to sleep at all. Just think how much more I could achieve in a day? Stephen occasionally asks, 'When are you going to slow down? Is every day going to be like this?' And I always reply, 'I do hope so.' To be honest, I'm convinced that the work keeps me mentally agile, physically more fit and engaged with the world. And as I always say, if I sit still too long I'll rust.

Michael asked me recently, 'Mum, what keeps you up at night?' I think he was expecting some deep, philosophical response but mine was simpler than that: 'Mostly Stephen's snoring.' I was only partly joking and of course have restless nights like anyone else. Often around the dinner table I joke with the boys about what they're going to do with me when I get older and whilst other people say, 'I never want to be a burden to my children', I'm the opposite and have made them promise that they'll never offload me. Ever since I was a child, when my mum took me to visit an ageing relative in a care home, for some strange reason I've had a complete and utter dread of the place! Some of the care homes I visit these days are like 5-star hotels, but I still want to avoid it if I can. I've even gone to the extent of ring-fencing money to have care at home. We call it the 'nurse fund'. Michael has even worked out where to put the stairlift in the house!

Despite any tribulations in life, I've always had an optimistic attitude that I've been able to use to my advantage in many situations. As my mum used to say, 'In life, always surround yourself with positive people, or you'll end up like the naysayers'. Overall, I'm OK, happily fulfilled and hugely grateful for the cards that life has dealt me.

I said in the opening chapter that so much of my life has

involved being in the right place at the right time, coupled with a great big dollop of luck. Well, lady luck hasn't run out yet and, to quote the Stephen Sondheim song –

'Good times and bum times, I've seen them all/ And, my dear, I'm still here.'

ACKNOWLEDGEMENTS

The older I get the more I appreciate my friends and colleagues who have supported me through many years of my life:

To Anne Thompson, my long-standing friend in Northern Ireland; to Merrill Thomas, who was always there for me, day and night, during Caron's fight against cancer; and to Jackie and Richard Caring, who are the most wonderful supporters of Caron's Foundation and on top of that give us experiences in life that we would never normally have.

To my colleagues at *Rip Off Britain* – I call them the 'A-team' – they work so hard to give us such a successful programme. Extra thanks to Carla Maria Lawson and Dan McGolpin who have just recommissioned the series until 2019; to two of our ITV bosses, Helen Warner and Emma Gormley, who keep the *Loose Women* in check; to all the girls at *Loose Women* who provide so much fun and laughs;

and to my make-up girls, who pick us up in the morning and put us together.

To Laurie Mansfield, my manager and still the wise Buddha; to my agent, Jo Carlton of Talent4Media, who keeps me together daily; and to Ray Sharp, who gets me everywhere on time!!

To all the people across the country who raise money in many different ways and kindly donate to the Caron Keating Foundation regularly, which we truly appreciate, especially 'Hard Rock' who for ten years have supported the Foundation by organising fabulous annual events and, in turn, helping so many people suffering from cancer.

To Mary Clifford Day, my secretary who really comes to my rescue regularly; to Elizabeth and Richard Husband, who advise us on how the grants should be distributed by our charity; to Neil Miller, head gardener at Hever Castle, who planted 300 of Caron's roses in the castle grounds and gives all the money he makes through gardening talks to the Foundation; and to Michelle and John Carlton-Smith who are great eating and drinking pals, both in France and in Kent.

Most of all, to John Blake publishing who have given me the opportunity to tell my story and had the faith in me to allow me to get on with it! To my Editor, Ciara Lloyd and to Virginia Blackburn who helped me remember all the stories.

Finally, to all those friends, family and acquaintances who bring so much to my life, thank you.